"I could not put this book down. Surely the most needless tragedy in the body of Christ is bored Christians. Following Jesus is the wildest ride on earth. It's time we took off the seat belts."

Beth Moore
Best-selling author, speaker and founder of Living Proof Ministries

"'Aslan is not a tame lion,' wrote C.S. Lewis. Mark Buchanan shows us what this means. The undemanding *God-in-a-bottle* genie, Who exists to serve *us*, is a modern heresy. It's the *God of the Bible* who's actually calling the shots! We are the servants of a fierce King—One who is gracious but never manageable. *Your God Is Too Safe* reminds us again and again what it means that 'Jesus is God—and we're not!' Strangely, it's *dangerous faith* in our untamed Savior that leads us to the joy we crave. The breath of life rises off of the pages of this book!"

Randy Alcorn, author of *The Treasure Principle*, *Lord Foulgrin's Letters*, *Dominion*, and *Deadline*

I dedicate this book to my BMW—Beautiful Marvelous Wife: Cheryl, thank you for your purity of heart and deep prayerfulness. You are to me living proof that the things unseen matter most and shape us most; and to my children: Adam, Sarah, and Nicola, thank you for your laughter and wonder and hope. You continually remind me that I walk on holy ground. I love all of you.

YOUR GOD IS TOO SAFE

Rediscovering the Wonder
of a God You Can't Control

MARK BUCHANAN

Multnomah•Publishers *Sisters, Oregon*

YOUR GOD IS TOO SAFE
published by Multnomah Publishers, Inc.

published in association with the literary agency of Ann Spangler and Associates,
6260 Viewpoint Drive NE, Belmont, Michigan 49306.

International Standard Book Number: 1-57673-774-8

Scripture quotations are from:
The Holy Bible, New International Version
© 1973, 1984 by International Bible Society,
used by permission of Zondervan Publishing House

The Holy Bible, King James Version (KJV)

Multnomah is a trademark of Multnomah Publishers, Inc., and is registered in the
U.S. Patent and Trademark Office.
The colophon is a trademark of Multnomah Publishers, Inc.

Printed in the United States of America

For information:
MULTNOMAH PUBLISHERS, INC.
POST OFFICE BOX 1720
SISTERS, OREGON 97759

Library of Congress Cataloging-in-Publication Data
Buchanan, Mark Aldham.
    Your God is too safe : rediscovering the wonder of a God you can't control / by Mark
Buchanan.   p. cm.   Includes bibliographical references.
    ISBN 1-57673-774-8 (pbk.)
    1. Spiritual life—Christianity.   I. Title.
BV4501.3.B83 2001   00-012051
248.4–dc21

03 04 05 06—10 9 8 7 6 5

CONTENTS

FOREWORD

THE CHRISTIAN LIFE HAS *LIFE* AS ITS SUBJECT, NOT *CHRISTIAN*.
Life is the noun; *Christian* is only the adjective. Not that the adjective is unimportant. It is, in fact, necessary, for life is subject to many distortions and illusions, betrayals and reductions. The adjective *Christian* is intended to set *life* apart from the diluted, deviant, or counterfeit forms that seek to pass themselves off as the real thing.

But the adjective doesn't seem to be working very well these days. Instead of giving the noun a salty zest, it often flattens it to something hardly distinguishable from bland survival. This is not good. In this book about the formation of the Christian life, however, the adjective is used very well, indeed.

An accurate understanding of the formation of the Christian life requires three things: stories well told, Scripture sharply imagined, and language skillfully used. All three are essential.

Stories. A story is the verbal form that most adequately conveys our actual, day-to-day, ordinary lives—who we are and the way we live. These days, virtually all the words used to account for what we are and mean—test scores, census figures, medical data, psychological profiles, academic transcripts, economic status, work performance, religious affiliation, racial category, political opinion, moral behavior—are abstractions and generalizations that lump us into impersonal file drawers. They are observations of outsiders that have little to do with who we really are. Only story provides the diction and syntax that reveals the unique particular, the inner identity, and the intricate web of relationships that account for who we are—our *life*.

Unfortunately, most of the attention we receive in contemporary society is indifferent to story; that is, to the way we actually live, our personal uniqueness. Most of the people who seek to understand us and tell us what they understand are not interested in *us* at all, but in something *about* us that they can use to their profit or fix for a fee. The more such de-storied language gets inside of us, the less storied we become. Life leaks away.

The formation of the Christian life requires stories well told.

Scripture. Scripture reveals God present and at work in our world and our lives. The revelation is given in the context of a multitextured, meandering, and somewhat baggy account of ancient Israel and early church, at the core of which is the crisp, focused life of Jesus. Most of the Christian life has to do with who God is and what He does in Israel, the church, and Jesus. Scripture is our primary access to this massive, all-encompassing, all-involving revelation. All the terms and details of our lives are worked out in the presence of God's life in responsive relation to Jesus.

But we live in a time and place in which we feel that we are or ought to be "on our own." And we are technologically so far removed from Bible times that whatever went on in that world, however true it might have been, seems totally remote. Understandably, then, we are impatient with those arcane details packed into the pages of our Scriptures. "Give us a summary of the truth," we say, "some 'biblical principles' by which we can live." But we can no more summarize and generalize God's revelation in Scripture than we can our own lives. Summary reduces. Generalization reduces. But we want *life.* The personal and lived details are essential. God is *person,* and we cannot respond to Him as category or function or idea. If we are to live fully and well, we have to know whom we are living with and for. When Scripture is depersonalized, we lose access to the very ground beneath our feet.

The formation of the Christian life requires Scripture sharply imagined.

And language. Language is the primary means by which life develops and matures. God, the Lord of language, spoke the world and our lives into being. Jesus, the Word made flesh, used language to proclaim the existence of the kingdom of God, call disciples, forgive sin, heal bodies, rebuke injustice and hypocrisy, express love, and teach the truth. Our words, spoken and written, continue to make, form, and shape life. Nothing about us is more life generating, life deepening, and life enriching than our use of language.

It follows that the widespread degradation and trivialization of language that marks our present culture constitutes a major threat to *life.* When language is taken over by those who sell, propagandize, bully, demean, mislead,

and gossip, life is cheapened to a commodity; people are reduced to cus-
tomers. And so it is of critical importance that the men and women who care
fervently about life—life-in-formation, the Christ-formed life—be passionately attentive to the use of language. When the Christian life is spoken or
written in tired clichés and sentences sodden with saccharine, the adjective
Christian diminishes the *life*.

The formation of the Christian life requires language skillfully used.

Mark Buchanan has used stories, Scriptures, and language to provide
those of us who have set out to "walk before the Lord in the land of the living" (Psalm 116:9) with a magnificent, cogent, and God-honoring manual of
the ways in which we are formed by our Lord and the Spirit into life, life, and
more life. His language, taut and sinewy, makes a tight weave of stories and
Scriptures that not only tells us what this formation is, but also sets the words
free to enact the formation, attracting us into what he calls the "holy wild,"
where there is both space and reason to bless and be blessed.

EUGENE H. PETERSON
PROFESSOR EMERITUS OF SPIRITUAL THEOLOGY
REGENT COLLEGE, VANCOUVER, B.C.

I'VE TRIED IT, AND IT DON'T WORK

I 'm stuck.

That's the impulse behind writing this book: my own affliction with chronic spiritual fatigue; my own dwelling in the doldrums of the heart; my own realization that I was spiritually stalled, held in place by a dead weight of apathy, sloth, doubt, and fear.

I had begun well. My conversion to Christ combined—at least in my over-literary imagination—the best of the legendary conversions.[1] Like the apostle Paul, my arrogant defiance was knocked out of me by the accosting of the risen Christ, who blinded me with light and then removed the scales so I could truly see. Like Augustine, I was wooed Christward by what seemed to be a child's voice. Like John Wesley, my heart was suffused with the strange warmth of heaven's peace. Like C. S. Lewis, I was hauled, almost kicking and screaming, headlong into the kingdom by the sheer intellectual potency of Christianity.

I hit the ground running. Immediately, I volunteered for everything, any-thing, that I felt vaguely interested in and marginally qualified for. I led youth group; I helped with music; I taught Sunday school; I wrote the church newsletter; I became a camp counselor; I served as a mentor to several young men.

But something, somewhere, went awry. The zeal fizzled. The fire in my bones became only an ache in the joints. My running became plodding. My lightness became heaviness. My joyfulness became jadedness. I joined the ranks of the murmurers and faultfinders—those who didn't like the music or the sermon or the color of the azaleas behind the church—and I found their number legion.

And I got stuck.

At first, it wasn't so bad being stuck. I had, from before my conversion, well-practiced habits of cynicism and self-indulgence. This was territory I knew instinctively and traversed with agility. I didn't have to work at it.

At the end of Mark Twain's *The Adventures of Tom Sawyer,* Tom and his friend Huckleberry Finn discover a large cache of stolen treasure, and the two become rich. A kindly woman, the Widow Douglas, takes Huckleberry in to give him a proper home and education. Huckleberry is part hobo, part hillbilly, part wild boy. He scrounges for food, wears smelly rags, and sleeps in a pig shed. But under the watchful and diligent care of the Widow Douglas, he gets scrubbed up and buttoned down. He has a warm, clean bed to sleep in every night, fresh clothes to wear (with shoes!), hot meals to fill his stomach, and a school to go to.

But he chafes under it. So before long, he shucks it all and goes back to pig sheds and poaching. That's the life he knows. That's the life he doesn't have to work at. As he tells Tom about life with the Widow Douglas:

> I've tried it, and it don't work, Tom. It ain't for me; I ain't used to it.
> The widder's good to me and friendly; but I can't stand them ways.…
> I got to go to church and sweat and sweat—I hate them ornery sermons.… I can't *stand* it.… I'd got to talk so nice it wasn't no comfort—I'd go up to the attic and rip out awhile, every day, to git a taste in my mouth, or I'd 'a' died, Tom. The widder wouldn't let me smoke; she wouldn't let me yell, she wouldn't let me gape, nor stretch, nor scratch, before folks.… And, dad fetch it, she prayed all the time! I never *see* such a woman! I *had* to shove, Tom—I just had to.[2]

It don't work...It ain't for me...I ain't used to it. That was me in the things of the Spirit. Gossip and grumbling were my mother tongue, and this new language of praise and exhortation was as foreign and inflected to me as Cantonese. Self-seeking was an inborn and sharply honed instinct in my blood, and these much vaunted Christian virtues of humility and servanthood were as stiff and constricting as a Victorian corset. My money was my money—and hard earned—and there was never enough of it anyhow, and this principle of tithing seemed usury. And doesn't the Bible condemn that?

Like Huck, I seemed only to be able to live this new life by yielding to an outwardly imposed, sternly enforced regimen of starchy, dreary, wearying rules. I had to walk in a lockstep of legalism.

But I couldn't stand it.

It was too easy to slip back into the old habits of mind and living. Going back was, in fact, *natural.*

Yet I stayed in the church. I continued to lead, teach, help, attend. I never renounced my faith. I had times of fresh resolve and redoubled effort. But it wasn't sustained.

And I was tired. I was tired of teaching an unruly group of kids who couldn't seem to care less. I was tired of the mere busyness of the church. I was tired of trying and failing. I was tired of not trying. I was tired of being tired. I was tired of being compliant and yet tired of being defiant. I had chronic spiritual fatigue, and as I looked around, it seemed the condition was epidemic.

I was stuck, and though I was often lonely in it, I wasn't alone.

BUT I NOTICED SOME WHO WERE NOT STUCK. THERE WAS PASTOR Gager, who, nearing eighty, was so joyful he sometimes seemed giddy. He was spiritually robust and mature and grew ever more seasoned but was always fresh. Every time I talked with him, he told me what the Lord had spoken to him that day and how excited he was about it. Then he'd scrunch up the loose skin on his forehead so that his disheveled white eyebrows touched in the middle. He'd skewer me with his eyes, lay a slightly shaking but still strong hand on my shoulder, and say, "Mark, what is the Lord speaking to you?"

There was Hazel Coneen, who, many years widowed, lived in a cramped, single-room apartment, a kind of monk's cell, surrounded by pictures of her children, grandchildren, great-grandchildren. Her furniture was sparse and tacky. Hazel had ankles swollen to a stumpy thickness. She often had trouble breathing, her words threadbare from the effort of it. But whenever I asked her how she was, Hazel would exclaim, "Oh, Mark, I am so wonderful. God's faithfulness is new every morning. It's true. It's really true." I could see that, yes, for her it was true.

There was Ernie Brown, stricken with multiple sclerosis in his thirties. Now in his midforties, it took him a half hour to eat half a sandwich. His words came out like slag and shrapnel, his speech shattered by his erratic breathing. Sometimes I would have to ask him four times to repeat himself. One day, I mustered up the courage to ask him what his sickness had taught him about God. Without hesitating and with utter clearness he said: "God is good."

These people weren't stuck.

So I've set out to discover two things. First, why do so many of us get stuck? Why are we so susceptible to weariness and jadedness and evasiveness—what I call the awkward, backward, wayward life? Why does our life in Christ so often gather moss rather than bear fruit?

Second, why do some people not get stuck or break free if they do? Why does their life in Christ grow richer, freer, more fruitful? Is there a cure for chronic spiritual fatigue, and if so, what is it?

That's what I've set out to ask. More importantly, that's what I've set out to answer.

LUKE TELLS A STORY THAT DRAMATIZES WHAT I'M TALKING ABOUT here. The story is told in Luke 24:13–35. Jesus, only that day risen from the dead, joins two of His disciples—one named Cleopas—as they walk to the village of Emmaus. They are downhearted and dim sighted. They fail to recognize Him. He asks what they are discussing. In their gloom they tell Him about "Jesus of Nazareth," a "prophet powerful in word and deed before God and all the people." They speak of the hope they had pinned on this man Jesus, about how the religious rulers handed Him over to be crucified, and about the rumors—told by women and more troubling than consoling—of His resurrection. One thing is for sure: The tomb is empty, bodiless.

Jesus listens and then speaks. "How foolish you are," He says, "and how *slow of heart* to believe all that the prophets have spoken! Did not the Christ have to suffer these things and then enter His glory?" He goes on to explain from the Scriptures how Christ's death was a fulfillment of prophecy.

When they arrive at the village, the two men persuade Jesus, whom they still don't recognize, to eat with them. He does, and as Jesus breaks the bread, gives thanks, and gives it to them, "their eyes were opened and they recognized him, and he disappeared from their sight. They asked each other, 'Were not our *hearts burning* within us while he talked with us on the road and opened the Scriptures to us?'"

The heart condition of these disciples is twofold: slow and burning. That is a strange affliction—and common. One definition of Christ's followers might be "those people of the slow, burning heart." Sorrow and hope, awe and self-pity, wonder and worry, belief and doubt all mix loosely in us, tugging us one way, jostling us another. Jesus walks the road with us. But we can look straight at Him and not recognize Him. Jesus opens the Scriptures to us, for us, and often something happens within—a warming at times, a scorching at others. And just at those moments when finally the scales fall from our eyes and we see that, behold, it is Him, it is Jesus!—at that wondrous moment, He often up and vanishes. Our encounters with the risen Christ are mostly like that: enigmatic, fleeting, mere glimpses, little ambushes. And we're left with the question: "Didn't our hearts burn within us? Didn't they?"

The burning heart keeps us going on the journey. The slowness of heart makes the journey wearisome. A burning heart inspires us to run. A slow heart discourages us sometimes from even trudging. And sometimes it tempts us to run, yes, but away. Slowness of heart and the heart that burns within—both are inbred and crossbred, and we're not reasoned very far in or out of either. We need to be more cunning than that, and more innocent. It will usually call for resting when we think we should be striving, and wrestling when we just want to sleep.

❧

PART OF WHAT I HAVE SET OUT TO DO IS TO DIAGNOSE OUR
slowness of heart—to lay the blackened, wizened thing on the table and find
where it bloats or clots. To diagnose where we're stuck and why we're stuck
and why it is so difficult for us to recognize Jesus even when He's standing
right beside us. Part 1 of this book is devoted to this diagnosis. I begin by looking at what I call living on borderland—the barren but crowded place between
two worlds, between the lost and the found, the old and the new, the damned
and the redeemed, where so many of us get stuck. I explore some of the reasons we live there, some of the excuses we make for it. I look, in short, at our
slowness of heart.

In 1961, J. B. Phillips wrote a book called *Your God Is Too Small,* a thin,
sharply worded and prophetic call to give up our modern fetishes and idols,
the cherished but foolish myths we have about God. We have made God man-
size, Phillips argues. Or smaller. In our hands, God has become our image
bearer, rather than we His. The god we worship is a shallow repository of all
our idle wishes and half-baked whims. Phillips exposes those tendencies,
explodes those myths, and then issues a call to return to the true God of mystery and sovereignty and intimacy, the God revealed in Jesus Christ.

This book is called *Your God Is Too Safe.* I am not trying to rewrite Phillips's
book, and in truth, what I have set out to do is significantly different from
what he has done. But we have this in common: the conviction that bad theology always produces bad living. If we get stuck, if we stay stuck, the root is
almost always theological and spiritual: how we see God or don't see God. It
comes from wanting a god other than God—a god who is nice, innocuous,
pampering, who forgets not our confessed sins, but our besetting ones.

More and more we see God as safe. In one sense, of course, it's true. God
is safe. He is the one in whom we find refuge, our hiding place, a shield about
us. He is the God of all comfort. He is the God of peace.

But that's not what I mean when I say we've made God too safe. I mean
that we want Him to be comfortable rather than comforting. I mean that we
want Him to be peaceable, to keep His peace, to be docile, rather than to be
peacemaking and peace giving. And instead of being our hiding place, we

would prefer that God be our ace in the hole. And if that doesn't work, we'd prefer to hide from Him.

And there is a kind of self-perpetuating downward spiral in all this. We often get stuck because we want a god who is too safe. And then we find, in the soft logic of our half-baked theology, that a too-safe god has no power to get us unstuck. His arm is too short for that. And He doesn't care anyway: He validates our borderland dwelling. He's the household deity of lapsed disciples. He's the god of our understanding, the god who always understands. He doesn't so much forgive sin; He accommodates it. He's the god who makes anything more than living on borderland seem imprudent, fanatic, ill advised.

THAT'S THE PROBLEM, STATED SIMPLY, YET MANIFEST IN A THOUSAND subtle ways. That's what part 1 will address and explore.

But diagnosis without prescription is a cruel thing. So the second half of this book seeks to be curative. I look at the secret that men like Pastor Gager and Ernie Brown and women like Hazel Coneen—and many more—have discovered: the way to keep slow hearts burning. There are men and women— you know a few—who live in the holy wild, the place far beyond the borderland, where God is God, not safe, but good.

How do you get to that place and go deeper, ever deeper, into it?

Part 2 will explore the ways men and women of all ages, through all ages, keep the fire in their hearts ever brighter, ever hotter, burning away its slowness—who fix their eyes on Jesus and throw off the sin that so easily entangles and run the race with perseverance. Who live in perpetual wonder with the God they can't control.

And they're not stuck.

Part One

⤗

LIFE IN BORDERLAND

SIGMUND FREUD ARGUED THAT GOD IS ONLY OUR HUMAN
yearning and dread, ancient as night, projected outward and upward.
God is the Father we need, and yet need to kill. We invented Him to
assuage our fears, yet seek to destroy Him as the object of our fear. He
is our primary wish fulfillment and our most menacing rival. He is the
Oedipus complex writ large.[1]

Freud was wrong. But he had an instinctual rightness about
one thing: we are deeply ambivalent toward God. Sometimes we
flee Him; sometimes we seek Him. But our motives in either case
are complex, mixed.

And at times the gap between the god we want and the God
who wants us is vast beyond bridging.

Chapter One

THE REFUGE OF THE STUCK

A little town called Busia wedges up against the border between Kenya and Uganda. Busia has a scattering of ramshackle buildings, a nest of narrow, dusty streets. The air is hazy from the smoke of open fires. The streets are overcrowded with hawkers and money changers—as you walk, toothless or toothy men thrust at you bundles of money for exchange, soapstone dishes, wood carvings, beadwork, baskets. You must set your face like flint and walk steady, not too fast.

Busia is a place of crossing. It is, actually, a place of double crossing. You cannot take a car from one country to the other. You have to walk the dusty earth between them. You go through the Uganda customs—a wood hut that splices together two lengths of steel mesh fence crowned with coils of barbed wire. The man in the hut wants to know why you were in his country, why you're leaving it, what you're taking with you, what you're leaving behind. He frisks you. He'll take a bribe if you want to avoid all this. Then you step into a brick building with several men who shuffle and stamp papers. Put money in their palms—especially American—and you can speed things up here, too.

You step out of the brick building, thinking you've made it, thinking you're in Kenya.

You're not. This, as I said, is a double crossing. Kenya has its own customs office, its own brick building with its own huddle of men shuffling and stamping papers. In between the two brick buildings—the Uganda one, the Kenya one—is a patch of ground. It's not large: maybe 100 yards wide, 300 yards long. It's borderland, no-man's-land, claimed or defended by neither country. All laws are suspended here. Shoot a man, rob him, beat him: The guards on either side would watch, stolid, unmoving.

There are two borders, then, two crossings to make. The Uganda one, the Kenya one. The two borders are testimony to an ancient blood feud between countries. They are brothers who refuse to speak to one another. And in between these two borders, this double crossing, is borderland.

It is strange and frightening to walk through here. There are no laws to restrain anyone from doing anything. Stranger still, the place is thronged with people—peddlers, hawkers, beggars. It's a carnival of the wayward and the waylaid. Why? Why would anyone choose to dwell here?

Why would anyone choose to be stuck?

Because, actually, it's safe. It's familiar. It's ground that can be staked out, marked off, well trod, packed down. It holds some things in and keeps some things out. It may take endurance to live there, but not much else: It's the endurance of inertia. Life there requires no discipline but falls into neat routines. It's domesticated lawlessness. It's chaotic, but predictable. Borderland might be dangerous, but even more, it's safe.

Borderland is a political and geographical reality. But it's also a metaphor. There is a blood feud that divides Christ's domain from the world's, and a cross marks the crossing. Salvation is stepping over the boundary from our old life, the old land: freedom from its rule, its laws, its gods. It's coming home from the far country. But sanctification is the journey into the new land: learning to dwell gladly in the Father's house.

It's a way of life that's hard to learn. The shape of the new land is, first, cruciform. It's dangerous, difficult terrain. There are feasts, yes, but also graveyards, badlands, boot camps. It calls us to a constant dying. Borderland seems safer, a land of exile when the homeland is war torn. So we refine an aptitude for lingering, malingering: for borderland dwelling. For standing out in the muddy field, as smoke mixes with twilight, and refusing to come join the Father though He pleads with us.

This book is about moving off the borderland. But it is also about mapping the borderland, naming its contents and discontents, tracing its contours, cataloguing its life forms and its deadliness. It's an attempt to try to understand the borderland's lure and its hold. Because often, very often, our experience of Christ and our life in Christ is a stunted, wizened-up thing. It doesn't live up to the rhetoric. It's like hearing music muted through water, kissing through canvas. It hardly seems worth the effort.

We don't want to go back. But neither are we particularly motivated to go forward. We're stuck on borderland. On the day my brother was baptized, several years ago now, a man came up to him, a stalwart member of the church, and said that he had been waiting for twenty-eight years for God to do something with his life. And he was still waiting. Twenty-eight years. Twenty-eight years on borderland. I don't know that man, but I have the grim certainty that were I to track him down, I would find him still waiting.

But this—this inner deadness, this spiritual sleepwalking, this chronic stuckness—happens all the time and all around us. We know it, and often, in desperate attempts to ward it off or drive it away, we grope for immunities, remedies.

We go to Bible college, hoping that will inoculate us against spiritual languor, will create in us robust faith. But many theological schools and Bible colleges are built on borderlands. There is the danger in such places that we will learn much about God and at the same time grow distant from God; we will study the intricacies of doctrine, but lose passion; we will become eloquent at God talk, but cease talking *to* God.

We go to church, we sing, we pray, we listen to the Word read and preached. Maybe we take notes. Maybe we even lead some of it. And maybe our slow hearts burn within us. But walking away—just strolling to our car in the church parking lot, fifty-seven steps away—the conviction, "He's alive!" dribbles down like water held in the hand. Monday morning, it's still hard to get out of bed.

≈

I'M SEEKING TO UNDERSTAND THE WEARINESS THAT SPREADS ITSELF over and soaks its way through so much of modern Christian living. I'm trying to diagnose the spiritual chronic fatigue syndrome in our churches. I'm seeking to comprehend our temptation to sleep when we are called to pray, to wield swords when we should bear crosses, to go shopping when we should be fighting, to either boast or gripe about what is sheer gift, to be loose-lipped with others' secrets and tight-lipped about God's Good News. I'm attempting to document the story, so varied yet so monotonous, about missing the grace of God. I'm setting out to tell, sympathetically but also ruthlessly, about our faintheartedness, and halfheartedness, and fickle-heartedness. I'm writing about life on the borderland.

THERE IS A DREADFULNESS ABOUT GOD. THIS IS SELDOM SAID. It is where I want to begin. We often cherish a pious delusion about ourselves: that we truly desire God and that all that's lacking to pursue deepest intimacy with Him is adequate skill, sufficient knowledge, proper motivation. But is that so? I've lived with myself long enough and been among God's people long enough to know that our hearts are as slow as much as burning, that we have a fondness for parades and masquerades of holy living, but little appetite for the real thing. Down in our bones, mingled with our blood, silent and potent as instinct, is a dread of God. Part of our essence is a longing to flee. There is a fear of God, the Proverbs tells us, that is the beginning of wisdom, the threshold for knowing God. But that's not what I'm talking about. I'm talking about something more primal: a deep down craven terror, a black hole of unknowing.

We know that we should desire intimacy with God. The better and saner part of us does. But there is in each of us a dark impulse toward separation, a love of distance. We want to see God, not face-to-face, but in rough silhouette, to hear, not the thunder of His shout or the sweetness of His whisper, but only rumors of Him, faint and faraway echoes.

The story of Moses and the people of Israel is instructive. After God delivers the tablets of the Law at Sinai into Moses' hands, the people witness the storm-stirring powers of God:

> When the people saw the thunder and lightning and heard the trumpet and saw the mountain in smoke, they trembled with fear. They stayed at a distance and said to Moses, "Speak to us yourself and we will listen. But do not have God speak to us or we will die." (Exodus 20:18–19)

This is primal fear. The voice of God, the presence of God, holds not comfort but terror. We fear God the way we fear tigers and tyrants, cyclones and cyclopses: a power swift and capricious. So we want it muffled, mediated, caged. We settle for—no, demand—echoes, rumors, shadows. We long for hearsay about God, but do not ourselves want to hear God say anything. We want priests or envoys, some kind of go-between: someone else to handle the fire, to risk death or deforming or deafening in the encounter with the living God. This perhaps is the secret agenda of most pulpit committees: to find someone who will keep God afar, make God safe. *Speak to us yourself, and we will listen. But do not have God speak to us....*

Why are we like that? There is no easy explanation. Part of it, an obvious and large part, has to do with God's holiness and our unholiness. In Exodus 33 we are told that God shows Moses His glory, but Moses must hide in the cleft of a rock and is only allowed a glimpse of the Lord's back because if he sees God's face he will die. We too have an instinctual knowledge of our unworthiness and cower in the rocks as God's glory, in a whirlwind, flashes by. Or we are like Adam and Eve, who, in the shamefulness of their sin, hid from God as He came walking through the Garden in the cool of the day.

But there is something else, something more—or less. Jesus said He would not entrust Himself to man because He knew all men and knew what was in them (John 2:25). He knows our drowsy indifference to matters of highest importance, our rabid passion for matters that are trivial. He knows we get angrier at missing a bus or being delayed on a runway than we do at crimes of genocide. He knows we rejoice more in winning a game of pinochle than we do in the news that the hungry are fed, the lost are found. So Jesus doesn't entrust Himself to us.

But we return in kind. We don't entrust ourselves to Jesus. Because we half-know what's in the Man. Jesus is not fickle, but He's unpredictable. God is on the loose through Him. We don't mind the magician's tricks—water into wine, bread crumbs and fish bones into banquet, lame men into dancers, mute ones into minstrels—but these field marshal commands of His— "Follow Me!"—we can do without.

Follow You? I don't think so. Follow You where? Have You made hotel arrangements? Did You purchase cancellation and travel insurance? What am I to wear? No, Jesus. I'm going to sit right here between worlds. I'm going to live here on borderland until You come up with a better offer.

Until it's safe.

So here we sit, whiling our days away in this flat, empty place of in-betweenness.

Most Christians I know are stuck. We feel caught in jobs we barely endure and often despise, in relationships that plunder us and baffle us and deepen rather than remove our aloneness, in activities that are soul wizening in their triviality and yet insatiably addictive. We squander jewels and hoard baubles. We experience harrowing emotions over mere trifles and can barely muster a dull ache over matters of shattering tragedy. We feel we've no time and no energy for the things that we know matter deeply, even eternally, but waste much time in silly and stultifying diversions: We are impatient with our child's longing to spend ten minutes with us at bedtime, but then fritter away an hour in idle telephone chatter or two hours watching the latest studio-produced inanity on video. We gossip, even though we've made repeated resolves not to. We envy, resent, judge, avenge, sulk, and overeat. We read *People* magazine—maybe even *Playboy*—and *FutureShop* flyers, but not our Bible much. We feel that everyone else has more money, longer vacations, newer cars, nicer clothes, and fewer things going wrong with their hot water tanks, automobiles, and children than we do.

We wonder where the freedom is for which Christ set us free. And this secret fear haunts us: *Is everyone else fulfilled, and I'm the only one who's not?* Or even worse: *Is no one fulfilled, and we are all just playing out a charade that we are?*

Meet, for example, James. James has an amazing gift with music. He can play nearly anything—strings, woodwinds, horns, percussion. Music soaks his bones and spills out of his ever agile hands, his rich and supple throat. He can dazzle and delight, even mesmerize. Yet he also has a real passion to lead people into God's presence—Jesus must become greater, James must become less.

But James also struggles with self-bullying and self-pity. *No one*, he thinks, *really understands me. No one really appreciates me. They snatch up what I give and never say thank you, and if they speak it's only to complain about what I did wrong. It's never enough, or it's always too much; it's overdone or it's underdone. That man who doesn't sing is obviously disapproving. That woman who walked out halfway through is obviously protesting. And why should anyone thank me anyhow? I'm useless, inept, worthless. Who am I kidding thinking I have something to offer anyone? That other musician over there can render these songs with more subtlety and integrity and beauty than I ever could. It must be nice being him.*

And so it goes.

Or meet Daphne. Daphne is attractive, intelligent, articulate. She is artistic, poetic, funny, fun, compassionate. She paints exquisite pictures. She has a sweet voice and a sweet way. People are easily drawn to her, and not just because of her beauty. She is charming without a hint of coyness.

But Daphne carries, well-hidden beneath the brightness of her smile, the lightness of her ways, a crippling weight of inadequacy. She is haunted, sometimes to the point of paralysis, by fear of rejection. Everything she is or does seems to fall pitifully short of some looming, rigid but undefined standard of approval. Her whole life is lived under the hovering chill shadow of a stamp marked REJECT. At any moment a hand—whose?—could slam it down hard and score its sharp letters indelibly into her delicate flesh. She wants to offer her artistic gifts to the church, but is afraid that no one would want them, understand them, notice them—or, if they did, would scorn them. She hears the pastor speak often, too often, about not succumbing to the fear of man. Daphne feels like she is congenitally flawed in this area: that the holy courage and conviction the pastor so glibly endorses is, by some jest of God, forever denied to her.

Or meet Jean, who is not pretty and not charming and not gifted. Who resents people like Daphne, and who would laugh, in a bitter, mirthless way, if she ever knew how Daphne really felt. *What right does she have to feel sorry for herself? She should try living in my skin for a day.* Jean has covered her anger and anguish with a raw jocularity. She acts like she doesn't care. She makes barbed jokes, most of them about herself, jibes at her own appearance or ability. If you compliment her—and to be honest, few do—she deflects it with self-mockery. Inside, though, she's dying. The person in the Bible she identifies with most is the man in the parable of the talents, the man who only gets one talent, buries it, plays it safe, and then is punished. That story, she thinks, is not an indictment of the man; it's an indictment of God. It is a story of God's stinginess and capriciousness. It's a story about the poor getting poorer, the luckless more down on their luck. It's a story about God's way with her.

Or meet Ben. Ben went to a men's conference three years ago, and God spoke to him, broke him. He was the man from Laodicea, thinking he had it all. And God revealed his nakedness and poverty, his sickening lukewarmness. Ben repented, in tears. He made firm resolve to be, by God's grace and strength, better: a better husband, a better father, a better employee, a better neighbor, a better man. In his heart, he scored the earth with a fixed boundary. He stepped over and swore he'd never go back. When the worship team closed with "I Have Decided to Follow Jesus," Ben, who's never been much for all this swooning music in church, sang with such gusto that he thought he might burst his lungs, rupture his throat. The joy in him was physical, a surging, gushing force, cleansing and filling.

But that was three years ago. Ben came home, made an earnest and honest effort to live out his resolve. But somehow, somewhere, bit by bit, old ways accumulated: salty speech, griping at the office, impatience in traffic, irritation toward his children. And, in all, an ennui: boredom and frustration, mixed together like water and ash into a thick, musty paste, encrust all his doings. He doesn't feel very Christian. Worst of all, most of the time he doesn't care.

These stories could be multiplied and then multiplied again. Joseph Campbell wrote a book, a kind of repackaging of Jungian philosophy, called *The Hero with a Thousand Faces*. It's about each culture's and subculture's embrace of a Christlike archetype. It should be the story of the church: Christ's face reflected in all our faces, His life embodied in all our lives. The manifold and many-splendored character of Christ in us and among us—the hero with a thousand faces. But there is another story in our churches, maybe more common: *The Failure with a Thousand Faces*.

This is where many of us live, this wet, gray city, this lifeless tundra, this austere waiting room where we sit hopeful and afraid, longing for good news, expecting bad. Where if we hear Christ at all, it is His Emmaus road rebuke: *How foolish you are, and how slow of heart to believe.*

This is borderland.

Maybe you're stuck here.

Chapter Two

THE GOD WHO'S
NOT SAFE

W ho is the god of borderland? *What is his name, and the name of his son? Tell me if you know!* (Proverbs 30:4). Who is the one who gives theological sanction to our dwelling there? This is his name: the god who is too safe.

The too-safe god makes us into borderland dwellers. Conversely, borderland dwellers make god too safe. Either way—whether we get lured into borderland because we seek a god less wild than the real God, or we end up on borderland by a different route but justify getting stuck there by fashioning a god who begs us to stay—the net result is the same: If you are on borderland, your god is too safe.

Second Samuel 6 has a famous story. David, secure in his kingship, ensconced in his new capital, brings the ark to Jerusalem. And as it comes, David dances. His dance is a kinetic outburst of sheer joy. It is a pantomime of trust and surrender. *Offer your body as a living sacrifice, holy and pleasing to God, for this is your spiritual act of worship.* So David dances.

But things go tragically awry. There's an accident: An ox stumbles, a cart lurches, the ark of the covenant totters, slides, threatens to tumble to the ground. Uzzah the priest is right there, though, and his instincts are razor sharp and lightning quick. He's ready for just this kind of thing. He's vigilant and diligent, hands hovering in anticipation. When the moment of crisis comes, Uzzah is prepared, saving the day. Liturgical impresario, him, master of ceremonies.

God smote him dead.

Why? Uzzah simply tried to keep the ark from tumbling to the ground. He tried to keep the flag from touching the dirt. This is good, we'd think. What any of us would do under similar constraints: the right and noble thing. But God kills him for it. Why?

Uzzah is a strange hybrid: an iconoclastic bureaucrat. He's a rule-flouting stickler, a nit-picking maverick. He makes radical breaks with convention, then rigidly adheres to his own conventions. Uzzah's idea of carrying the ark on an oxcart was in clear breach of divine command. God had given detailed instruction about how the ark was to be transported: slung on poles and hefted by priests. Freighting the ark on an oxcart was a Philistine notion. It must have seemed to Uzzah more convenient, efficient, elegant, innovative. The latest fashion in worship accoutrements. *Why didn't God think of it? Well, we'll amend that.*

It was always the hankering of the Israelites to be like the other nations. It's always been the hankering of the church, too. *If everybody's doing it out there, it must be an improvement on what we do in here.* Whatever keeps us current, that's the thing.

Uzzah was a novelty hound. But that in and of itself doesn't appear to be the main problem. He was also a tradition monger. He had, indeed, a pharisaical disposition: to contrive or embrace the innovation, and then insist on it, kill or die for it. So Uzzah gets an oxcart and fusses so painstakingly over every little detail—makes such a binding tradition out of his newfangled innovation—that he forgets the one thing needed: worship. This is supposed to be about worship.

Here is where Uzzah gets me. I'm a pastor. I am "responsible" for the church's worship. I am paid to make sure it all glows and flows and steps on no one's toes. And, frankly, it's hard to preside and participate at the same time. It's hard to lose myself in the presence of God when I'm the one appointed to not lose my head. Somebody's got to make sure the songs move in the right thematic flow, in the perfect emotional key of elation or exhortation or solemnity. *Is that guitar's B-string a half note flat? Is that background singer doing unison when she should sing a one-sixth harmony part? Why are they doing another song when I told them the offering had to be taken before half-past?*

What if the ox stumbles and the ark falls off? Who will reach out their hand and steady it? Who will protect God? Somebody's got to pay attention here. Not everyone can dance.

Dead.

Uzzah teaches us, at great personal cost, a valuable lesson about God. God is not safe. God is not a household deity, kept in our safekeeping. And—be warned—God's safety is not our business. Our role on this earth, be it prophet, king, priest, or bank teller, is not to keep the Almighty from mishap or embarrassment. He takes care of Himself.

It is, the writer of Hebrews says, a fearful thing to fall into the hands of the living God. He's dangerous, not safe at all. And yet there is something far more fearful and dangerous than to fall into His hands: to *not* fall into His hands. But perhaps the most fearful and dangerous thing of all is the sin of Uzzah: to think that our job is, should God stumble, to ensure He falls into our hands.

The safest thing to do with a God like this is not to play it safe with Him. It is to never get so caught up in keeping the traditions or hastening the innovations that we forget to throw ourselves headlong into His brusque and tender embrace. It is to never get so busy protecting God that we fail to take refuge in Him. It is to never become so preoccupied in our Keep God Safe march that we forget to dance before our God with all our might, heedless of borderland's rules, tripping the light fantastic all the way into the holy wild.

Uzzah was struck dead by God. But in ways that matter most, he was dead already.

I TALKED TO A WOMAN RECENTLY WHO SAID THAT WHEN SHE FIRST became a Christian, someone told her to imagine Jesus sitting beside her when she drove her car. Then she could talk with Jesus. So she did this. What she found for the longest time is that this was no sweet lullaby time, being crooned over and coddled. No, she had shouting matches with Jesus. "Sometimes," she said, "I would be hollering at Him. Just screaming my head off. I really needed Him to talk straight with me, and I was angry about a lot of things. 'Why is it always Your way, Jesus? Why always in Your time? Sometimes, frankly, Your way and Your time seem lousy.'" Some of the psalms read like that, a sustained shriek at God.

I had dinner once with some people who were uncomfortably surprised to learn I was a pastor. After a moment of awkward silence, the lady ventured a broad theological claim: "Well, that's nice. I've always felt that churches serve an important role in society. They are safe havens. People should be able to go into a church and escape reality for a little while."

I couldn't resist: "You know, somehow I missed all that when I last read the book of Acts."

Your God is too safe.

The safe god asks nothing of us, gives nothing to us. He never drives us to our knees in hungry, desperate praying and never sets us on our feet in fierce, fixed determination. He never makes us bold to dance. The safe god never whispers in our ears anything but greeting card slogans and certainly never asks that we embarrass ourselves by shouting out from the rooftop. He doesn't make us a kingdom of priests, only a colony of Uzzahs.

A safe god inspires neither awe, nor worship, nor sacrifice.

A safe god woos us to borderland and keeps us stuck there. He helps us escape reality.

In C. S. Lewis's most famous Narnia chronicle, *The Lion, The Witch and the Wardrobe,* the children—Peter, Susan, Lucy, and Edmund—enter Narnia through a wardrobe in their uncle's home. Edmund has already given allegiance to the witch and sneaks off to join ranks with her. The other three children go the home of the Beavers, a wary but hospitable pair. Mr. and Mrs. Beaver tell the children that they will take them to see the King, Aslan.

"Is—is he a man?" asked Lucy.

"Aslan a man!" said Mr. Beaver sternly. "Certainly not. I tell you he is the King of the wood and the son of the great Emperor-Beyond-the-Sea. Don't you know who is the King of Beasts? Aslan is a lion—*the* Lion, the great Lion."

"Ooh," said Susan, "I thought he was a man. Is he—quite safe? I shall feel rather nervous about meeting a lion."

"That you will, dearie, and no mistake," said Mrs. Beaver; "if there's anyone who can appear before Aslan without their knees knocking, they're either braver than most or else just silly."

"Then he isn't safe?" said Lucy.

"Safe?" said Mr. Beaver; "don't you hear what Mrs. Beaver tells you? Who said anything about safe? 'Course he isn't safe. But he's good. He's the king, I tell you."[1]

Safe? Don't you hear what I'm saying? Who said anything about safe? 'Course He's not safe.

But He's good.

I did a funeral once for a lady who was a Christian, but few of her many children and grandchildren were. I thought I spoke the gospel clearly and boldly. Afterward, a woman came up to me. "Thank you," she said. "That was so *nice* what you said. It was really *nice*. I'm religious, too. The family always ask me to pray for the weather when we go golfing."

I reckon this: the idol of the nice god, the safe god, has done more damage to biblical faith—more damage to people coming to faith—than the caricature of the tyrant god ever did. The despotic god, howling his rage, wielding punishment with both ransacking destruction and surgical precision, at least inspired something in us. We were afraid. We wanted to appease. But this Milquetoast-Pampering deity is nothing but a cosmic lackey, an errand boy we call on to make our golf games pleasant or to help us escape reality for a little while and then summarily dismiss. Worship him? Revere him? Die for him? Believe that he died a cruel and bloody death for us? You must be kidding.

It is a strange habit of ours, that we fling so widely to the extremes but rarely find the middle. God's wrath and sovereignty we easily caricature into tyranny. And God's kindness and tender mercies we just as easily transmute into mere niceness. Meanwhile, the God who actually is—the God whose ways of speaking and acting and being are disclosed to us in Scripture—continues through Christ, "full of grace and truth," to come among "that which is his own." And, as before, "his own do not receive him" because they "do not recognize him" (John 1:10, 11, 14). Scripture elsewhere tells us that the "ruler of the air has blinded our eyes" to the truth. But one of the main ways the devil has done that is through the cult of the safe god. The safe god has pretty much killed the power of recognition in us, and so when the real God comes into our midst, we mostly don't even bother to look up.

The safe god has no power to console us in grief or shake us from complacency or rescue us from the pit. He just putters in his garden, smiles benignly, waves now and then, and mostly spends a lot of time in his room doing puzzles. Who would leave borderland for another kind of god? The excuse I hear most often when people continue in a confessed sin is: "I think God understands. The kind of God I worship isn't all hung up about this." It's as though God were a half-daft old uncle, hair sprouting from his ears, a bit runny about the eyes, winking at our little pranks and peccadilloes.

Well, that's nice.

But God isn't nice. God isn't safe. God is a consuming fire. Though He cares about the sparrow, the embodiment of His care is rarely doting or pampering. God's main business is not ensuring that you and I get parking spaces close to the mall entrance or that the bed sheets in the color we want are—miracle!—on sale this week.

His main business is making you and me holy. And for those of us who love borderland more than holy ground, whose hearts are more slow than burning, that always requires both the kindness and the sternness of our God.

Historians tell us the cult of Mary arose in Catholicism because the medieval portrait of God was so dark and punishing—the wrathful Father, always at the edge of a tantrum—that the common folk needed a sweet, understanding mother to turn to, to hide behind, to intervene for them. In Protestantism, I think we've simply substituted the safe god. But the biting irony is this: Neither the safe god nor the tyrant god are the real God. The God who truly is, who seeks you and me, who desires our holiness, is far more loving and comforting than the safe god. And the true God is far more fierce and fearsome than the bullying and petulant god of our imaginations. But His anger is not irritability: It is the distillation of His justice, His hatred of evil. It is what we would want, even demand, from a good God.

Moses captures the paradox well. After the people of Israel witness God's awesome power and beg Moses not to let God speak to them, Moses responds, "Do not be afraid. God has come to test you, so that the fear of God will be with you to keep you from sinning" (Exodus 20:20). *Do not be afraid...so that the fear of God will be with you to keep you from sinning.* As A. W. Tozer remarked, we take refuge *from* God *in* God. Only a God we fear and yet do not need to be afraid of can make our slow hearts burn. Only this God can dislodge us from borderland. Only this God wants us to be holy and has the power to make us so.

The safe god is only the patron deity of rainless golf games. He doesn't even do that well.

IN THE BOOK OF JUDGES, AN ANGEL OF THE LORD VISITS GIDEON. Gideon is threshing wheat in a winepress. Winepresses are lousy places for threshing wheat—the wind can't sweep through clean and brisk and carry off the chaff—but they're good places to hide. Gideon's hiding. He's hiding from the Midianites—a nation of raiders who swoop down on the Israelites every harvest season and plunder their grain after the hard work's been done.

The angel addresses Gideon: "Hail, Mighty Warrior." This is, of course, ridiculous. Gideon is a coward and says as much himself. But the angel is not hailing what Gideon is now. He hails what Gideon is to become.

You probably know this story: Gideon is made the general of an army that, through God's odd recruitment program, amounts to a meager 300, and they are sent out against 135,000 Midianites. They are equipped with clay pots, torches, and horns. That's it. No weapons, no shields. And they come up against seasoned fighters who are bristling with armaments and have a cavalry of camels as well. But Gideon leads his men to victory—complete victory. That's a famous story, deeply cherished.

But there is one part that we usually forget. Before Gideon is fit to be God's general, to be a mighty warrior, he has a task *he* must do: destroy the idols in his own backyard. And after destroying them, he is told to build in their place, on their ruins, a proper altar to the one true God.

"And Gideon took ten men of his servants and did as the Lord told him. *But because he was afraid* of his family and the men of his town, he did it at night rather than the daytime" (Judges 6:30, emphasis mine). It is a fearful thing to fall into the hands of the living God, this God who claims us so completely, uncompromisingly, that He often puts us at odds with family, with the men of the town. This God brooks no rivals and orders us to tear them down with our own hands. This God calls us out of secluded winepresses and into open battlefields.

Why leave borderland to follow Him? Why ruin the idol of the safe god and risk our good standing in the community? Why, with a mere promise from this God, take our little ragtag army and go up weaponless against a ruthless, sprawling, well-armed foe?

Why? Because the safe god is actually your worst enemy. He is in the pay of the Midianites. He breeds cowardice. He plunders your fields. He keeps you stuck, complacent, bored, angry, threshing your meager wheat where the wind never blows.

And the God who is *not* safe hails you as mighty warrior and wants to show you wonders and fully intends to rout the ancient oppressor and set you free.

The Lord is with you, mighty warrior. Now go, tear down the idol of the safe god, this flimsy, gimcrack invention cobbled together from faintheartedness and softheadedness. On its ruins, build a real altar to the true God.

Safe? Who said anything about safe? 'Course He's not safe.

But He's good.

Chapter Three

COUNTING
DEAD FISH

Bette Midler topped the music charts a decade ago with a song about God's watchful care. "From a distance," Bette sings, her voice swinging from cocktail lounge croon to roadhouse belt, "God is watching us." The song's popularity, I think, was based on something other than its musical qualities. It expressed a deep and culturewide theological sentiment: We want a God who provides but doesn't intrude, who protects but never demands, never judges, never meddles. We want a God who keeps His distance and doesn't crowd us.

I've been talking about the unhealthy way we sometimes fear God and so try to make Him more safe. Maybe you think that this fear I've described, this cringing, flighty fear, was a uniquely Old Testament response to God, when He was more prone to show up in storm and fire, dressed in tempest. Maybe you think that in the New Testament, when God appears as Jesus—meek and mild, the one who calms the storms but doesn't stir them—such fear naturally dispels.

But then there's the apostle Peter, who figures prominently into a Gospel story that can be read in two distinct, contrasting ways. It's the story where Jesus calls Peter, James, and John. Jesus goes out on the fish boat with the weary, empty-handed fishermen, and urges them to try their nets again. Peter protests but does it anyhow. And, lo, the nets teem with fish. Peter looks at Jesus and then falls on his face. "Depart from me," he says, "for I am a sinful man" (Luke 5:1–11).

This can be read piously. We might take Peter's protest at face value: Peter is a sinful man, and he comes to fresh, stinging awareness and confession of the fact. Peter realizes who Jesus is—His majesty, His power, His divinity—and in that instant sees his own smallness and dirtiness, his life as a shabby chronicle of failures and half-starts, of lapses and losses. Shame drives him.

But Luke makes this reading hard to sustain. Luke makes a cynical, wary reading more plausible: This is one place in the Gospels where a hermeneutic of suspicion is almost demanded. Because this is what Luke records in the scene just prior to the fish boat encounter:

> Jesus left the synagogue and went to the home of Simon [that is, Peter]. Now Simon's mother-in-law was suffering from a high fever, and they asked Jesus to help her. So he bent over her and rebuked the fever and it left her. She got up at once and began to wait on them.
>
> When the sun was setting, the people brought to Jesus all who had various kinds of sickness, and laying his hands on each one, he healed them. Moreover, demons came out of many people, shouting, "You are the Son of God!" (Luke 4:38–41)

Presumably, Peter witnesses all of this—it happens on the doorstep or in the living room of his house. But where is the falling on his face in sudden agonizing awareness that he is a sinful man standing before the one whom even the demons declare to be the "Son of God"? Peter just keeps on drinking his after-dinner coffee, glancing at the classifieds for a good used rototiller. Nothing seems out of sorts for him, out of the ordinary. No need here to fall on his face.

So why, on the fish boat, does Peter suddenly recognize the power and holiness of Jesus?

Imagine the moment—the exhilaration of it, that dizzy, giddy sensation of pay dirt and breakthrough. Finally the drought has ended, the rain has returned. All the cherries pop up in a row—click! click! click!—and the windfall rushes at him. The numbered balls roll out; he compares them with the creased lottery ticket in his hand, gaping, gasping: "Those are my numbers! Mine!"

Imagine the moment. Fish scales fleck Peter's hands like gold dust, diamond shavings. *Ah, wait till the wife hears. We'll take that dreamed-of vacation down at the seaside resort of Joppa. Hey, maybe we'll buy an RV. Or pay off the house. Hmm, I wonder. I wonder if the wife will let me buy that Boston Whaler I've been eyeing down at the marina, the one with swivel seats and locking rod holders and depth sounder and that pop-up canopy for when it rains.*

Imagine the moment. Laughing, laughing, heart light and huge with laughter, the weariness of the long night falling swiftly away. Peter, in his laughter, looks at Jesus. Maybe Peter's about to recruit Jesus, make him a partner with, say, 10 percent of the profits to begin. Maybe…

But there's a strange look in Jesus' eyes. A wild, burning, dangerous look. And Peter gets a hunch about what's coming: that Jesus' calling is not to follow Peter. His role and task in life is not to advance Peter's career, enhance Peter's reputation, thicken Peter's wallet. Peter sees all that in Jesus' eyes. He sees that Jesus is not the man who exists simply to come onto our fish boats and fill up our nets. Peter must know what Jesus is about to say: "Follow me." Which means—ah, why does it have to mean this?—*leave everything.* The fish. The boat. The nets. The safety. The security. The prospects.

Leave everything.

Now imagine the moment. Peter falls on his face, begs Jesus to leave. *Depart from me.*

Somebody's got to leave. Either Peter leaves everything, or Jesus leaves Peter.

That happens every day somewhere. Jesus comes onto our boat and fills up our nets—a job promotion, a new house, a new car, a big raise. And our prayer is: "Oh, Lord, depart from me." Which means: Don't take it away. You leave me alone, Jesus, so that I don't have to leave this behind. Go away and don't interfere with my unbridled pleasure-taking in it.

But I'll call if the fishing gets scarce again.

I have noticed a distinct pattern in my own life and in the lives of those I serve as a pastor. The pattern is this: When we have before us a decision that is to our own benefit—the offer of a job that pays more and confers more clout, the opportunity to buy a bigger house or a newer car, the decision to invest or spend an inheritance—few of us rarely seek honest, prayerful counsel. These are, we contend, private matters, deeply personal, nobody's business but our own. But when we're in trouble—facing the loss of our job, foreclosure on our house, the misappropriation of an inheritance by a wicked cousin—ah, then suddenly we are begging Jesus and begging His people to come on board and help, please help, to fill the nets.

I have never had anyone, not one person, ask me to pray about and give guidance in how best to handle their investments. That's remarkable when you think about it. It is unmistakably clear that mammon and God are in pitched battle. Where our treasures are, there our hearts are also. If there is one area in which I would have expected my pastoral counsel would be much sought and highly prized, it's in the matter of money—how best to be a steward and a giver of it, how to keep our lives free from the love of it. But it's simply not so.

Yet I have had many come to me asking for my prayers, thoughts, comfort, and direction—to mediate the presence of Jesus Christ, to help them know the mind of Christ—as they've faced bankruptcy. Mainly what I'm asked to pray for is that the bankruptcy can be averted or the worst of it can be mitigated, that though the boat capsize and all the nets tear, yet still will there be a few fish flopping in the rags.

I, too, operate in this pattern. I have little interest in knowing the will of God concerning my windfalls, but much interest in having the provision of Christ in my pitfalls. I want to be rescued but not bothered, comforted but never disrupted, soothed but not disturbed.

I love borderland, actually. Borderland is the fish boat I know. I know every creak and warp in its planking, every patch on its sheets, every splice in its nets. I know its smell of fish oil and fish guts, brine, bilge water, salt air. I know how a constant rubbing has worn the ropes ragged and the gunnels smooth, and I find an inexplicable comfort in this. I know what a twist and downward plunge of the nets means, what a circling of birds overhead means, what a line of spindrift along the water's surface means. I know this fish boat, and the only reason I want Jesus on board is if He plans to be part deckhand, part shaman: the one who, by shrewdness or magic, fills the nets.

Curious: The apostle Peter goes back to his fish boat three years later. Jesus has been crucified. Jesus has been resurrected. Jesus has appeared to His disciples, including Peter. He has told them not to be afraid. He has told them not to doubt. He has breathed the Holy Spirit upon them. He has given them authority and a promise and a clear commission: Go, preach to all nations, and teach them. I will be with you always, in all things. As the Father has sent Me, so I am sending you. Go!

And Peter goes…back to his fish boat.

So Jesus comes along the beach one day and replays with Peter and his companions the whole scene of the boats and fishes and overflowing fishnets.

Afterward, Jesus appeared again to his disciples, by the Sea of Tiberius. It happened this way: Simon Peter, Thomas (called Didymus), Nathaniel from Cana in Galilee, the sons of Zebedee, and two other disciples were together. "I'm going out to fish," Simon Peter told them, and they said, "We'll go with you." So they went out and got into the boat, but that night they caught nothing.

Early in the morning, Jesus stood on the shore, but the disciples did not realize that it was Jesus.

He called out to them, "Friends, haven't you any fish?"

"No," they answered.

He said, "Throw your net on the right side of the boat and you will find some." When they did, they were unable to haul the net in because of the large number of fish. (John 21:1–6)

Peter recognizes then that it is Jesus and jumps into the water to get to Him. The other disciples come, too, and they have breakfast with Jesus, using some of the fish. Then Jesus turns to Peter: "Simon, son of John, do you truly love me more than these?" (John 21:15).

And then Jesus does it again: "Follow me." Leave it, all of it, and follow me. But what was Peter doing on that boat again, anyhow?

Borderland, that boat is. Refuge of the slow hearted. The charter trip for those who want life predictable, quiet, settled, safe—who want, not to go out to the deep, wild sea, but to hug the shore. Who prefer a safe God who keeps His distance.

Every Sunday I get up in front of five hundred people and find myself preaching from a fish boat to people on fish boats. It doesn't matter that we finished last Sunday committing, with fresh and joyful resolve, to live in the power of the Resurrection and to go out into all the earth and make disciples. Sometime around Wednesday—or, for some of us, between the church foyer and our parking stall—we found ourselves almost mindlessly wandering toward our fish boat, climbing on, setting sail.

Why do people get close to God? Why do you? When I subject my own motives to the sharpest and roughest scrutiny, I find, very often, that the God I'm looking for is the God who follows me—comes onto my fish boat, fills up my nets. But I fear the God who becomes concretely personal in Jesus, who confronts me with a stark command, barren of option: *Follow Me.*

But what about all this stuff, Jesus—these boats and fish? Why did You give me all these fish at this particular moment? Why didn't You ask me to follow You last night, when I hated my job, when I would have given anything for an excuse to walk away from it? Why do You do that, Jesus? Why get everything going my way and then ask me to forsake it?

Follow Me.

Follow You where?

Where I lead you.

To do what?

What I tell you.

For how long?

He doesn't say, but we know He means forever.

There's only one certainty about this. We know what we'll get if we refuse: to sit on wet stones and count dead fish.

WE USUALLY APPLAUD ANY GESTURE OF INTIMACY TOWARD JESUS. If the impulse to flee is from our fallen nature, then surely any impulse to approach, to draw near, is a sign of redemptive health. If "depart from me, Lord" is the motto of the sinful man, then "come to me, Lord" must be the life verse of the holy one.

Maybe.

But maybe not.

Watch James and John. They approach Jesus and implore Him to do whatever they ask of Him.

"What is it you want Me to do for you?" He asks.

"We want to sit on Your left and Your right when You come into Your kingdom," they respond.

Jesus basically tells them no.

A few verses later, a blind man sits by the road as Jesus passes by with His entourage. Picture him: grubby and shabby. He's dirty from not being able to look in a mirror and see himself, from not knowing that a cowlick in his hair needs smoothing down with spittle, that little bits of encrusted food need scrubbing off his face. And long ago he stopped caring anyhow. His blind eyes are dead and gray like stones, thick at the edges with oozing. But he hears Jesus pass by, and an old longing stirs up.

"Jesus, Son of David," he bellows, "have mercy on me!"

Simple, desperate, direct. But there's a problem: Those who "lead the way" (maybe it's James and John) tell him to shut up.

But he won't. No, he's going to keep right on shouting, disrupting the parade, disturbing the peace—shouting down all those who make rules about who can and who cannot come to Jesus. And Jesus hears, and Jesus invites him to come forward.

"What is it you want Me to do for you?"

There's that question again, word for word.

The blind man answers, "I want to see." Jesus, who refused James's and John's request, grants this man's. Jesus gives him his sight. Luke's account says that he then "followed Jesus, praising God" (Luke 18:35–43).

Let me ask again: Why do you want to get close to Jesus? *What do you want Him to do for you?* Some come so that they can lead the way, sit at His right or at His left. But some come simply so that they can see and follow and praise.

Let's admit it: Jesus is powerful, and power lures, mesmerizes. It sings like a siren and drives like a galley master. It caresses like the brush of angel wings and stings like the bite of adders. Henry Kissinger called power the great aphrodisiac. Why do we get close to people with power? Why do men and women vie for positions in the prime minister's cabinets? Why do they jockey for status among the president's advisors? Presumably, some just want to serve and see power as the fount from which they can, the fulcrum upon which they can move the earth. But others, maybe most, find the power hypnotic, addictive.

And so here is Jesus, full of power, asking, "What is it you want Me to do for you?" We typically applaud people who want to get closer to Jesus. But that in itself tells only half a story. The movement toward Jesus begs interpretation. The motives need to be searched, parsed.

"What is it you want Me to do for you?" Jesus asks.

So much depends on our answer.

Chapter Four

ANOTHER SIGN
OF JONAH

I sometimes picture the prophets rendered in portraits and sculptures all housed together in a vast, hushed art museum. A museum guide walks a crowd through the gallery:

On your left is the sculpture of Isaiah, carved by the strong, deft hands of Michelangelo. Note the huge, hulking form, how Isaiah's torso swells and twists with muscle. His passion for God strains through every cord and sinew. See how his eyes, even in marble, blaze fire.

Now, to your right is a painting of Jeremiah by, of course, Rembrandt. Study his use of dark, mournful colors, how the shadows convey an atmosphere of hauntedness and grief, how potently the strong brush stroke evokes the inner divisions of Jeremiah.

Next to him is Peter Paul Ruben's Elijah. The artist's bright, tumultuous style, his use of blurred contour to convey brisk motion perfectly captures the prophet's wild muscularity, his fierceness, his boldness, his terrible aliveness.

And on this wall, Daniel. Notice how the Dutch master Jan Vermeer has painstakingly rendered Daniel's calm serenity and shrewd piety in solid Spartan color, and note, too, his careful attention to detail in the backdrop of the Persian court.

Ah, next to him, Ezekiel. You will recognize Picasso's cubist style: the skewed, scattered jumble of shapes, the disarray of lines and forms, and how compellingly it conjures that prophet's tormented greatness, his cockeyed dignity.

Over here, Eduard Munk, in the same garish, churning style as his more famous painting *The Scream,* has attempted to capture Hosea's lovesickness for his wayward wife.

Ladies and gentlemen, that almost concludes our tour. But saving the masterpiece for last, I invite you to step over here and draw near to the framed portrait in the far corner. There you will behold a stunningly realistic depiction of the prophet Jonah.

And here awaits a surprise. In the frame marked "Jonah" is not a portrait, but a mirror. Jonah is us.

If borderland has a king, his name is Jonah. Jonah is that land's tribal chieftain, its mascot and spokesman. He writes its shifting decrees, renders its vague judgments, presides over its noisy assemblies, embodies its evasive spirit.

Yet Jesus identified Himself with Jonah. You know the scene. One day some Pharisees and teachers of the law asked Jesus for a miraculous sign. *Impress us, Jesus. Convince us, Jesus. We've heard rumors of Your sleight of hand with water and wine, Your conjuring tricks with bread and fish, Your banishing stunts with demons and pigs. The word's out that You're Messiah, but we demand credentials. Give us a sign.*

Jesus rebukes them: "A wicked and adulterous generation asks for a miraculous sign! But none will be given it except the sign of the prophet Jonah" (Matthew 12:39).

Jonah? *That* runt, *that* rebel, *that* sulking, self-serving malcontent? Jonah and Jesus? As the Pharisees were so fond of pointing out, Jesus never could choose His friends very well.

I know what you're thinking: *That's not what Jesus meant.* The sign of Jonah is an image of Jesus' dying and rising (Matthew's emphasis, in chapter 12); the sign of Jonah is a warning to Israel that, though even wicked Nineveh repented at the preaching of Jonah, they are in danger of refusing one "greater than Jonah" (Luke's emphasis, in chapter 11).

But I wonder. I wonder if, in part, Jesus' willingness to identify Himself with Jonah—and in front of Jonahlike Pharisees, no less—isn't exactly the point. I wonder if the sign of Jonah is an image, not just of dying and rising, not just of hearing and heeding, but also of incarnation and crucifixion—of Jesus coming to be with us, to share in our fallen humanity, to empty Himself, to become sin for us.

You mean *Jonah?* The one who runs from God? The one upon whom God wants to pour out grace, through whom God wants to extend grace to others, but who resists, rebels, runs? Jesus and Jonah? Well, if the Incarnation and the Cross represent Jesus' willingness to stand alongside with, and finally to die in the place of, those who are God's enemies, what better mascot could Jesus have than Jonah? Jonah is us—a borderland dweller, a slow-hearted disciple, keeper of the Keep God Safe Society.

No sign will be given you except that of the prophet Jonah.

BUT LET'S BE FAIR. JONAH HAS GOOD HISTORICAL REASONS, good personal reasons, for fleeing God. God wants to send him on a nasty mission: to Nineveh, the capital of Assyria. Assyria was a nation cruel and blood-thirsty, both capricious and calculated in doing evil. The Assyrian's specialty was sacking and burning. They were a looming threat for the northern kingdom of Israel, and within seventy years of Jonah's ministry they would carry Israel into exile. They were not good people. Think of someone who has hurt you, betrayed you, threatened to devour you. Think, if you can, of someone you hate or have good reason to. That's an Assyrian. Jonah is sent to their capital.

The story of Jonah stirs up a dark suspicion we have about God. The suspicion is: *God will always ask me to do the thing I least want to do, to go to the very last place I desire to go. If I say I won't go to the prairies or India, God is sure to send me there. If I tell Him I hate Bosnians or Tutsis or French Canadians, that's exactly to whom He'll send me.*

Let's state the suspicion in theological terms: *God is a hard man, harvesting where He has not sown, gathering where He has not scattered seed.*

This suspicion—that God is out to get me, to humiliate me, to deprive me, that He *really did say* I couldn't eat from any of the trees in the Garden—is what lies mostly behind our impulse to flee God. What kind of God is God?

"Well," Jonah answers, "He wants to send you to the hellish Ninevites. And if you bolt, He'll loose the hell of storms and swallowing sea beasts upon you."

That's the suspicion. Is it so?

I heard Paul Yonggi Cho speak a few years back. Yonggi Cho is pastor of the largest church in the world. Several years ago, as his ministry was becoming international, he told God, "I will go anywhere to preach the gospel—except Japan." He hated the Japanese with gut-deep loathing because of what Japanese troops had done to the Korean people and to members of Yonggi Cho's own family during World War II. The Japanese were his Ninevites.

Through a combination of a prolonged inner struggle, several direct challenges from others, and finally an urgent and starkly worded invitation, Cho felt called by God to preach in Japan. *Oh, You're a hard man, harvesting where You have not sown.* He went, but he went with bitterness. The first speaking engagement was to a pastor's conference—a thousand Japanese pastors. Cho stood up to speak, and what came out of his mouth was this: "I hate you. I hate you. I hate you." And then he broke and wept. He was both brimming and desolate with hatred.

At first one, then two, then all thousand pastors stood up. One by one they walked up to Yonggi Cho, knelt at his feet, and asked forgiveness for what they and their people had done to him and his people. As this went on, God changed Yonggi Cho. The Lord put a single message in his heart and mouth: "I love you. I love you. I love you."

Sometimes God calls us to do what we least want to do in order to reveal our heart—to reveal what's really in our heart. How powerful is the blood of Christ, Reverend Cho? What are the limits of forgiveness, anyhow? How far does the gospel of peace, the ministry of reconciliation, reach? Can it heal hatred between Koreans and Japanese? Can it make a Jew love a Ninevite? Can it make you be reconciled to...well, you know who?

Ah, maybe that's the problem. As it turns out, Jonah is not afraid God is too hard. His suspicion actually runs in exactly the opposite direction: God is too soft.

"O LORD, is this not what I said when I was still at home? That is why I was so quick to flee.... I knew that you were a gracious and compassionate God, slow to anger and abounding in love, a God who relents from sending calamity" (Jonah 4:2–3).

What use is it denouncing murderous Ninevites if they can simply repent and God will show them mercy? What kind of God would do such a thing? He's neither tame enough nor tough enough.

He's not safe either way.

The portrait of God that emerges from the story of Jonah is a God both too hard and too soft—too hard on us and too soft on our enemies. He's stern toward His children and indulgent toward strangers. He scolds all the wrong people, pampers all the wrong people. He gives fatted calves to prodigals, but not so much as a goat to His dutiful sons.

Maybe we understand Jonah very well, understand his impulse to run. It's hard to draw close to a God and be perfect as He is perfect and holy as He is holy, when He so clearly doesn't cherish what we cherish or hate whom we hate—who won't share our fetishes or grievances or prejudices. When He's too soft and too hard. When He's not safe.

Put starkly: It's hard to obey a God like that.

OBEY. I USED TO THINK JONAH'S CENTRAL LESSON—ITS MORAL, the nugget to mine for sermons or Sunday school—was how important it is to obey God. After all, disobedience is costly for Jonah: a sea storm, a near drowning, a fish belly. And, in the end, the same unbending command: Go!

But I don't think that's the story's main thrust. For one thing, God uses Jonah's disobedience rather effectively. The reluctant prophet becomes the accidental evangelist. He boards ship with pagan sailors to Tarshish. Jonah's not interested in these men. He's avoiding not just God but everyone. He goes down into the hold of the boat to sleep. But God sends a storm. The sailors, decent men, try everything to save the boat from going down. Then, when all that fails, they wake up Jonah and ask him to pray. That doesn't work either. They cast lots to find out who's causing the trouble and—wouldn't you know—the lot falls on Jonah.

"Who are you?" they ask. "Where do you come from? What do you do?" (Often pagans have to force us to identify ourselves.)

Jonah answers with what sounds like staggering smugness: "I am a Hebrew and I worship the LORD, the God of heaven, who made the sea and the land" (Jonah 1:8–9).

They keep trying, with all strength, courage, ingenuity, to save the ship and themselves, but nothing doing. So, at Jonah's bidding, they toss him overboard. Earlier, these men prayed earnestly to their own gods (1:5). But in our last glimpse of them—we see their boat, their faces, blur and darken as the water surges up above Jonah's sinking body—they fear and make sacrifices and vows to Jonah's God, the Lord, the God of heaven, who made the sea and the land. God uses Jonah's disobedience, openly confessed, as an opportunity to reveal Himself to pagan sailors (1:10).

God is not interested in our obedience so much for His sake. He can just as well use our disobedience. Obedience is for our own good.

But in the end obedience by itself is not much good.

Under compulsion, Jonah finally does the will of God. He trudges off to Nineveh and preaches as he's told. He is obedient. But he's more miserable in his obedience than he was in his disobedience. In the ocean's depths, in the fish's belly, in his disobedience, Jonah feared death and prayed for deliverance (2:7). But under the wilted vine, with Nineveh saved, in his obedience, Jonah longs for death and prays for God to deal it swiftly and unflinchingly (4:3).

"Trust and obey, for there's no other way to be happy in Jesus than to trust and obey." Jonah didn't write that song. Jonah doesn't sing that song. Jonah hates that song.

Is God solely, or mostly, interested in our obedience?

Oh, God wants our obedience. But actually He wants something deeper down than that. Bare obedience can harden us to God more than disobedience can. If you doubt it, compare the older boy with the younger one in the parable of the prodigal; compare the Pharisees and religious rulers with the tax collectors and prostitutes in the stories about Jesus. Or just look at Jonah. Obedience by itself can make our heart withered and bitter and barren as a husk.

What is God mostly interested in? Strangely, anticlimactically, it has to do with *concerns*—with what our hearts fix on, with what stirs us in the depths and makes us rise to the heights. What are we *concerned* about? Is it what God is *concerned* about? Both Jonah's disobedience and his obedience rise up from the same source: *from what he is concerned about.* He's concerned about himself. He is looking for the path of least resistance, the way of greatest convenience. He'll do whatever he must—obey, disobey, go to Nineveh, flee to Tarshish—to get God off his back. He'll find the thing that God disrupts the least and do that. The last thing Jonah wants is for God's concerns to be his own. The last thing Jonah wants is the too soft, too hard God to get too close. Jonah just wants to dwell on borderland, undisturbed and safe.

I'm just old enough to remember that at one time, not long ago really, the central task for the faithful preacher of Jonah was to convince hard-bitten, science-bred parishioners that there are fish in the sea big enough to swallow a man whole and to explicate just exactly how a man could survive intact three days inside such a fish. The main hermeneutic for the book was not theology, but ichthyology. So now let me confess my secret heresy: The fish question is beside the point.

The real puzzle of Jonah—its perpetual source of wonder and doubt—is this: Why is God so deeply concerned about not just Nineveh, but this man Jonah? This sulking, griping, stingy, self-absorbed little man—why him? Why would God pursue him to the ends of the earth, to the bottom of the sea, to the outskirts of Nineveh? Why should God keep trying to roust him off his borderland? Why would God keep chasing a man who flees Him?

Why doesn't God just honor Jonah's wish and leave him alone?

Because God is too concerned.

I BOUGHT A RHODODENDRON BUSH TWO SUMMERS AGO. I PAID $8.99—a cut rate, because it was well past planting season and the plant's leaves had a blight, a charred brittleness at their edges. But the earth around here is endlessly fertile, and I figured it would do fine. I was right. I planted the rhododendron in my front yard, and it flourished. The leaves turned a waxy dark green, and the next spring it flamed bright with pink-red flowers. A burning bush.

I live in a cul-de-sac that's perfect for playing road hockey—flat, wide, little traffic. Teenagers from all over the place descend on the street on summer evenings and engage in noisy, tussling hockey games. One morning after the neighborhood teens had been playing road hockey the evening before, I went out to water my rhododendron. I looked down and saw that a large branch from the bush had been raggedly broken off. I picked up the branch, and a wave of bitterness and anger came over me. *Should I phone the city, I wondered, and have hockey banned on my street? Should I go out when those teenagers return this evening and scold and threaten them?*

"Mark," the Lord said, "do you have any right to be angry?"

"I do."

But the Lord said, "That's just a cut-rate bush that you neither made nor tended. You merely planted it, and it grew. But these boys are My creation, made in My image. Should I *not* be concerned about them?"

Should God *not* be concerned about Nineveh or New York or Duncan, British Columbia?

Should He *not* be concerned about teenagers playing road hockey, breaking bushes?

Should He *not* be concerned about smug, sullen prophets?

Should He *not* be concerned about middle-class, middle-aged pastors who stew over broken rhododendrons?

Should He, plain and simple, just *not* be concerned?

More and more, I see how my whole view of God—and my relationship with Him—depends on how I answer that.

Equally, it depends on my refusal to answer. For borderland has many former prophets who now are only bitter men, quarrelsome, sun-scorched, angry enough to die, or too dead inside even to be angry anymore.

Chapter Five

WHATEVER HAPPENED TO WONDER?

L ast night the world shifted," E. B. White wrote many years ago in the *New Yorker.* "There was a total eclipse of the moon, and the weather conditions were such that most people could have watched it from their front lawns. But most people watched it on television."

It is strange that technology has done so much to diminish us. It has, of course, done much, staggeringly so, to empower us. It is, in fact, a harbinger of both freedom and captivity. Sometimes the two are so tightly entwined that it's hard to know where one ends and the other begins. Movies are being made now with the massive help of technology that play on our encroaching fear that this cornucopia of whizzing, whirring, shiny things could be our downfall. The modern catastrophe movie usually has at its center some evil mastermind tweaking a computer, rummaging around in someone else's database. It's as though Revelation's bowl of plagues is a software virus, an electronic version of mad cow disease. Like Delilah, technology has wooed us in order to kill us.

We've pinned so much hope on machines. The yearning and wishing we once attached to relics, saints' bones, and talismans, we now give to gadgets. The energy we once poured into prayer, we have shunted over to computers. And in truth the machines we keep coming up with are increasingly more wonderful. They speak to us, and we speak back to them. They work, unceasing and uncomplaining, while we play, eat, sleep. They can save the little girl whose back was broken in a car accident from being a cripple for life, save the man with a clogged and bloated heart from sure death. The blind see; the lame walk; the hungry have good things to eat. That is technology's blessing.

But here's an irony: Machines are so wonderful that they have killed wonder in us. Here's another: They are such an answer to prayer that they have almost eliminated our sense of the need to pray. And another: They are stunning monuments to the power of our imagination and have come close to obliterating our imaginative powers. We now watch eclipses on television or simulate them on interactive CDs. The screen has replaced the heavens.

The fallout from this is very great. We have largely lost our capacity for wonder and imagination. All blame for this, of course, can't be laid at the feet of technology. Though technology has been a catalyst for it and a crowning of it, the loss of imagination has been a long time in the making. Many forces have shaped and filled it or, perhaps better said, *emptied* it. Whatever the exact causes, this is certain: Imagination is anemic today, and nowhere is this more evident than in most of our churches. We fear imagination, believing it somehow undermines the purity of truth. We think it threatens the integrity, the intactness and exactness, of our finely wrought doctrines. So we build in our churches intellectual ramparts against it. When was the last time you saw good art in a church?

There's almost no awareness that maybe imagination is the missing link between having a doctrine and living it. What's at stake is our ability to know God and worship Him. "If you want to change a people's obedience," the language scholar Paul Ricouer said, "you must change their imagination." Yes. A good case could be made that Jesus' primary way of reaching the lost was appealing to their imaginations—vivid, simple stories about life in the kingdom, the character of God, the nature of grace, forgiveness, joy, illustrated with object lessons. Jesus didn't simply say that God was welcoming and forgiving; He told about a father who had two sons.

The religious rulers never did this. They had, I think, too little imagination. And they refused the opening of imagination required to hear Jesus, to see Him, to receive Him. They were wonderless. Common people were often "amazed" by Jesus—His words, His works, His presence. He Himself was often "amazed." And the priests and Pharisees and Sadducees? They were often annoyed, angry, threatened, threatening. But never amazed.

Revelation and imagination are actually *pago* and *verso,* two halves joined. Revelation is God's method of disclosure, but imagination is the primary way we receive it. "The heavens declare the glory of God; the skies proclaim the work of his hands" (Psalm 19:1). But we are blind and deaf to God's glory revealed in the skies if we only watch the heavens unfold on television.

It takes imagination. Consider all the men and women of massive, piercing intellect who study the stars in all their infinite vastness and intricate smallness, but don't ever hear God setting them to sing like a Harlem choir, loosing them to jig like a Riverdance troupe, festooning them across the sky like Matisse hanging his artwork out to dry. It's not that these people don't have enough brains. Maybe they have too much.

Maybe they lack imagination.

If you describe a kiss in sheer physical terms, it sounds repulsive. Two people press their moist, creased facial orifices together, cinch tight the sphincter muscles to draw the flesh around the orifice into a bulbous mound, and exchange saliva and breath. It takes imagination to transmute that into an act of intimacy and eroticism. It takes the power to see beyond and beneath the stark physicality of it. Those who look at the stars and see only dead rock and gases are like men who have spent their lives analyzing kisses and have never kissed anyone.

We do that; Christians do, churches do. Look at Communion. Communion is tasting death and tasting life. Communion is the taste of flesh and blood and the foretaste of heaven's banquet. But most churches in my Baptist tradition have made it into describing a kiss without ever kissing. We take communion once a month. We pass around little thimbles of grape juice, little scraps of mastov bread. We read some Scripture, we pray, we drink, we eat. We sing. We leave.

I once went to a church where, before we did the eating and drinking, the pastor held up a piece of bread. "This," he said, "is only bread. It was made from flour and water, baked in an oven. We buy this at the grocery store. This is *not* Christ's body, and it *doesn't become* Christ's body. It is only a symbol. But when we eat it, we should remember Christ. Take and eat." Then he held up a tiny cup of grape juice. "This," he said, "is only grape juice. It was made from grapes, crushed, poured into bottles—but not fermented. You probably drink this at home all the time. This is *not* the blood of Christ, and it *doesn't become* the blood of Christ. It is only a symbol. But when we drink it, we should remember Christ. Take and drink."

Describing the kiss without kissing. I took, I ate. I took, I drank. But it was just eating and drinking and not a very satisfying eating and drinking at that. The bread was dry and flavorless. It made me thirsty. But the thimble of grape juice only stirred my thirst more, certainly didn't quench it. I left hungry. I left thirsty. I just left.

Jesus said, "This is my body. Take and eat. This is my blood. Take and drink." He didn't explain it. In fact, all attempts to explain it have been mere descriptions of kissing. He just stated it and left it to our imaginations to figure out how it was so. He left it to us to remember—to vividly remember— His life and death and resurrection and ascension. To experience right now, right here, His presence. To anticipate with a wild yearning our seeing Him again, eating this meal *with Him* in heaven. And to leave full.

It takes imagination.

ONE OF THE WAYS WE KEEP GOD SAFE AND WHILE AWAY OUR DAYS on borderland is by winnowing out mystery. Mystery is not explained—*this is bread, only bread.* Mystery, rather, is entered into through imagination—*this is My body.* The holy wild is pervaded with mystery.

But not borderland. Borderland is wonderless. There all is explained, explainable, contained, controlled.

Author and theologian Os Guinness was once speaking in Australia, and afterward a Japanese CEO approached him. He said to Guinness, "When I meet a Buddhist monk, I meet a holy man in touch with another world. When I meet a Western missionary, I meet a manager who is only in touch with the world I know." And then Guinness adds this comment: "You could say that many, many Christians are atheists unawares."[1]

This is a bitter irony. That a faith based on staggering mysteries—the Trinity, the Incarnation, the Cross and Resurrection, the imparting of the Spirit—should have become shorn of mystery, so plodding and prosaic, so mundane and managerial is a bitter irony. It's an irony that Jesus' famous statement to Nicodemus, you must be born again, has in our hands been turned into a slogan and a formula. Out of Jesus' mouth, in Nicodemus's ear, that statement proclaimed a staggering mystery. It was the ultimate antiformula.

"The wind blows wherever it pleases," Jesus goes on to tell Nicodemus, who struggles in his literalism and rationalism to understand. "You hear its sound, but you cannot tell where it comes from or where it is going. So it is with everyone born of the Spirit" (John 3:8). This is no formula. This is a description of the in-breaking and surprising move of God. This is something we can't work for, work up, predict, direct. It doesn't slot neatly into a program. You just hear it coming and fling yourself headlong into the hurricane.

But this leaves too much unsettled, doesn't it?

So we've taken refuge from mystery in numbers, formulas, three-point sermons, seven-step regimens, ten tips for fuller faith, thirty days to deeper prayer. We have become masters of the how-to manual. We have become the makers of sermons that, like sitcoms, pose a problem and with pithy or witty one-liners wrap it up in less than a half hour.

Evangelicals scowl at those who treat the Bible as myth or metaphor. When I first became a Christian, the favorite sport among budding evangelical theologians was Bultmann bashing. Rudolf Bultmann was the diminutive German professor who became notorious for his program of "demythologizing" the Bible. He argued that the Bible was mostly a series of legends, rooted in a mythological worldview. The Bible was not history, he said, but merely devotional literature, parables of religious sentiment. To get at the core of this sentiment, to really hear the Bible's message, Bultmann said we must strip off the outer form. A miracle story, for example—say, the feeding of the five thousand—is not an eyewitness report of an actual event. Rather it's a declaration of piety and faith. It's a description of spiritual hunger and nourishment. Jesus never fed anyone *literally*. No, this is a statement of the church's faith, that those who find themselves in the "wilderness," empty and needy, who have come to hear the words of Jesus, will discover that they are filled. And those who are in the church, the disciples, the followers of Christ, who are overwhelmed by the world's emptiness and neediness and are tempted to send them away, will discover that if they bring what they have to Jesus, however meager, He will use it and multiply it. The story itself—hungry people rending and chewing real bread, their mouths shiny with the oil of broiled fish, the ground littered with flakes of crust and the white filigree of fish bones—never happened. That's just a mythic husk, a way of dramatizing a psychological yearning and experience. We can shuck that story now. It may have once helped believers to get the point, but now it just distracts us.

The whole Bible, Bultmann argued, needed a thoroughgoing demythologization, a ruthless and rigorous paring away of its thick rind of fairy tales.

Bultmann led theology nowhere. He led it, in fact, to borderland. Intending to bring some kind of intellectual credibility to the church, he instead deadened it. His was a program of enforced sterilization, an engineered barrenness. Some claim he did more to empty the churches of Europe than communism and materialism ever did.

And he was, after his heyday, an easy target. Like a boy in a medieval village joining other boys flinging rotten vegetables at a heretic in the stocks, I hurled my overripe accusations at Bultmann's head. I was gleeful and prideful, brimming with my own sense of rightness. What I at first didn't notice was how I, a "Bible-believing" evangelical, was practicing more and more a biblical hermeneutic, an interpretative method, that was just as harmful in the long run as anything Bultmann was attempting.

It was what I call the "de-mysterious-ization" of Scripture. If Bultmann treated miracles as parables, I was learning to treat parables as puzzles to be solved. If he handled history as metaphor, I was learning to handle metaphor as a code to be cracked. My main interpretive task, as I understood it, was to distill from the Bible principles, technique, a series of points to ponder or steps to take. It was to compress the infinite into the numeric, corral the miraculous into the pragmatic, tidy the messy earthiness of the Bible into a neat-edged moralism, parse its poetry into prose—or worse, propositions. In short, it was to banish mystery.

I suppose there is something typically North American about this. We are impatient of anything that's not immediately understandable and obviously practical. We are, after all, the culture that invented and perfected the philosophy of pragmatism: *It doesn't matter if a thing is true or not as long as it works.* Mystery—the bread and wine *as* flesh and blood—is anathema to this view. Mystery is not amenable to method. It's not pragmatic. What we want are sermons and seminars, books and workshops, on how-tos: how to have a great marriage, for instance, or how to manage our money so we can tithe 10 percent.

The problem is that not that we want great marriages or more discipline with our finances. Of course we want these; our wanting it is good, and our having it will require practical help.

The problem is that these things take imagination as much as, or more than, technique. The problem is that our fondness for reducing mystery to method, for quantifying and calculating truth, often steals away the very gift we're seeking to bestow. When we marry, we make a promise of such extravagant self-giving, such audacious daring, that we have little hope of fulfilling the promise apart from an imaginative seeing of one another. A technique—say, "creative communication"—might help in this, but it might also mechanize the relationship and leave it colder than ever.

My own marriage, my own ability to live the vows I took, has been deepened through imagination. Through several years of counseling couples soon to be married and couples whose marriages were in trouble, I kept being drawn back to two biblical stories, both in Genesis: the story of Adam and Eve and the story of Jacob and Rachel and Leah. Each time I approached these stories, they became more alive for me. More and more they possessed the power of what historian Barbara Tuchman calls "A Distant Mirror": true stories that contain, and reflect back, my own story.[2] They mingle history with diary, the ancient with the contemporary, the disclosing of long ago and far away with the exposing of the here and now.

My wife is Eve, the first woman. She's the one created for me because God saw that it was not good for me to be alone. All creation might parade before me; I might know it and name it, but no one else besides her is suitable for me. She is the one taken out of me, broken out of my side, the part of me I lose only to gain back a millionfold: bone of my bone, flesh of my flesh. She is the one I leave mother and father for—forsaking my need to pay tribute to or my desire to take vengeance upon those who bore me and bred me. She is the one I join to. She is the one I seek to stand naked with and feel no shame.

Yet she is the one I also know as sinner, eater of the forbidden fruit, and who knows me this way. She is the one who, rather than standing naked with me and feeling no shame, covers her nakedness before me, as I do before her. She is the one who, with me and yet against me, hides from God. She is the one I blame for my troubles. She is the one whose desire is for me—desire to both appease me and to control me—and whom I seek to rule over. She is the one who resents me for her travail, whom I resent for my thorny, sweaty, toilsome life. She is not only bone of my bone and flesh of my flesh, but now also the other.

She is Eve.

And she is my Rachel and my Leah together. She is the one I worked seven years for, and my love for her was such that those years were like a day. And finally, the day of being united as one arrived. We celebrated, and we went to our tent. But in the morning—maybe not the first one, but some morning—I awoke, and beside me was not Rachel, but Leah: a woman I didn't know, didn't choose, a stranger. She had been switched. I had been duped.

I worked for Rachel, the woman I chose, and one morning woke up beside Leah, the woman I didn't choose. The other one. The changeling. Could I learn to choose the one I hadn't chosen, to love Leah?

These stories took imaginative hold over me. I found that they had power to console and convict me like no pep talk or lecture ever could. They guided me in surprising ways, awakening long-dormant intuitions. They spoke things to me, about me, that provided answers to long-sought questions. They took me outside myself when I was stuck in self-pity, inside myself when I was adrift in self-denial. They showed me the roots of my anger or unforgivingness or suspicion, and showed me, too, the source of my longing and hope. Time and again, they called me back to a fresh resolve to live my vows, a fresh energy for doing that.

I would still be married apart from this. I just think I wouldn't be married as well. That takes all the imagination I've got.

THE WORST CONSEQUENCE OF LOSING OUR IMAGINATION, OUR wonder, is that we no longer see the Christward life as an adventure. We see it as a duty, a chore, a list of dos, don'ts, and how-tos. We think the point of life is to stay as safe and undisturbed as possible. We think borderland is not a bad place to live. The stories we read in Acts about the church "turning the world on its head" (Acts 17:6)—well, what would that kind of thing do to our tax-exempt status?

Once, speaking at a camp, I held up two video cases for a group of about seventy teenagers to see. One was the case for the first Indiana Jones movie, where the archaeologist-adventurer goes flinging across continents, brawling with a host of rivals and enemies, swimming oceans and scaling stone walls, in a race to find and take the ark of the covenant. The cover had a picture of Indiana's sweat-soaked face, a cut wet with blood across one cheek. Around him were pictures of a Nazi villain, a hooded cobra, a ship under siege.

The other video cover showed a sewing machine with a swatch of cloth clamped beneath its chrome foot. The swatch was rough-hewn on one side, neatly stitched on the other. It was a training video for using the machine.

I asked the young people, "When you look around at churches today, which of these videos would you say best captures the essence of the Christian life?"

Every single one of them said the sewing machine training video.

Maybe the greatest gift we could give our young people is to go get ourselves wonder struck.

Chapter Six

SEEING IS NOT BELIEVING

D oubt juts large in borderland. Its shadow falls at dark, odd angles, cockeyed to the light. And its depths are riddled with a labyrinth of tunnels. Some of them, seemingly, have no bottom; they just twist and twist, fall and fall. Call out, and all you hear is your own voice, swelled huge with echo.

Who hasn't scrabbled, belly chafing, through doubt's tunnels? Who hasn't spent long sojourns stuck in some crook of its maze? We find ourselves wandering in unexpectedly, without planning. We were doing fine, sturdy and resolute in our belief, and then something happens, or something doesn't happen, and doubt surrounds us. It can leech all of that fine, hard resolve out of us, whittle away our steadfastness.

I am often surprised to find how my doubts can mingle so freely with my faith. Even at moments of most intimate prayer, a doubt—like a fly tapping and buzzing against the windowpane—can flicker at the edge of my thinking. *You are just talking into the air.*

The nature of doubt is best glimpsed in the story of Thomas:

Now Thomas (called Didymus), one of the Twelve, was not with the disciples when Jesus came. So the other disciples told him, "We have seen the Lord!"

But he said to them, "Unless I see the nail marks in his hands and put my finger where the nails were, and put my hand into his side, I will not believe it."

A week later his disciples were in the house again, and Thomas was with them. Though the doors were locked, Jesus came and stood among them and said, "Peace be with you!" Then he said to Thomas, "Put your finger here; see my hands. Reach out your hand and put it into my side. Stop doubting and believe."

Thomas said to him, "My Lord and my God!"

Then Jesus told him, "Because you have seen me, you have believed; blessed are those who have not seen and yet have believed." (John 20:24–29)

I think Thomas is gaunt, his face stark and raw edged like a Palestinian landscape. Sharpness of bone, hollowness of flesh. And something else, something in the eyes—a shrewdness, a wariness, a caginess. He is sparing with words. He watches. He listens. He can unnerve you with his silence, with the depths and layers of it. *What is he thinking?* His silence is more inflected than Cantonese.

Thomas is a doubter, *the* doubter—doubt's patron saint. His name comes conjoined, hip to bone, feather to wing, with that unshakable epithet: Doubting Thomas.

The Bible never describes Thomas this way. It describes his moment of doubt. But it is one moment, only one, and he moves quickly beyond it. His identity, despite our perception and description of him, is not rooted in that moment. There is much that is praiseworthy about him. When Jesus, hearing of his friend Lazarus's sickness in Bethany, tells the disciples that they are returning there, some of them protest: *People want to kill You there, Jesus.* But Thomas speaks up. "Let us also go," he says, "that we may die with him" (John 11:16). These are hardly the words of a chronic doubter.

Yet Thomas's moment of doubt has comforted and troubled us so much for so long—has reflected back to us our own stubborn and fragile faith—that our remembrance of that moment has for most of us eclipsed everything else about the man. It is a truth about Thomas that, dwelt upon obsessively, has become a myth, a character lapse that has become his all-defining character trait.

This is unfortunate, but not entirely. After all, Thomas's doubt itself is pithy, earthy, real. His is a doubt that often taunts us. It is a doubt that stands between the world's believing and disbelieving. Because his doubt is this: Is Jesus really risen from the dead? Has He really conquered death, with all that such conquest means? Or is the claim that He is risen just the deluded wish fulfillment of a few men and women made unstable by grief, needing to invent resurrection to console themselves, to vindicate their naive faith?

Is this not our doubt, too? Is this not *the* doubt? To second-guess and explain away Christ's resurrection is, of course, the vogue of academia, a virtual growth industry. It has been for a long time. That's neither particularly surprising nor particularly interesting. But this is: Even dear Mrs. Smith, so reverent and faithful and faith filled, so abounding in good works and unshakable in her convictions—feels, from time to time, the chill of this doubt's shadow. It is, in fact, this doubt—doubt that He is alive—that Jesus rebukes His Emmaus-bound disciples for: "How foolish you are, and how slow of heart to believe."

Doubt—in the Resurrection, in the presence of Christ, in the goodness of God, in the power of God—is a primary alibi for borderland dwelling. Why venture out into the holy wild—why go to the trouble, take the risk, incur the cost—if we're not sure how this will work out in the end? Why follow Him if He's being so vague about the details?

Unless I see.

Thomas's doubt is ours, too, our nemesis and companion, our secret haunting.

UNLESS I SEE IT WITH MY OWN EYES, TOUCH IT WITH MY OWN hands, *I will not believe.* This is the heart of the matter. This is what stands between Thomas's believing and his doubting: *unless I.*

I know what he means. I can have all the personal testimony and logical airtightness and empirical verification in the world, but unless I see it, touch it, have an experience of it, a shade of doubt exists. Nothing—not the witness box, not the lab report, not the field dispatch—substitutes for the power to convince that my own seeing and touching can deliver. "Unless I" is the doubter's mantra.

I read of miracles in the Bible. I hear of miracles today. Not long ago a close friend of mine was in church, and a woman got up during testimony time and tearfully and joyfully praised God. Only moments before, the Lord had healed her completely of an eye problem that had plagued her most of her life.

I believe these accounts. And yet. And yet, *unless I...*

And who can fault Thomas for his refusal? After all, though Jesus had foretold His resurrection, look who attests to it—the "other disciples." That means the likes of Peter, James, and John. Thomas has seen too much fickleness in those men. Peter? He's an unstable mix of headlong rashness and fleet-footed cowardice. He dashes into things, then thrashes his way out of them. He's the son who says yes and means no. James and John? They're filled with hot-tempered brashness—wanting to call down fire on hapless Samaritan villages—and petty rivalry—spatting over who gets to sit next to Jesus in heaven. Here are Peter, James, and John, words tumbling out, jumbling up, in a breathless welter of half-baked testimony: *Jesus is alive! Alive! We've seen Him ourselves!*

Oh, really?

We live in an age not of skepticism, but of credulity. The cult of scientism—which itself was a sign of the age's credulity—is waning, giving way to ever new and extravagant forms of mysticism, irrationalism, just-believism. This is widespread in our culture, and it's widespread in the church. Recently I have heard numerous reports of people in church worship services having silver teeth turned to gold or of gold dust sifting down, *ex nihilo,* onto their skin, then disappearing. These events are touted as miracles, a touch of God. What am I to make of them?

I question them. I doubt them. I take the position that "unless I see...." Sometimes doubting is not a lack of faith but rather an expression of it. Sometimes to doubt is merely to insist that God be taken seriously not frivolously, to insist that our faith is placed in and upheld by something other than seeming conjuring tricks. There is in these accounts of gold teeth and gold dust a kind of nostalgia at work for the old god-of-the-gaps, god as necro-mancer. Thomas stands as a bulwark against that. These things might be true occurrences. But they need to be sifted, probed, tested. We need to bite them to see if they're fool's gold or the real thing. Beyond that, even if they are genu-ine occurrences, they need to be unfolded theologically and biblically. Most—maybe all—miracles in the Bible have a discernible social function. Even floating ax heads and water turning into wine, though not as socially worth-while as the blind seeing and the lame walking, serve clear enough social pur-poses. But gold teeth, evaporating gold dust?

Biblical faith is not sentimental, not sloppy or vague. It excludes more than it embraces. Biblical faith progresses in an alternating rhythm of yes and no, a taking hold and a letting go, a believing and a doubting. Peter represents the part of our heritage that says, "I will believe though I have not yet seen." But Thomas represents the other, equally needed part of our heritage: "Unless I see, I will not believe." More than ever, the strength of evangelical faith must draw from both sides of the heritage.

The word *skepticism* has an interesting etymology. It means to look at a matter closely, to scrutinize, to study with great care and in minute detail. Based on this definition, what the church needs is not less but more skepti-cism. I met a man who told me he didn't believe the Bible because he was a skeptic. I asked him if he had read the Bible.

"No, not really," he said. "I told you; I'm a skeptic. I don't believe it."

This is not skepticism. This is its opposite—a refusal to investigate, to scrutinize, to ponder deeply. One thing skepticism is not is an excuse for eva-sion, an alibi for idleness. It is not a self-imposed boundary to keep you from embarking on any deep and meaningful search. *I have just bought a pair of oxen, and I cannot come.* This form of skepticism is only a subtle way of lying to our-selves, like telling ourselves that the world is flat to avoid the burden of launching dangerous and costly voyages beyond the horizon.

Any true skeptic worthy of the name is both hunter and detective, stalk-ing the evidence, laying ambush, rummaging for clues, dredging the river bot-tom, wiretapping phone lines, setting traps. A skeptic is passionate about discovering truth and wants to believe, but safeguards against the hypnotic power of that wanting. So he tests.

Thomas was a true skeptic. He doubted not to excuse his unbelief, but to establish robust belief. He doubted so that his belief might be based on something more than rumor and wishful thinking.

He doubted, not to justify staying on borderland, but in order to find a firm path out and into the holy wild. For the place God calls us into isn't doubt free—how can any place where we walk by faith and not by sight be that? No, the holy wild is where we have driving and haunting doubts, God-hungry doubts that pull us to our knees, force us to the Word, make us wrestle all night and not let go until He blesses us. The holy wild throngs with true skeptics.

But not borderland. It is filled with armchair doubters, dressing up excuses as theology, content with the safe god but, ironically, forever disappointed in him.

DOUBT HAS ITS LIMITS. IT CAN BE FAITH'S TONIC, A CLEANSING and invigorating force. But doubt can quickly turn corrosive or cancerous, burning or mutating healthy tissue. It can become a way of holding God for ransom. Our lives can degenerate into a fruitless and futile round of "Unless I see, unless I touch, unless I have the experience, I will not believe." Indulged too long, doubt becomes just a parlor game.

And for what? Most people can attest, and the Bible confirms, that even spectacular displays of divine power don't always or forever secure faith and faithfulness on the parts of those who witness them. The raising of Lazarus is, again, a prime example. Many witnessed it and believed. But the Pharisees and chief priests had a much different reaction: Though they apparently never questioned the reality of the miracle, they saw Jesus' ability to perform such miracles as a threat to their power, so they launched plans to kill Him (John 11:45–49). Philip Yancey makes the observation that miracles, especially in the Old Testament, almost always created *distance* rather than intimacy between people and God. And those who saw Jesus' miracles and believed hardly came off as unshakable and unswerving in their decision to follow Him.

In Michael O'Brien's potent novel *Father Elijah,* the central character, after whom the book is titled, ponders repeatedly the mystery of his own belief and doubt. His faith has led him to radical acts of self-denial and risky acts of self-sacrifice. Over and over his faith has been bolstered by miracles. Yet just as sturdy and solid as his faith is, he is also subject to violent storms of despair and doubt. His doubts are as big and dark and menacing as his faith is bright and vast and promising. Perhaps that's a general principle: The depth of our doubt is roughly proportional to the depth of our faith. Those with strong faith have equally strong doubts. That principle bears out in the other direction as well: People with a trivial and shallow faith usually have trivial and shallow doubts. And if you ask them, *Who is this god you doubt?* you'll likely find this: He's safe.

Father Elijah, this man of deep faith and deep doubt, is haunted by a realization, what he calls "the fundamental problem of his soul." He had been given everything and it did not suffice. The reflection continues:

> He had been graced to see the actions of God as few men had seen them. The consolations poured out upon him were extraordinary.... And yet...and yet, the ancient scar of Adam dragged him inexorably back, again and again, to his desire for certainty.... He longed for a trace of explanation.
>
> He knew full well that if it were given he would soon need a larger one after that, until in the end no explanation would fill the yawning abyss of his doubt.[1]

Here lies the basic flaw of all doubt: It can never really be satisfied. No evidence is ever fully, finally enough. Doubt wants always to consume, never to consummate. It clamors endlessly for an answer and so drowns out any answer that might be given it. It demands proof but will doubt the proof proffered it. Doubt, then, can become an appetite gone wrong; its craving increases the more we try to fill it. Christ's concluding words to Thomas are not so much an endorsement of "mere belief" as a warning that the quest for "proof" is not the path of blessedness. "Because you have seen me, you have believed; blessed are those who have not seen and yet have believed" (John 20:29).

And what, anyhow, is the connection between seeing and believing? Jesus tells Thomas *after he sees* Him to stop doubting *and believe*. Belief is still called for, still demanded. Seeing does not remove the necessity of belief. Seeing is not believing.

We walk by faith, not by sight.

IN ANOTHER MODERN NOVEL, JOHN UPDIKE'S *ROGER'S VERSION*, a reworking of themes in Nathaniel Hawthorne's *The Scarlet Letter,* Roger Lambert, a jaded, debauched theology professor argues with Dale Kohler, a gangling, earnest young evangelical who is bent on proving the existence of God mathematically. Dale argues that we need some logically airtight demonstration for the existence of God to counter the bravado of scientism. And more: If we could prove God's existence, he contends, we could rout the devil. Roger asks Dale who he thinks the devil is. "The Devil," Dale replies, "is doubt."

Roger's response to this is both ingenious and disturbing:

> Funny...I would have said, looking at recent history and, for that matter, at some of our present-day ayatollahs and Fuhrers, the opposite. The Devil is the absence of doubt. He's what pushes people into suicide bombing, into setting up extermination camps. Doubt may give your dinner a funny taste, but it's faith that goes out and kills.[2]

As the story progresses, it becomes clear that the devil is both doubt and its absence. Roger the Doubter, Dale the Assured, both do terrible, godless things—adultery, incest, abortion. And for both this marks them out: a dauntless, swaggering pride.

Doubt and faith, mix either with pride and the concoction is toxic. Those proud in their faith, those proud in their doubts—both are terrors. But Thomas, he *is* the patron saint of real doubt, because with him, believing and doubting are marked by humility.

ALL OF THIS MAKES THE NATURE OF THOMAS'S DOUBT AND Christ's answer more poignant. What, after all, does Thomas want to see and touch? What does Christ show him? What is the evidence sought and then offered for the Resurrection?

Wounds. "Unless I see the nail marks in his hands and put my fingers where the nails were, and put my hand into his side, I will not believe." And Jesus says to Thomas, "Put your finger here; see my hands. Reach out your hand and put it into my side. Stop doubting and believe" (John 20:25, 27).

Christ demonstrates His victory over death, not with feats of strength, not with more frequent and more spectacular miracles, but with wounds—nail holes, spear marks. *Behold, the lamb who was slain.*

It is no accident that the more squeamish our culture becomes about wounds—denying death, cloaking sickness, hiding away the old and the decrepit—the more we are plagued with doubt about the Resurrection. We shun wounds, and our doubts breed. We take offense at a God who associates with suffering, blood, and heartache. We want God to prove Himself by some other means: by windfalls and whirlwinds, boons and blessings. We yearn for the carnival God, with His dazzling stunts and sleight of hand tricks and potions for quick cures. We like the God who feeds the crowd and fills the fishnets. We like the Banquet Impresario God, the Caterer King. But we're wary of the God of Scripture: He's too much into roughhouse and stern measure for our tastes, too prone to battlefields and bone breaking, too beholden to the fellowship of suffering, and altogether too preoccupied with the disguise of weakness.

How many times have we heard the lament, "I can't believe in a God who would allow so much suffering in the world"? Yet here is the strangest of paradoxes: To actually see wounds, to actually touch them—not just to sit in our warm, antiseptic homes and offices and learnedly debate about them—is often the strongest antidote for doubt. *This* claim can be empirically tested. People in history—Saint Francis, Mother Teresa, Father Damien, Dr. Paul Brand—who have had the vocation of touching real flesh-and-blood wounds and seeing them as Jesus' wounds have had robust faith. They have lived far from borderland.

Put your finger here. See My hands. Stop doubting and believe.

DOUBT, WHEN HONEST, SHOULD SET US ON A QUEST FOR THAT which is true and real, for that which we can not only give intellectual assent but, more than that, can entrust our very lives to. Thomas's doubt led to this place. Jesus shows His wounds to Thomas, tells Thomas to see, to touch. He sees, but he doesn't touch. He knows when enough is enough. And here is the real sign that Thomas is not some poseur, some mere academic trend chaser: His seeing gives way, not just to belief, but to worship. "My Lord and my God!" he proclaims.

Recently I had lunch with Dr. Philip Wiebe, a professor of philosophy at a prominent evangelical university. Among his many distinctions, Wiebe is a Shroud of Turin scholar. He is convinced—and convincing—that the shroud is the genuine burial cloth of Jesus and that it is intrinsic evidence of His resurrection. He argues the point in a detailed, scientifically sophisticated manner and can answer the most stubborn objections without any logic twisting or special pleading. His case seems without crack or warp.

This poses its own set of problems. What if the much-contested shroud is no hoax? What if it can be demonstrated that this is indeed the burial cloth of Jesus, that it bears the imprint of Christ's gaunt image scorched, by the unique event of His rising from the dead, into the delicate fibers of its linen? Again, is this all faith is—*seeing* the evidence? To reduce faith, as modernist theologians have often done, to free-floating sentiment, lacking root in historical event, is mistaken. To tell a dying man that the Resurrection is only a "symbol" of new life is like giving a starving man a picture of food and thinking he should be satisfied. But to reduce faith to mere empiricism, a verification procedure, is also a mistake. In Jesus' parable about the rich man and Lazarus, the rich man dies and goes to hell. From there he pleads in his torment with Father Abraham to resurrect Lazarus from the dead and send him to warn his five brothers. "If someone from the dead goes to them," the rich man reasons, "they will repent." And Abraham replies, "If they do not listen to Moses and the Prophets, they will not be convinced even if someone rises from the dead" (Luke 16:30–31).

Wiebe told me about another scholar who had written an article that calls into question the resurrection of Jesus, claiming that those who encountered the risen Christ were in altered states of consciousness and were, in effect, only *seeing things.* Wiebe had begun an exchange of views with this scholar. The battle was joined.

I asked, during our lunchtime conversation, "Do you envision this man ever being so convinced by the evidence that he believes—and, more, that he worships and cries out in wonder, shame, joy, 'My Lord and my God!'?"

Weibe laughed a sad, wry laugh. "No," he said. "No, I don't."

That's not honest doubt. That's something very different—intellectual dogma, doctrinaire agnosticism, hidebound ideology, scholarly trivial pursuit. That's only an excuse for slowness of heart. That's only an argument for being stuck on borderland.

That's the refusal to be convinced even if someone rises from the dead.

Over that, I'll take Thomas and his doubt any day.

Chapter Seven

WRESTLING TOWARD SURRENDER

Self-composed marriage vows make me nervous. Usually they end up vague and mawkish, Gibranesque inanities posing as profundities. Or they are hard-nosed bargains and cutthroat contracts covered with a thin veneer of poetry.

A couple I was going to marry insisted on writing their own vows. I asked that they let me review them. One phrase in particular stopped me cold: "I promise to be true to myself."

"Um," I said, "I'm pretty sure you don't want that in the vow."

"I'm pretty sure we do," the man said.

"Maybe you're very different from me," I said. "There's a part of me, I'm glad to say, that is joy-filled, generous, trusting, trustworthy. But there's another part of me—maybe the larger part—that's slothful, lustful, greedy, miserly, apathetic. I could go on. Which part should I be true to?"

It occurred to me then that to take traditional marriage vows is to pledge, in essence, that I *won't* be true to myself. I will be true to another. I will be true to God. But in order to do that, I will often have to deny myself—deny my impulse to run, to retaliate, to sulk, to self-indulge, to self-destruct.

I promise to wage war on myself, defy myself, die to myself.

One way to describe the trouble we're in is that too many of us for too long have lived by a promise, binding as a vow, to be true to ourselves.

This is the myth of self-reliance. Being self-reliant, being true to ourselves, is at the root of our fallenness. We fell because we trusted ourselves. We will never be saved until we come to the end of ourselves and fall upon the mercy of God. We must trust Him. We must be true to Him.

But self-reliance also plagues the redeemed. We are painfully aware of this, of how much we withhold and withdraw from the hands of God, how much we clutch our lives and our plans in our grubby, fumbling little hands because we dare not relinquish such treasures to God. Most of borderland's inhabitants are proudly, stubbornly self-reliant.

We often treat God as the Lord of the predicament and Master of the pinch. He is there to bail us out, to whisk us away, to vindicate and rescue us. He is the God of our binds and squeezes, but rarely the God of our *lives*. Until a crisis hits, we really do not want God crowding in on us. We want Him to keep a safe, cool distance, hovering in the shadows until summoned, usually to assist us in being true to ourselves.

The story of Jacob is instructive. Jacob was a conniver, a charlatan, a kind of ancient sideshow pitchman. He swindled almost everything he got. His life is a chronicle of backroom deals, disguises, sleights of hand. His is a portrait of self-reliance, of a man who is true to himself and no one else. Jacob is the quintessential borderland dweller. No, more: He's its events promoter and poster boy.

But the moment of reckoning in Jacob's life, the moment that gives him greatness, is when he wrestles with "a man" and is wounded and blessed by him: "After [Jacob] had sent [all his family and servants and herds] across the stream, he sent over all his possessions. So Jacob was left alone, and a man wrestled with him til daybreak" (Genesis 32:23–24).

The precondition for Jacob's full and terrible encounter with "the man" is his complete aloneness. All his things are removed to the other side of the river. He is naked, with shame. See Jacob standing there, a lonely man, getting old. His skin, once stretched tight over sharp bones, has become thick and soft, loose and heavy. A paunch gathers beneath his clothes where there was once a flat hardness. *Getting old.* The night is as vast as forgetting but haunted with remembering. The huge sky has a breaking weight to it. It's full of stars, uncountable. *Uncountable.* Those stars in their infinite beyondness, beyond reach, beyond numbering, are a threat and a taunt to Jacob, an emblem of his failure. And all his success, all the success in the world, can't cover that failure.

The night before the encounter, Jacob prays. He prays in a kind of vague desperation. He has to meet his brother Esau who, twenty years before, Jacob had cheated out of birthright and blessing. Then Esau was angry, murderously angry. And Esau is a big man, the kind of man to whom you bring jars with lids on too tight, and who can pop them open with one effortless twist; the kind of man who carries pianos down stairwells single-handedly. Jacob fled Esau's anger. And now he prepares to face him again. He's expecting—and he should—that the intervening years have not softened Esau, have not soothed his bitterness into melancholy. Some wounds are not healed by time, but are infected by it. Jacob expects that with Esau.

Jacob prays. But it's a nice, pious, conventional prayer, with just the right measure of humble posturing and you-owe-me-this demands:

> O God of my father Abraham, God of my father Isaac, O LORD, who said to me, "Go back to your country and your relatives, and I will make you prosper," I am unworthy of all the kindness and faithfulness you have shown your servant. I had only my staff when I crossed this Jordan, but now I have become two groups. Save me, I pray, from the hand of my brother Esau, for I am afraid he will come and attack me, and also the mothers with their children. But you have said, "I will surely make you prosper and will make your descendants like the sand of the sea, which cannot be counted." (Genesis 32:9–12)

Is Jacob imploring God or wringing out a business deal from Him? Is he dust-eating lackey or hardballing blackmailer? Is he boasting or thanking, pleading or threatening? He's *so good* at this kind of thing, this smooth talk and fast talk and doublespeak. Like this line: "He will come and attack me, *and also the mothers with their children.*" That last clause is a fine touch, the work of a master. Jacob suffers no qualms about sending the women and their children first, in point man position, as a buffer for himself. Well, we'll just trust God on that one.

We've heard this prayer before at the beginning of the church business meeting, which, right after the "amen," descended into pitched battle. We've probably said this prayer just before setting out to do exactly what we planned on doing anyway. That's how Jacob prays this prayer. Jacob is Jacob, and he's not one to think prayer does anything, means anything. Prayer is...what? A pretty, pious decoration. A hedge on the bet. The rubber stamp of providence on business as usual. A way of getting my will to be done, in heaven as it is on earth.

So Jacob prays. Then Jacob schemes about how he's *really* going to work things to his own sweet advantage. Jacob is Jacob. And the real plan involves bribery and flattery, diversions and delays, sweeping Esau away in a flood tide of gifts and groveling. Jacob calculates everything down to the last detail; he anticipates Esau's questions and reactions. Jacob plans, yet again, an end run. "For he thought, 'I will pacify him with these gifts I am sending on ahead; later, when I see him, perhaps he will receive me'" (32:20).

But there's that next passage: "So Jacob's gifts went on ahead of him, but he himself spent the night in the camp. That night, Jacob got up and took his two wives, his two maidservants and his eleven sons and crossed the ford of the Jabbok. After he had sent them across the stream, he sent over all his possessions. So Jacob was left alone" (32:21–24).

So Jacob was left alone. He stands in deepest solitude. He stands separated from all that crowds and clutters his life, stands bereft of all that gives substance and importance to it. He stands on two good legs. He stands alone.

Well, he's used to being alone, standing alone, being true to himself. Isn't that what life, shorn of its fakery, is all about? *I'm alone. I had better look out for me, take care of me. If I don't, who will? God takes care of those who take care of themselves. Where is that Scripture anyhow? First Jacob something. That's a good Scripture. When I get out of this mess, I'm gonna have that etched into a plaque and hang it on my wall, under my degrees, beside the photos of me posing with senators and movie stars.*

So Jacob was left alone. No wives, no children, no servants. No television, no cellular phone, no magazines. Nothing. It would take him a moment to settle into that aloneness. His mind would race: *Have I thought of everything? Maybe I should have instructed so-and-so a little more on how to inflect his speech to Esau. I wonder if two hundred female goats were enough? Oh, I know what I should have done! I should have put a jeweled necklace around the neck of every fiftieth animal.*

Maybe Jacob even has a brief thought: *Is there something else, something more, than this aloneness?*

And then, *he's* there—*the man.* An ambush. The hard, two-fisted grappling. The surging strength of adrenaline, the heart drumming in the ears, the sweat-slipping skin, the crushing, stinging, wrenching, clawing of hand on flesh on bone. The breathiness and breathlessness. The aching.

At first, Jacob tries to win. Of course. He is used to wrestling. He's done it in one form or another all his life. He started heel grabbing in the womb and has gotten more skilled at outmaneuvering his opponent ever since. When it's clear he won't win—when the man proves to have more tricks than Jacob and wounds him in the hip—Jacob resorts to another well-practiced stunt: demanding he get something out of this. He did this when Laban, his father-in-law, wounded him by tricking him out of another seven years of labor. Jacob deftly turned that around to his own advantage and used those seven years to plunder Laban's livestock.

"I will not let you go," Jacob says to the man, "unless you bless me."

In response, the man asks Jacob a question. "What is your name?"

Who are you? Who are you really? Will you dare say: I am Jacob, the heel-grabber, the man who trusts no one, takes from everyone? I am the man at the center of the universe. I am the lord of the borderland.

"Jacob," he says.

No, you're not.

"Your name will no longer be Jacob, but Israel, because you have struggled with God and men and have overcome."

The man gives Jacob a new name, a name that fits and yet doesn't. *Israel. He who wrestles with God.* It characterizes who Jacob is—the wrestler, the overcomer—and yet calls him into a fresh identity, calls him to discover whole new dimensions of wrestling (see Colossians 4:12 about Epaphras always wrestling in prayer) and overcoming (see Revelation 2 and 3 about those who over-come). In this dimension, he who would be first will be last, but he who would be last will be first; God's power is perfected in weakness; and real life comes through dying. *Your name is now Israel.*

Then Jacob has a request: "Please tell me your name."

But the man won't. He only responds with a question, unanswered: "Why do you ask my name?"

Why do you ask My name? When Jacob walks away from this encounter, he knows he has seen, face-to-face, and knows he has struggled with, limb-to-limb, no mere man: "I saw the face of God," he says. So this is God. *But why do you ask My name? Who do you say I am? What is it you want Me to do for you?*

Do you really want to know the one whose name you do not invent and impose, the one who names Himself, the one who will not grant you every little wish just because it is *you* wishing it, the one who will not conform to your image but who has made you in His and is now forming in you, some-times by hammer blows, grapplings, hip wrenchings, the image of Christ? The one who says, "You must follow Me. Deny yourself. Take up your cross and follow Me"? Do you want to know *that one,* His name? Or are you con-tent simply with your own vague or talismanic names for Him—the God of *my* understanding? The God who helps me to be true to myself? The God who is safe?

Why do you ask My name?

Then we're told that *the man* blesses Jacob there. There. Not in some undefined and undisclosed future, not in some general and generic way. But right there. Only we're not told how Jacob is blessed.

But here are some guesses.

Maybe the blessing is the wound. Jacob limps now. The man who stood and walked so well on his own two feet now walks wounded. The man who has lived crooked his entire life now literally walks crooked, but maybe he's beginning for the first time to walk straight. This scar in his flesh, this twist in his bone, perpetually reminds Jacob of his dependence. Every step is now a jog of the memory, a physical insignia that *this is the way; walk ye in it.*

Maybe the blessing is the question: *Why do you ask My name?* Maybe that is what is given to Jacob—a haunting, a Holy Grail, a quest, and a question that Jacob will spend the rest of his life *wrestling* with.

Or maybe the blessing is what happens next. As morning breaks, Jacob walks away from his encounter with the man across the open plain. The rising sun, screened through a gauzelike strata of cloud, crisscrosses his body with light. His limping leg rakes dew from the sere grass beneath him, and the moisture is cool and cleansing like a foot washing, like an anointing. He looks up. There is Esau, looming huge and dark against the rising sun. And, Jacob being Jacob, he kicks everything into gear—the bribery, the flattery, the minuet of manipulation. The only change in plans is that, rather than his taking up the rear, he now leads the way:

> [Jacob] divided the children among Leah, Rachel and the two maidservants. He put the maidservants and their children in front, Leah and her children next, and Rachel and Joseph in the rear. He himself went on ahead and bowed down to the ground seven times as he approached his brother. (Genesis 33:1–3)

And there is a surprise: Esau loves him. God answers Jacob's prayer—Jacob's shallow, manipulative, conventional prayer. In fact, God does more than Jacob asks or imagines: "But Esau ran to meet Jacob and embraced him; he threw his arms around his neck and kissed him. And they wept" (33:4). The prodigal comes home and finds, of all things, a welcome embrace.

Jacob has just walked away from wrestling *the man* and exclaimed, "I saw God face to face, and yet my life was spared." And now Jacob looks at his brother Esau and exclaims, "To see you is like seeing the face of God."

The face of God—the face of one who we thought was an enemy, who we thought was against us, who we thought we had to approach warily, in gestures of self-abasement and self-promotion and self-protection, with gifts to appease and cajole. Instead, we find one who runs to embrace us and kiss us and weep over us. *Prepare the fatted calf, for the lost one has been found.*

Jacob's story portrays a man who experiences redemption and reconciliation, not through his own cunning or coercion, but through wounds from the hand of another. Not by self-reliance, but by God-dependence. Not by being true to himself, but by coming to the end of himself. In the ruins of his own efforts and ambitions, he meets God, who comes to meet him out of the holy wild. "Come," He says. "Follow me."

How common is his story. I have met so many people who were never really blessed until they strove against God, were wounded, were given both a new identity and a haunting question, and who discovered in the most unlikely place, the most unexpected face—the face of God. These are people who never really danced until they limped. They are people whose self-reliance has been shattered, who have wrestled with *the man,* and who have found Him both brusque and embracing, wounding and blessing, and always stronger than they are. Not safe. But good.

What amazes me is how many people meet God through tragedy. A man's young wife dies of cancer. A woman's husband has a paralyzing stroke the week after his retirement, the day before their long-awaited trip to the Bahamas. A child is disabled in a freak bicycle accident. A family's house burns to the ground along with everything in it. They had intended to get insurance. They really had.

And suddenly they are alone, everything removed to the other side. And a man wrestles them until daybreak.

What is your name?

Why do you ask My name?

Chapter Eight

THE RIGHT THING IN A WRONG WORLD

I n the town where I live, a little girl is dying. Her name is Kaitlyn. My
daughter Sarah attended preschool with Kaitlyn, and on the days when I
picked Sarah up, I would often find her and Kaitlyn playing together, at the
swing set pushing one another in great stomach-fluttering arcs, or in the
sandbox, piling pail upon pail of crumbly sand into a kind of replica of a
ruined acropolis. They were two vigorous, joyful four-year-olds, prankish,
coltish, giddy, quick to laugh, dance, cry, sing.

One day, Kaitlyn's mother, Bonnie, came to pick her up, and something
was terribly awry. Bonnie wrote this to me:

> Have you ever had a day that you know has changed your life forever,
> a day that you would do anything to black out, just fast-forward past?
>
> February 28, 1997. I arrived at the preschool. Kaitlyn was stand-
> ing in the playground, looking down at the grass. One of her play-
> mates said several times, "Kaitlyn, your mommy is here." I spoke to
> her and there was no reaction, so I approached her and lifted her chin

up with my finger. When I did this, I realized something was wrong. Her eyes were vacant, and she had no recognition of me. I immediately called for the preschool teacher. Kaitlyn began to waiver. I knelt down beside her and laid her across my lap. The teacher called her name and did other things to get her to respond. Her eyes were open but not focused; they rolled to the right. She remained limp. The ambulance was called. I carried her inside and started to lay her on her side. When I did this, she began to cry and call for mommy. When the paramedics arrived, I was holding her and kissing her and weeping. We were taken to the hospital by ambulance.... I was told she had a seizure but she would be fine. Tests were ordered.[1]

The tests agreed with the initial diagnosis: Kaitlyn would be fine.

But Kaitlyn wasn't fine. She grew more and more pale. Her speech started to slur, and she began to fumble things, stumble often. She got more and more clumsy. She couldn't hold things. She walked into walls and doorjambs, and she fell down a lot. Her speech worsened. Words started coming out in guttural chunks, in sharp jagged howls, in throaty grunts, in mournful groans. The other four-year-olds grew afraid of her. Some made fun of her.

The doctor kept ordering tests.

Then one day, Kaitlyn's mother and father got the news that they dreaded and expected: Kaitlyn is dying. She has Batten's disease, a rare and incurable congenital degenerative neural disorder. It means her muscles are petrifying. They are now hard like wood; they will soon be hard like stone. They will harden until one day she can no longer swallow or breathe. Kaitlyn's parents, her brother, her grandparents, her aunts and uncles and cousins, her friends, her church family all watch beautiful little Kaitlyn die a slow death, and they can do nothing.

Kaitlyn's mother is a Christian and has drenched her bed with tears. She has beaten her fists bloody on heaven's door, trying to get the owner to open it and give her bread. She attends a church full of godly, caring people. They pray. Other people at other churches pray. They pray for many things: strength for the parents, wisdom for the doctors, comfort for Kaitlyn. But mostly they pray that God will heal Kaitlyn.

God hasn't answered that prayer yet. In truth, few now think He will.

The people who live beside Kaitlyn won the lottery. More than six hundred thousand dollars. I know almost nothing about these people, except that they have a lovely house. The house, I was told, is already paid for. It has been for a long time. These people, I understand, had a good, abundant life even before their jackpot win. I'm not sure why they buy lottery tickets or, if they don't, why others buy lottery tickets for them. I'm not sure if they ever prayed to win the lottery or if they ever pray at all.

But they won the lottery. More than six hundred thousand dollars.

And, in the house next door, Kaitlyn is dying.

LIFE ISN'T FAIR. THERE IS A LOPSIDEDNESS AND RANDOMNESS TO its distribution of windfalls and pitfalls and pratfalls. Who will get sick? Who will get rich? Who will be beautiful? Who will be disfigured? Is there any sovereign logic to this? And sometimes—and this is more puzzling, more troubling—the lopsidedness doesn't seem random: It seems calculated, a cosmic booby trapping of someone's life.

I know a man who loves God and serves Him with deep and heartfelt dedication. He soaks himself in the Word of God and then pours it out. He lives far beyond borderland, deep in the holy wild. Yet nothing seems to go right for him. He is a self-employed tradesman. He has honed skills, wide expertise, years of experience. He works hard. The problem isn't getting work. The problem isn't people not liking the work he does. The problem is that many of the people who hire him don't pay him, or pay him much less than they agreed they would. There is always some reason or another. But after a few years of this, it begins to look like a cosmic conspiracy, like a Jobian wager God made with the devil to see if a good man would curse Him. To see if a man living in the holy wild with a burning heart could be tempted back to borderland, slow hearted, defeated.

The money problems are only part of the difficulty. Disaster seems to lay ambush for this man. On any given week he can be served with an eviction notice for nonpayment of rent, have the utility company threaten to cut off his heat and lights if he doesn't pay his bill in twenty-four hours, have one of his children do something to break his heart, have no food to put on the table, and in the middle of all that have either the car break down, the water heater explode, another client fail to pay him, or any number of niggling mishaps occur. It's like the plagues of Exodus—gnats, flies, locusts, frogs—one after the next, swarming, attacking, pestering, devouring.

And he's one of the good guys.

Recently I asked him how he was doing. "Things have been better," he said. "But I'm trying not to get my hopes up."

Life isn't fair.

The psalmist knew the experience and wrote about it with refreshing and disarming frankness:

As for me, my feet had almost slipped....
For I envied the arrogant
    when I saw the prosperity of the wicked.
They have no struggles;
    their bodies are healthy and strong.
They are free from the burdens common to man;
    they are not plagued by human ills....
Surely in vain have I kept my heart pure;
    in vain have I washed my hands in innocence.
All day long I have been plagued;
    I have been punished every morning.
(Psalm 73:1–5, 13–14)

My friend could have written this.

YET THERE IS ANOTHER STORY THAT IS MAYBE MORE PERPLEXING, more embittering. It begins, "A father had two sons...." You can call them the older and the younger, the prodigal and the frugal, Esau and Jacob, Cain and Abel. Let's make them daughters and call them Jane and Becky. The dilemma is this: The father, from all appearances, likes Jane and not Becky. He seems to pamper and dote on Jane, scorn and scold Becky. Everything Jane does meets with applause and leads to greater recognition and approval. Everything Becky does somehow crumbles. If Jane touches something, it turns to gold. If Becky touches something, it turns to dust. Is this not the father's doing? Is this not the classic case of the parent playing favorites?

Look closer. Both Jane and Becky are faithful. They both tithe. They both serve in ministry in some way. They both love the Lord, though neither one perfectly. In fact, if it were up to you to decide which one appeared more devout, more faithful, more prayerful, more sincere, and to dispense favor accordingly, you would pick Becky. Jane is...well, Jane can be manipulative and meddlesome. She can be downright gossipy. She has a sly, shifty way of getting what she wants. She has an uncanny ability to flaunt, beneath a suitable cloak of humility, her accomplishments. She can manage to take credit, without appearing to connive at it, for good things she's hardly had anything to do with. She can manage to slip blame, without seeming to contrive it, for bad things she's mostly caused.

As Jane grows older everything just gets better and better for her. Her children are intelligent, attractive, popular. They get good grades in school and are both confident and respectful among adults. Her husband just got another promotion, and with it a bonus: his company's paying for the whole family to go to DisneyWorld in Florida. Jane's decided to have a new sunroom added onto the house while they're away.

"I wanted to do the addition last year," she says, "but we just couldn't afford it after we got the new van. But Robert's promotion comes with [voice lowers to a mock conspiratorial whisper] *a very substantial financial incentive,* so we're better positioned this year for a little indulgence. Not that it is an indulgence. We're finding that as the kids get older, we could really use the extra space. And my plants in that one corner just don't do that well, so they'll appreciate a sunroom. Do you know what the real blessing is? Because the work will all be done while we're in Florida, we don't have to live with all that dust and noise and mess, not to mention all those workers tramping in and out. Isn't God good?"

Becky has to wonder. Becky's children are not particularly intelligent, attractive, or popular. Becky's children have crooked teeth. Her husband, who works as a hardware salesman and hasn't seen a raise in his meager salary for five years, can't afford to get those teeth straightened. Their oldest son just got suspended from school for a week because he started a fire in the cafeteria garbage can. Their daughter is overweight and has a bad complexion and at twelve is already so depressed that every morning mother and daughter have a screaming match just to get the girl dressed and out the door. Today Becky's husband came home and said his company issued a memo announcing that because of another year of losses, eight workers will be laid off after Christmas. Becky has a queasy feeling inside, a dark intuition about who one of them will be.

Sometimes Becky wonders if she's done something wrong, something to offend God, to anger Him, to place herself outside the circle of His blessing. She frets about her past. Was it that time in the seventh grade when she wished Gilbert Jones dead? Or the time as a teenager when she and her three friends played with a Ouija board? Or the time, two years ago, when she lied to the pastor about why the family had missed six weeks of church? Was that it? She worries that she is not praying right or praying enough, repenting properly, serving with entirely good motives. Then she feels anger at the idea of a God who would punish her for such trivial lapses. Then she feels guilty for getting angry at God. Then she thinks of Jane and feels bitter. Then she feels guilty again for feeling that way toward Jane and wonders if God is punishing her for her envy.

> Then the LORD said…, "Why are you angry? Why is your face downcast? If you do what is right, will you not be accepted? But if you do not do what is right, sin is crouching at your door; it desires to have you, but you must master it." (Genesis 4:6–7)

That is God's brusque response to Cain's sulking. Cain sulks because, by all appearances, God likes his brother Abel and not him. In fact, God's apparent proclivity to favor one family member over another is almost a leitmotiv in Scripture: Jacob over Esau; Joseph over his brothers; David over his brothers and over Saul; the prodigal son over the frugal one; the Jews over everyone else; then the Gentiles over the Jews. And that's an embittering thing for those who are on the downside of it, the brunt end of it.

A man from my church who teaches at the local Christian high school called me one morning in early September and asked if I had any insight to pass on to him about the Cain and Abel story. The senior class that year was using as its motto, "I *am* my brother's keeper"—the reverse of Cain's angry rebuttal, after he has killed Abel, to God's question about where his brother is. I confessed to this man that I had not read that passage in a long time. I asked him to give me a few hours; I would read and ponder the story, then call him back.

So I did. I read it, and read it again. I thought about it. And then I read it once more. The man who called me had put no particular pressure on me, but I felt pressure nonetheless, and the pressure was this: to distill out of this story some tight and tidy moral bromide. I strained to unearth a clean, glinting nugget of truth, a timeless ethical principle. But the more I read it, the more I started to feel Cain's anger. I started to feel the rightness of his feelings, the wrongness of his situation. I started to sulk with him.

I phoned the man back. "Listen," I said, "I'm a bit embarrassed here, but the best I've come up with is this: *Life isn't fair. Get over it.*"

The man thanked me and hung up. I don't think he was impressed.

But Cain haunted me. He dogged my steps, shadowed my moves, hovered over my thoughts.

> The LORD looked with favor on Abel and his offering, but on Cain and
> his offering he did not look with favor. So Cain was very angry, and
> his face was downcast. (Genesis 4:4–5)

And well he should be. What is this favor of the Lord—the seeming fickleness, arbitrariness, inscrutability of it? The book of Hebrews, of course, puts an interpretive twist on this episode: Abel made his offering with faith, Cain without it. But the writer of Hebrews probably knew that from some other source: It's difficult to exegete it out of the story itself. Other than the hint that God rejected Cain because he had failed to do what is right, the story is devoid of clear reasons for God's choice. It is stark in its details, plain in its telling. All we know is that Cain worked the soil; Abel kept flocks; and they both brought an offering from their work. God liked Abel's and liked Abel. He liked neither Cain nor his offering.

Not long after I began to live deeply with this story, I had a moment of epiphany. I don't remember what exactly triggered it, if anything. It might have been hearing about the missionary who returned from a lifetime of self-giving work in a Chinese orphanage to enjoy a modest retirement, only to be diagnosed with cancer and swiftly die. Or it might have been the incident of a pastor I knew who had served God and His people in faithfulness and fruitfulness for forty years and who, a year away from his retirement, was hit by a car while riding his bike on a sunny spring morning and died of massive internal bleeding. Or it might have been Kaitlyn.

I don't remember. But the epiphany was vivid. The epiphany was that Cain and Abel's experience—where one enjoys God's favor while the other doesn't—is one of the deepest realities about life. This is the way the world comes to us. This is the way many of us experience life. I'm cursed or I'm blessed; I'm chosen or I'm rejected; I'm favored or I'm scorned. And though we would like some solid sense that life fits an obvious ethical pattern that is cosmic in scope—in which bad people have bad things happen to them and good people reap good things—we're at a loss to find that pattern.

God breaks in on all this with a word so unconsoling, so unsympathetic, so curt and cold and cut-and-dried that it stings worse than the blow that incited Cain to bitterness: *Do the right thing. Sin would take you down in a minute. Quit your sulking. Stop this self-pity. Do rightly and justly, and don't give sin an inch.* We look for tender empathy, some therapeutic soothing and wooing, and instead get this brusqueness, this sternness, this drill sergeant bark.

You know the story. Cain doesn't do the right thing. His sulking gives way to grudge, and that to vindictiveness, and that to rage. And then Cain kills his brother in the very fields that he's grown his food in, the very fields from which he gathered his spurned offering to God. He spills Abel's bright, hot blood on that earth. *If God doesn't want the fruits of my soil, if He won't open His mouth to receive them, then let the soil open its mouth to receive Abel's blood* (verse 11). And then Cain refuses responsibility for what he has done.

God punishes Cain, sets him adrift, makes him a wanderer, an outlaw. But God also shows grace to Cain. He promises Cain protection and marks him with a sign of it. Cain heads east of Eden, a marked man, scarred with wandering and warning, bearing stigma, and yet also marked with the insignia of God's guardianship. He is a cursed man and a blessed man. He is rejected, banished, cast out, but also protected, kept, watched over.

If my years of pastoral experience guide me in any way here, I would venture that God's protection of Cain is as embittering to those who loved Abel as God's favoring of Abel was embittering to Cain. Why doesn't God let Cain suffer the full crushing brunt of his actions? Why let him off so lightly? He's a killer—a cold-blooded, premeditated, first-degree murderer. Yet there's no real justice rendered here, no capital punishment, no eye for an eye, no life for a life. No jail term. Not even bail. Just a perpetual exile. And God steps in to ensure that no vigilante action or frontier justice is ever exacted against Cain. The killer gets to go free, on the loose. He might be your neighbor. Your kid might go to school with his kid. And you can't do a thing about it, and those who loved Abel can't do a thing about it. Bitter news, this.

Life isn't fair. And in the thick, swarming midst of life's unfairness, our options often narrow down to something so simple it seems cliché: *Do the right thing. Have the right attitude.*

Bitter news, this. And that is the main danger in a world of unfairness: bitterness. The danger is to indulge our bitterness, to feel justified in it, to feel justified in the deeds that spring from it. The danger is that we will, *on principle,* refuse to do the right thing. After all, we reason, has God done the right thing? Isn't God a hard man, reaping where He has not sown, gathering what He has not scattered?

I HAVE NEVER BEEN INVOLVED IN A CHURCH DISCIPLINE ACTION that has come out well. When it was all said and done, everyone—including me—seemed soured by the business. Those who received the discipline felt they were misunderstood, mistreated, that the church acted without grace or love. Those who had been hurt by the offender felt the church had tiptoed, kid-gloved, pampered the wrongdoer and had insufficiently upheld their cause. Many watching from the sidelines have thought that we have either soft-pedaled righteousness or trampled grace. We have acted too harshly or too cautiously; we have been legalistic, or we have failed to take sin and holiness with biblical seriousness. We're Pharisees, arrogant and accusing and rigid—or we're Sadducees, arrogant and accommodating and slippery-soft. We're crusaders or we're kowtowers. Almost everyone is angry about the outcome. Some in their anger withdraw their services. Some stop giving. Some stop coming. I have yet to lead the church through a disciplinary action where all of the above, in some measure, did not happen.

For years I put this down to my own inadequacy, my callow youth and shallow experience, my sometimes patched together knowledge of Scripture or makeshift interpretations of it, my fumbling grasp of original languages, my half-baked wisdom, my thinly mustered courage and thinly veiled frustration, my slipshod ability. All of that may be true. But in recent years, I have been less inclined to think the problem lies in these things—in me.

The problem is that life is unfair. Unfairness is genetically coded into it. And so sometimes the innocent are murdered, and the murderer is protected.

So what is right? If that is the stark command to Cain—*Do what is right*—what is right? What is right in a world where little girls get sick and die and genocidal despots live in luxury? Where hard working men go bankrupt and swindlers go on swindling? Where slumlords and warlords get rich off the spoils and good people are left to scavenge? Where all the wrong people, it seems, suffer?

What is the right thing?

The writer of Hebrews mentions Cain and Abel. He says the difference between them distilled to one thing: faith. Abel had it, Cain didn't. "Without faith," the writer of Hebrews warns, "it is impossible to please God." Then he builds his case with example after example of those who lived by faith. What is curious about the list is how many people are mentioned who must have carried within them a keen sense of life's unfairness. "Some faced jeers and flogging, while still others were chained and put in prison. They were stoned. They were sawed in two. They were put to death by the sword. They went about in sheepskins and goatskins, destitute, persecuted, mistreated.... They wandered in deserts and mountains, and in caves and holes in the ground." And then this: "None of them received what had been promised" (Hebrews 11:36–39).

Yet all of them lived by faith. Without faith, it is impossible to please God.

Faith is the right thing.

This seems altogether too simple. But of course the simplest ideas—thankfulness, kindness, generosity, faith—are the most difficult to live out. To continue to trust God, to give ourselves into His keeping, to entrust our riches, our first fruits, our children, our homes to Him—well, what if we did that already and were stricken with multiple sclerosis or went bankrupt or got robbed or had a child go astray or lost our home to fire? What if life isn't fair?

The right thing is still, is always, faith. *If you do what is right, will it not go well with you?* That's what God says to Cain. Much depends here on how we understand the phrase "will it not go well with you." Is God promising Cain that if he does the right thing, he'll prosper in health, finances, relationships, intellectual pursuit, and physical achievement? Surely not. Abel did the right thing; he was killed. God loved Abel. God accepted Abel. God showed favor to Abel. But that favor was expressed only in accepting Abel's gift, opening His mouth to receive it. It was not expressed in protection. In fact, God provides far more protection to Cain than He ever did to Abel. He marks Cain to keep at bay the ruffians, the avengers. Why didn't God mark Abel that way and stay his own brother's hand of death?

Life isn't fair.

If you do what is right, it will go well with you. What will go well? I would like this to mean that God will stay the hand of death, disease, accident, injury, and illness, always, everywhere, right to the sweet, gentle end for me and those I love, and then that He will whisk us Enochlike to heaven. I would like it to mean that the rapists and serial killers and genocidal despots are brought to swift, unswerving justice. I would like it to mean that Kaitlyn lives a long, healthy life, marrying at twenty-three, bearing three children, burying her parents when they are in their eighties, retiring after a productive and fulfilling life of teaching or stone sculpting or genetic research, dying in her sleep in her early nineties, still mobile, her own children and grandchildren and great-grandchildren gathering to mourn her and celebrate her and sing hymns over her.

It will go well with you.

But of course, it doesn't mean that—the idyllic, undisturbed life. That might happen. It might not. Neither its happening nor its not happening affects *its going well with you.*

God's definition of *it going well* is unique, distinct, almost eccentric. His definition of wellness is not about health, finances, or job security. It's not about unfailing protection from the vagaries and dangers of a broken world.

It's not about life being fair.

It's about acceptance. It's about God accepting us as His own, the ones He loves. It's not about being spared from untimely or difficult death. It's about being spared the "second death"—the death of unbridgeable separation, the death that is at once coldness and burning, oblivion and torment, a writhing crowd of teeth-gnashers and the desolation of unending aloneness.

Because of Jesus Christ, we have received God's *unmerited* favor. And actually that favor has always been unmerited. *If we do what is right, it will go well with us.* The right thing is faith—to have faith in the one who doesn't always remedy life's unfairness, but who does far better: He redeems it—its unfairness, its brokenness, its disease and death, and He gives us back sevenfold all the years the locusts have eaten. *Today*—He says to repentant thieves, to trusting Abels, to dying little girls—*today you will be with Me in paradise.*

Ultimately, we are citizens of heaven, and we eagerly await a Savior from there. But meanwhile, in the shadowlands, we walk by faith and not by sight. Meanwhile (ambiguous word, that: mean-while—in the mean place, the between place, the unfair place), those who walk by faith discover that life rarely gets easier. It often gets harder. Safe? Who said He was safe? Fair? Who said He was fair?

The holy wild is wilderness. But if you walk and don't faint, you find what Job did: *Though He slay me, yet will I praise Him.* You find that the God who walks with us through the valley of the shadow of death is infinitely better than the dull, safe god who lulls us into borderland, seducing us with false comforts, spinning a cocoon around us that doesn't protect, only entraps, and from which we emerge wingless.

Bonnie, Kaitlyn's mother, again:

> God is doing a mighty work through this little girl. Why she has to be sick for it to happen is not for me to understand. All I know is that out of her life Jesus Christ shines. And those that dare to get close to her can't help but see it. "This sickness is not unto death, but for the glory of God, that the Son of God may be glorified through it." (John 11:4)[2]

Life isn't fair. But for those who live by faith—for Abel and Abraham, for Kaitlyn and Bonnie—it is well, it is well, with their souls.

Chapter Nine

SAINT PRIDE

A young man came up to me after I had preached on temptation one Sunday. I had spoken about the temptations of flesh but said that they were nothing in terms of their destructiveness and deceitfulness compared with the sins of the spirit. I talked specifically about pride.

"Pastor Mark," this fellow said, "when did you finally overcome your pride?"

He was serious.

The funny—or sad—thing is that my first impulse was to say, "Well, many years ago now, God came and removed every last shred and spark of it."

I managed a stale joke: "I'm not sure, but now that I have, I'm perfect."

There are some sins that we keep constant vigilance over. Pride is one of them. It's a shape-shifter, a master of masquerade. It often cloaks itself as humility—perhaps pride's most effective and attractive costume.

There was a movie made in the late nineties called *The Saint,* based on a television series from an earlier era. Val Kilmer plays a master of espionage and burglary. He's a man of many disguises—a Russian commando, a sniveling journalist, a mystic poet, an effeminate booking agent—but he always takes the name of a saint. His disguises are so thorough, so precise in detail, that they fool even those who know him intimately or who are on the hunt for him. In one scene he sits down right beside the man who has been obsessively tracking him for years. He looks straight at the man and asks him a question. The man has no idea it's him.

That's what pride is like. It keeps showing up in disguise, bearing a saint's name, mingling freely in the crowd, unrecognized by even those who seek it out. When that young man asked me about my secret to conquering pride, I had a surge of pride in thinking how very godly I must look. There it was, pride, sitting down right beside me and duping me again. Pascal once said that real humility is so elusive that when he wrote about it, he often felt proud of how eloquently he'd written.

Pride grows in most soils, most climates. There are few conditions under which it can't survive, even thrive. But there is one soil that usually withers pride. It's brokenness.

"Blessed are the poor in spirit," Jesus said.

"A broken and contrite heart," David said, "you do not despise."

Of course, brokenness can't be contrived. Should we try, it becomes just one more occasion for pride to flourish: *O God, behold your servant, how broken he is....* The real thing often comes at first like a curse. We wouldn't ask for it, don't welcome it. Who wants to be broken? There is a gift in brokenness, but it is well hidden, discovered in the depths of the thing, a treasure strewn among rubble and sewage.

Here is a curious thing: Brokenness—a broken heart, a broken spirit— molds our character closer to the character of God than anything else. To experience defeat, disappointment, loss—the raw ingredients of brokenness— moves us closer to being like God than victory and gain and fulfillment ever can. This is a paradox. I would think that, given that God is all-wise, all-powerful, everywhere-at-once, the opposite would be true. I would assume that as we experience power, we move closer to God; as we grow in knowledge, we grow in the likeness of God; as we attempt to control more things, we mimic God more exactly. But that just isn't the way it works out. We imitate most precisely the all-powerful, all-knowing, everywhere-at-once God when we are childlike, beggarlike, broken.

I am not recommending we pray for brokenness or seek it out. In fact, I think such praying and seeking undo the benefit that brokenness can otherwise give. Seeking it is akin to vandalism or arson, a willful damaging. Only sick people ransack or burn down their own houses. But ordinary people sometimes find, in spite of themselves, their house burned down or ransacked. And then the only thing you can do is pick through the wreckage for heirlooms.

Sometimes you walk away rejoicing that something you never really wanted but hadn't the strength to throw away has been destroyed.

ONE OF THE WORST MANIFESTATIONS OF PRIDE IS SELF-DECEIT. Self-deceit is the unwillingness, even the inability, to face our own evil, and if we do face it, we can't accept the real reasons for it. Instead, we have a large repertoire of lies to tell ourselves to ease our consciences, to save face, to explain away. We're good at lying to ourselves. Even when we're faltering and awkward at all other forms of pretense—when we couldn't lie to someone else to save our lives—we're almost always adept at duping ourselves, even when it means losing our life. In our skin exist both the country bumpkin, easily addled and awed, and the traveling mountebank, wily and wooing as a snake.

And here's a funny thing: The more sophisticated and educated we are, usually the more gullible we are. Solomon was reputedly the most knowledgeable man on earth. Perhaps because of that, not in spite of it, he was the most prone to self-deception. Few have sinned as extravagantly and excessively as Solomon. An educated liar, after all, has all the vast, complex repository of psychology and sociology to draw upon for his lying. Mix a little Freud, a bit of Nietszche, a dash of Jung, a dose of Mead into the pot, and we can excuse ourselves endlessly, almost effortlessly. Like shyster lawyers, we can nimbly evade the bone-stark truth with a flurry of qualifications, technical maneuvers, semantic quibbles, procedural rigmarole, logic chopping, hairsplitting, murky jargon, fluffy rhetoric, dodges, delays, diversions, revisions, aspersions. We pride ourselves—oh, there's *that* word again—on being able to see through every con man and pitchman, every quack and demagogue. We laugh derisively at the simple fools who fall prey to charlatans. We scoff at those who pay exorbitant sums for potions that promise to cure baldness, revive flagging energies, turn luck around. Laughing and scoffing at the fools, we meanwhile tell ourselves that sin is something other than sin.

Some years ago, Robert Redford made a fine movie called *Quiz Show*, about the game show scandal that rocked the U.S. television networks in the fifties. Ralph Fiennes plays Charles Van Doren, the highborn and erudite young professor who becomes a national icon with a string of wins on the show *Twenty-One*. Van Doren has amazing breadth and depth of knowledge. He can pop off, with agility and charm, the right answer to the most esoteric questions ranging over a huge variety of fields. Only one problem: He's being fed the answers ahead of time by the network moguls. The whole thing's fixed.

Richard Goodwin, a congressional investigator, gets suspicious and launches a low-scale federal investigation. He and Van Doren become sort of friends. In one scene, they're playing poker with some other men. Van Doren ups the stakes, and Goodwin looks him in the eyes.

"You're lying," Goodwin says in his grating, street-smart New Jersey accent. He is, of course, referring to more than just the poker game.

"Bluffing," Van Doren retorts in silky Ivy League tones. "I believe the word is *bluffing.*"

That is the trick of the sophisticated: to call lying, adultery, thievery, or whatever by some other name, something soft and elegant, even alluring.

Jesus said our condemnation stems from exactly this—a refusal to have our sin exposed. "This is the verdict," He says. "Light has come into the world, but men loved darkness instead of light because their deeds were evil" (John 3:19). Or as the apostle John says, "If we claim to be without sin, we deceive ourselves and the truth is not in us" (1 John 1:8).

David, the man after God's own heart, duped himself. He refused for a long, dark stretch to come into the light. He committed adultery with Bathsheba and got her pregnant. When his cover-up scheme failed, he had her husband, Uriah, murdered.

David lived with his lie for a year. During that time, he camped in borderland. At one point in his life, David had been forced by Saul's madness and jealousy to live in desert caves, in enemy territory, in border towns. But that was because of his integrity, his refusal to raise his hand against Saul. It was, as he says so often in the psalms he wrote, because of his righteousness that he was there. Those border towns were the center of God's will.

But for a year, David lived a self-imposed exile in a place far from the will of God. He was there because he couldn't be honest with himself. It was a refugee camp outside the presence of God. That's pride's land.

Scripture keeps no record of what he thought during that stay in borderland, and it's probably futile to speculate. But if we're honest with ourselves—that's what we're hoping to be—we know the labyrinth of excuse making he likely got himself into. A good part of this would consist of blaming: blaming Bathsheba for bathing naked in his view; blaming her husband, Uriah, for his failings as a husband, a warrior, a man; blaming his other wives for not understanding him, attending to him, satisfying him; blaming his courtiers for not safeguarding and preoccupying him elsewhere. He likely reviews the benefits of his deed: He feels attractive again, youthful. He's lost weight. He's finally married to the woman he *should* have married in the first place, the *woman God had intended* for him to marry. She really understands me. We have so much in common. When I'm with her, I feel alive.

And so it goes. Men after God's own heart claim no immunity from lying to themselves. Finally, a year later the prophet Nathan confronts David, and he repents. We have a record of that prayer of confession and repentance in Psalm 51. The entire psalm is remarkable, but this verse captures me: "Surely you desire truth in the inner parts; you teach me wisdom in the inmost place" (v. 6).

No clearer summary of holiness has ever been spoken. Holiness is just that. It is truth in the inner parts, God's wisdom spoken into the inmost place. When we search the deepest, most hidden regions of ourselves, we find truth, God's voice speaking.

For a long time—and this despite all Jesus' warnings to the Pharisees—I saw holiness as an outward thing. It was a matter of what I *did*. Of course, holy people act in holiness, but that's the least of it. Good behavior is the flower of a Godward life. But just as often, it's the mask of a self-centered one, a self-deceived one. Good behavior can be our true self exposed or our true self concealed. Good behavior can be the fullness of life that we discover in pursuing the God who is good. It can be the overflow of worshiping the God who is holy.

Or it can be merely the reduction of life that we settle for because we've embraced the god who is too safe. A god who is too safe, after all, doesn't care about true holiness: He just wants us scrubbed up, well groomed, without halitosis or scalp itch or dirt beneath our fingernails. Respectable. Presentable. That god is as easily fooled by rhetoric and charade as we are. He is pleased as punch by good behavior and sticks a little gold star on our lapels to reward us for it.

But what does the true God want?

Surely You desire truth in the inner parts.

Given the choice between an original piece of artwork—a Rembrandt, a Titian, a Van Gogh—or a cheap calendar or poster copy, we would without hesitation choose the original. We'd take the real thing.

Every day, God offers us the real thing—His holiness. Real holiness is truth in the inner parts, God's wisdom spoken in the inmost place. Real holiness is being naked and not being ashamed. Real holiness is coming into the light. Real holiness is telling ourselves the truth, no matter what. Real holiness is calling sin by its real name.

Pride always tries to foist off on us the cheap copy. It's the burglar feigning sainthood.

God offers us the original. God desires to actually make us saints, from the inside out.

Only one condition: You've got to humble yourself.

Chapter Ten

HOLDING ON TO
A HOLY MUST

T ypical day: awaken after a rough night. Siren wails and cat yowls, hot entangling sheets, a dull ache in the bones, a sharp pain in the back, tumult in the belly, angst in the heart—all were a riptide keeping you, exhausted, from reaching the solid ground of sleep. It's earlier than you want to get up. It's later than you should have. The kids need to be roused, fed, dressed, sent off to school. Everyone is tired. Everyone is irritable. There's not enough hot water for showers. Someone forgot to turn on the dishwasher last night. Lipstick-stained cups, smudged glasses, food-encrusted bowls—all need to be swished out beneath the tap, set on the table where they leave rings and puddles of wetness. Arguments erupt. Angry words are shouted. Things are hastily patched over and everyone scatters—the daily diaspora

Driving to work, you notice your husband didn't put gas in the car yesterday like you asked him to. You have to do it. At the gas station, you remember that you forgot to turn on the dishwasher again. You make a mental note to phone home after school and get one of the kids to do it. There's a road crew slowing traffic on the route you drive, and you miss a light because you have to halt for a fire truck. You are running late, and your nerves, like string caught on the hub of a spinning wheel, wind to a choking tightness. Your muscles, like wet cloth wrung by strong hands, twist into heavy knots. And it's not yet nine o'clock.

At work, you have three phone calls to return (two of them urgent), five e-mails requiring a response, a stack of paper you've been intending to get to all week, and a woman outside your office waiting to see you. You don't recognize her but think you should, and you're unsure if she made an appointment and you forgot it, or if she just arrived unannounced. Both possibilities annoy you. You get most of that sorted away, plus handle several other phone calls and e-mails and interruptions, and it's almost lunch, and you still haven't touched that stack of paper.

At lunch, mustard comes out the wrong seam of the little plastic packet and spatters over the front of your shirt. You rush into a clothing store and buy a new one. You put it on your VISA card because you're low on cash and doubt a debit card will clear. You return to the office. The afternoon is like the morning, except you have even less strength and enthusiasm for it.

You arrive home weary. The only mail is a pizza flyer and a VISA bill. Opening the bill, you are deflated: You had forgotten about the $350 brake job you charged last month. You order a pizza from the flyer because you're too tired to cook. You put it on VISA. Only when you go to set the table for dinner do you realize that you forgot to make your phone call: The dishwasher has still not been run. More swishing of plates, glasses, forks.

You eat quickly because your son has soccer practice and your older daughter has youth group and you have to drive them both. You have a meeting at seven. You hope, against reason, that it will end by eight-thirty so that you can pick up your daughter at church without making her wait and the youth pastor wait with her. At the meeting, you are so obsessed with watching the clock that you can't focus on the business at hand. You get more and more irritated at Sally's shambling, mawkish stories and George's bulldog fierceness and Harry's slippery persuasion and Betty's "I think we shoulds" and Larry's pretentious otherworldliness and his monomaniacal question, "Have we prayed enough about this?" Inside, you feel the fruits of the Spirit, one by one, shrivel and drop off the branch, pushed out by their opposites: loathing, sourness, worry, impatience, rudeness, rottenness, faithlessness, gruffness, wildness.

The meeting goes to nearly nine. You rush out, gravel flying scattershot beneath your spinning wheels (did you just hear the ping of rocks hitting Larry's car?) and arrive at 9:08 to pick up your daughter. Neither she nor the youth pastor are pleased. You drive home in silence because your daughter refuses to speak to you, and you are too angry and prideful and weary to apologize. You had earlier planned to read a bit before bed, but you're too spent for that. You get into bed, and though your body has a corpselike stiffness and heaviness to it, some angst in you, along with the cup of coffee you had at the meeting, keeps plucking you from sleep. Twice you have to get up, once to check for a file you need to take to work tomorrow, once to let the cat out. When morning comes, you can't remember ever getting to sleep, though the alarm wakes you with an abruptness like a coronary. You begin all over again.

Typical day.

WE'RE BUSY PEOPLE. THE MAIN EXPERIENCE OF MEN AND WOMEN and even children in North America is busyness, having far more to do any day, every day, all day, than we can possibly get done. We simultaneously scurry and slog through breathless, breakneck schedules. We flounder in a welter of meetings and errands, demands and delays, expectations and obligations. It's joyless. It's endless. Our leisure itself has become an anxious, rushed, fitful business. Our rest is restless. Maybe we implicitly acknowledged this reality when we stopped calling our time away from work a *holiday* and started calling it a *vacation*. What was once time set apart for Godward and God-filled refreshment, a holy day, became merely an evacuation, a vacating, a vacancy, a vacuity. It's an interval to flee, escape, avoid real life for a while.

Most of us, right now, need a vacation. Don't you want, just for a time, to disappear? Don't you feel like the proverbial sloth trying to mimic the proverbial ant? The phone ringing startles you like gunshot and fills you with a similar foreboding. Mercy seems like just another job to do. You lack motivation for the simplest tasks and can only perform them through a mix of Herculean effort and robotic plodding.

But will a vacation help? Mere vacations are just that, an emptying that often leaves us empty, a reprieve that brings short-term relief but no lasting refreshment. Too often I have returned from vacation only minimally restored. A day or two back into my routine and responsibilities, and I am just as caught up in the endless and wearisome toil that the writer of Ecclesiastes so vividly describes: "I hated life, because the work that is done under the sun was grievous to me. All of it is meaningless, a chasing after the wind" (2:17).

A pastor I work with returned from a recent two-week vacation, part of it spent lying on white sands beneath the ragged shadiness of palm trees, strolling through a maze way of bright, cluttered markets amid the din of hawkers' banter, and dining at candlelit tables covered in thick white linen, with the napkins folded like a sconce shell and the silverware handles embossed with tiny seahorses. It was paradisaical. I asked her, after a week back, how she was.

"Uhhh," she said. "Well, it was like I was never away. To be honest, I almost didn't come back."

And it's one of those vacations I dream about all year long? Is it really worth it?

What I need are more holidays, more holy days. But, deeper than that, what I really need is a Christlike sense of time and timeliness and timelessness. Christ undertook the most urgent work ever assigned, announcing the kingdom's arrival, restoring and redefining Israel's hope, enacting salvation for the whole world. Along with that, He cast out demons, healed the sick, raised the dead. He gathered and trained those who, after He was gone, would carry on His work of announcing, building, healing, teaching. And He did it all in a mere three years.

Yet He did it in an attitude of nearly unbroken serenity, almost leisureliness. He never seemed to be watching the clock. He could get tired, but He had no qualms about falling asleep just about anywhere, storm-tossed fish boats, for instance, or having luxurious dinners out. He could be wonderfully responsive to the demands of others—a gruff centurion, a panicked father, a desperate widow—but never got caught up in their anxiety. Just as often, He could without a twinge of guilt walk away from demands and expectations. When the disciples interrupted His prayers because "everyone is looking for you," He responded by saying, "Let's go somewhere else" (Mark 1:37–38). Or when news reached Him in Capernaum that His friend Lazarus was dying in Bethany, He stalled, dallied, came late. Even after He "set his face like flint" to go to His death in Jerusalem, He meandered. The journey was filled with interruptions, detours, rounds and rounds of storytelling.

When the architect Frank Lloyd Wright was a boy of nine, he walked with his uncle across a snowy field one cold, gray morning. His uncle was a driven man, bristling with impatience. The clock inside him boomed like a war drum, drove like a ramrod. Once across the field, the uncle stopped and turned around and called young Frank to come stand beside him. The uncle's tracks in the snow were like a stitch made on cloth: clean, straight, tight, evenly spaced. But young Frank's tracks were a skein: a looping, disheveled mess of wanderings and shufflings and backtrackings.

"Frank," the uncle said, "notice how your tracks wander aimlessly from the fence to the cattle to the woods and back again. And see how my tracks aim directly to their goal. There is an important lesson in that."

"I determined right then," Frank Lloyd Wright said years later, "not to miss most things in life, as my uncle had."[1]

No one now doubts that Frank Lloyd Wright had a sense of call and purpose that never stirred in his old uncle's blood.

Jesus lived like that. Jesus was the man of ultimate destiny, pursuing a cosmic goal, eternal in scope, high as the heavens, deep as the pit, gathering all nations and all generations, enduring the passing away of all things. But He never made clean tracks in the snow—or sand. He went here, He went there, moved by seeming whim, chance, need, second thought and afterthought, and some inward tug of holy instinct. His zigzagging journey was anything but the anxious rushing about that characterizes our own living. It was, rather, the manner of one whose life is completely His own possession and free to give to whomever He pleases, however He pleases, whenever He pleases. Or not to give it. "I lay down my life—only to take it up again. No one takes it from me.... I have authority to lay it down and authority to take it up again. This command I received from my Father" (John 10:17–18).

T. S. Eliot described middle age as the time in your life when people keep asking you to do more and more, and you're not old enough yet to have an

YOUR GOD IS TOO SAFE   103

excuse for saying no. I know what he means, and you may, too. Our tracks in the snow skitter off in a dozen directions, but it's not from enjoying the journey. We are in fact goal driven, but have set far too many goals. And we've lost the power to discern which ones are actually important. Few of us possess the inner compass, map, calendar, and clock Jesus had. How did He know when to go and when to stay? And He could turn on a dime, change His plans in an instant. First He won't help at the wedding in Cana, but then He does (John 2:4–5). First He won't go to the feast in Jerusalem, but then He does. He curtly tells His brothers, "The right time for me has not yet come; for you any time is right" (John 7:6).

Wouldn't that be something if we could live that way? Our four-year-old comes whining into the kitchen, "Mommy, mommy, give me something to eat."

"For you, any time is right," you retort. "The right time for me has not yet come."

The boss comes into your office and asks if you can take on extra work.

"No."

"Pardon me?"

"I said no. I have not been sent to do this kind of work. Let the dead bury the dead."

There was Jesus—vigorous yet relaxed, clear-eyed yet dream-filled, purposeful yet not driven. He was active, productive, and diligent, but never busy. A blind man hollering at the roadside could get His time, His touch. Hungry people interrupting His retreat day could receive His compassion and provision. But John the Baptist—the "greatest in the kingdom of heaven"—could languish in prison, listening to the scrape of the ax being sharpened in the next room, and receive barely a greeting card from Him. Jesus' life was His own to take up and lay down as He chose. But the time for that laying down and that taking up had to be right: not just any time, any chunk or sliver of *chronos,* but *the moment,* a sharp, bright pinprick of *kairos,* the tip of huge unseen forces converging.

And He accomplished a work that forever changed heaven, hell, and earth. And you.

AT THE HEART OF JESUS' MINISTRY WAS A HOLY *MUST*. HE MUST GO through Samaria. He *must* go to Jerusalem. He *must* suffer. Everything He did or refused to do centered around that. A true *must* both constrains and liberates. It brings wonderful clarity. It allows for great seriousness and great playfulness, and it makes for serious, playful greatness. Most of our drivenness and anxiousness comes from not really knowing what we *must* do. So we do a lot of things. We do them all with grim, fretful haste. We do them with panic but no zeal. We have to, after all, get *this* thing done and get on to the next thing. We're not really sure what it is we *must* do, so there's no time to pause over, to savor, to reflect on anything. Our tracks in the snow are a pinwheel of straight lines shooting off in myriad directions. We're never sure which, if any, is the *right* direction.

I just turned forty. I can already feel my flesh wanting to slip bone and muscle. I have a growing looseness in my reflexes and tightness in my joints. My body begs me for more exercise, but begs me to stop when I do. The other day I went prawning with a friend. As I reeled up a prawn trap, my arms burning with the unfamiliar work, I had to better position myself by stepping down from the boat's transom onto a ledge about a foot wide at the back of the boat. The ledge skimmed the water's surface. Ten years ago, I would have jumped down with both feet onto that ledge. A few years back I would have gotten down in one seamless, graceful, surefooted step. But the other day, I stood above that dark, depthless water, knowing it held a deathly coldness that could freeze blood, and, like Peter looking at the rising waves around him instead of at Jesus who bids him come, I lost confidence. I got down in an ungainly, old-mannish way. I crouched on my haunches, secured my balance on my arms and cautiously slid one leg down until it touched the ledge, then the other.

When did this happen? I wondered. *This getting old, this becoming afraid?*

So the question that grows for me is this: "Lord, what *must* I do?" When I was younger, the question was not important. I had vast energy, swaggering confidence, ample time. I had a sense of immortality and invincibility. If I addressed the issues of life's brevity and the investment of finite hours, I did so rhetorically, dramatically, a fillip or flourish in the midst of a sermon. "What is your life?" I would say, strutting across the platform, arms aloft in a brandishing gesture. "Do you not know that your life is like dew, like a mist?" But this was better oratory than soul searching or soul piercing. It came not from any burning or haunting within.

But it's starting to. Age brings with it an odd assortment of accumulation and diminishment. Some things—flesh, grief, disappointment, nose hair—gather to a thickness. Others—muscle, laughter, triumphs, scalp hair—wear to a thinness. Ambitions that in our youth stirred and drove us we either abandon or, fulfilling them, wonder why we did. Passions we once had hot in our belly—for waterskiing or watercolors, Russian novels or coin collecting—cool to a damp, heavy lump in our gut. And other things—fetishes, grudges, cranky or quirky habits, dark or petty thoughts—swell into obsession.

The easy thing is just to stop bothering about the sticky, prickly, puzzling question of life's meaning. The easy thing is to take up permanent residence in borderland, a place chaotically and mindlessly busy, the hectic trading house of the trivial. The easy thing is to adopt some hybrid philosophy that crossbreeds stoicism ("just grit your teeth and take it like a man") with hedonism ("you only go around this way once, so you'd better get while the getting's hot") with epicureanism ("leave me to my patch of sunlight, I'll leave you to yours") with nihilism ("nothing matters anyway, so just do what you want"). Those worldviews, so dominant in the world of the apostle Paul, still define our main options today, and usually in most people's thinking they're mixed and matched as needed.

But if you live that way, after a while you notice that your life has nothing at its core. It has no center. There is activity. There is opinion. There is busyness. But there's nothing to give real pleasure or deep meaning to the activity, nothing to ground opinions in truth and shape them into convictions, nothing to translate busyness into fruitfulness, nothing to convert selfish ambition into holy purpose. You realize you're stuck slow hearted on borderland. And you start to wonder if this is it, or were you made and called for something else?

If we are ever to get beyond mere busyness—which is mostly self-contrived camouflage, a way we keep ourselves from seeing our own life's hollowness—we need a center out of which to live. We need a deeply Christian philosophy: "For to me, to live is Christ and to die is gain" (Philippians 1:21). We need a *must*.

So what *must* I do? What is the one thing needed? Forgetting what is behind, we want to say with Paul, and pressing on, *I take hold of that for which Christ Jesus took hold of me* (Philippians 3:12).

I take hold of that for which Christ Jesus took hold of me. That is the rally cry of those who live their lives on purpose, beyond the burden and trivia of mere busyness.

What is that for which Christ has taken hold of you? Discern that, take hold of that, and you have cut to the heart of a holy must beneath all life's muchness and busyness. There is freedom here and great gladness. But don't be fooled: It will not be an easy life. Life off the borderland never is. Paul would attest to that. When the risen Christ sends Ananias to a newly converted Saul of Tarsus, Ananias balks, complaining that Saul is a dangerous man, bent on the destruction of Christians. Christ is gruff with Ananias, a field marshal scolding a timid soldier: "Go!" He commands. Then He gives Ananias an account, sharp and stark, of why He has taken hold of Paul: "This man is *my chosen* instrument to carry my name before the Gentiles and their kings and before the people of Israel. I will show him how much *he must suffer* for my name" (Acts 9:13–16, emphasis mine).

How striking the language here. Christ does not say, "And he *will* suffer much for my name," as though suffering were only an unfortunate and perhaps avoidable by-product of Paul's call. No. The suffering is a necessity: He *must* suffer. It is an integral part of why Christ has taken hold of Paul, central to Christ's intent for him: *I will show him how much he must suffer.* Christ's hold on Paul was twofold: Paul was both to carry Christ's name and to suffer for it. The carrying and the suffering could not be separated from each other.

Suffering is often part of a holy must, something Jesus intends to *show* us. Jesus' earthly father, Joseph, in his woodshop, must have once *shown* Jesus the unique ways of carrying out the work: how to hold a chisel to notch a joint cleanly, how to wield a hammer to set a nail firmly, how to draw a saw to slice the wood squarely. So now Jesus, in His shop, *shows* His apprentice Paul the unique ways of carrying out the work: how to expose his back to a whip to take a lashing, how to open his hands to have nails driven through, how to pour out his life as a drink offering when falsely accused and rejected by those he loves.

How to live in the holy wild.

And Paul learned well. The book of Acts and Paul's own testimony, especially in 2 Corinthians, recount Paul's hardships in unflinching and unsentimental detail. Paul tends to list these things—beatings, stonings, hunger, imprisonment, torments within and without—as credentials, trophies, badges, medals: the paraphernalia of accomplishment. He does this deliberately and explicitly in 2 Corinthians 11, where he compares himself with the false apostles who have infected and afflicted the church. Those men are boasters. They flaunt their pedigrees and parade their degrees. They conspicuously display the insignia of entitlement, strut the marks of achievement. And in case you missed the point, they're quick to tell you how very important and skilled and knowledgeable they are. Paul, in direct rebuke of this behavior, rattles off his résumé: "I have…been in prison more frequently, been flogged more severely, and been exposed to death again and again. Five times I received from the Jews forty lashes minus one. Three times I was beaten with rods, once I was stoned" (11:23–25).

I take hold of that for which Christ Jesus took hold of me. Paul lived a holy must. The irony and paradox of living this way is that your life will be your own, and you can lay it down or take it up as you choose. You can dress yourself, go where you want. And yet, when you are older, you will stretch out your hands, and someone else will dress you and lead you where you do not want to go (John 21:18). You choose and yet have no choice. You live from a center that looses and binds you, and you are both utterly free and wholly restrained. It is deeply fulfilling and full of sacrifice. It is carrying the name and suffering for it. That is the nature of a must.

It is miles away from borderland and a world removed from mere busyness.

Chapter Eleven

THE ETHICS OF A
DANGEROUS FAITH

I n order to escape borderland, it is not enough that you grasp a holy must,
maintain faith, or forsake your pride. Living in the holy wild also requires
a complete change of ethics. Before you slam this book shut in protest,
mumbling that you knew all along I was a heretic, let me explain.

A number of years ago, a wise man pointed out to me the root difference
between the ethic of Jesus and the ethic of the Pharisees. Usually we think of the
difference in these terms: The Pharisees had an ethic of externals, of ritual and
rigmarole, and Jesus had an ethic of the heart, of the heart's inner workings. The
Pharisees were concerned about not committing adultery, while Jesus was concerned about lust, the root of adultery. He was concerned with *adulterousness*.

That's true as far as it goes. Only it doesn't go very far. The deeper difference between Jesus' ethic and that of the Pharisees was this: The Pharisees had
an ethic of avoidance, and Jesus had an ethic of involvement. The Pharisee's
question was not "How can I glorify God?" It was "How can I avoid bringing
disgrace to God?" This degenerated into a concern not with God, but with
self—with image, reputation, procedure. They didn't ask, "How can I make

others clean?" They asked, "How can I keep myself from getting dirty?" They did not seek to rescue sinners, only to avoid sinning.

Jesus, in sharp contrast, got involved. He sought always and in all ways to help, to heal, to save, to restore. Rather than running from evil, He ran toward the good. And evil, in fear, fled. Look at Legion, the man under assault by a demon mob. Everyone else fears Legion, tries to banish him to tombs. But when Jesus shows up, it's Legion who is afraid, begging Jesus not to torture him. Jesus has come to seek and save that which is lost, not to destroy. He heals Legion and restores him to community. Jesus is not the least afraid of Legion's evil. Rather, the evil in Legion fears the holy power in Jesus and is subdued by it. Darkness always flees light.

Mark it well: Evil isn't safe in the presence of the God who is not safe. Nor—and this is the point—is evil safe in the presence of those who forsake the god who is too safe and follow the Christ. Legions all over the world live both in terror and in desperate yearning for those who dare to leave border-land and live in the holy wild. They're the ones who set the captives free.

Jesus got close enough to unholy people for the spark of holiness in Him to jump. He took the tax collectors, the rough fishermen, the harlots, the demon possessed, and gave back to them dignity and life. He gave back to Legion his real name. The Pharisees avoided these people lest they were infected with their sin and were overwhelmed by their evil.

The tragedy is that we have often preferred the ethic of the Pharisee to the ethic of Christ. We have become self-obsessed in our doctrine of sin, as though sin were merely a personal flaw like acne, plantar's warts, or crooked teeth. As though sin is merely about personal victory or defeat. We seldom see sin as a brokenness that's bone deep and creationwide. Sin ruptures our relationships: with God, with one another, with the creation. It ruptures our own deepest self. So sin needs more than a private remedy, a personal therapy. Overcoming sin requires more than avoidance. The ethic of avoidance proves altogether too frail an ambition. God desires restoration and reconciliation—of relationships, of creation, of our own true selves. That's the wider and deeper meaning of the Cross. As Paul declares in his letter to the Ephesians, "You who were far away have been brought near through the blood of Christ" (2:13). Brought near to what? To God. To each other. To the self God intended you to be. To being sons and daughters who all creation, waiting for, groans in eager expectation.

Christ's ethic sends us into the fray. It is about restoration, about healing the brokenness. Frequently, Jesus issued a sharp command: "Go!" There was a time in the early church when the worship leader, after pronouncing the benediction, would rush through the congregation, waving his arms in urgent gesture, shouting, "Go! Go!" The whole creation groaned, waiting for the sons of God to be revealed.

I once spoke to a group of young people and asked them to define a Christian. Here's what they said: A Christian is someone who doesn't smoke, doesn't drink or do drugs, doesn't have sex until marriage, doesn't use bad language. Of course, I am not suggesting a Christian does these things. But it's tragic that we instinctively define Christians by what they are *not,* by what they avoid. It's like being asked to draw a picture of someone and instead drawing everything around the person and leaving the portrait blank. In saying what Christians are not, we merely sketch the air around them.

Christ never did that. In Matthew 25, Christ, regnant and fierce, divides sheep from goats. How does He tell them apart? How does He separate true followers from false ones? He does not identify His disciples as those who didn't drink and didn't chew and didn't go with girls who do. What He says is: You are My disciple if I came to you naked and you clothed Me, came to you hungry and you fed Me, was in prison and you visited Me.

We are known by our fruits, not by our lack of tree fungus or leaf rot. We need to restore this ethic in our hearts and homes and churches.

Years ago, I attended a Bible study whose leader said that if you go into a bar, at any time, for any reason, you have stepped outside the bounds of God's will and forfeited His protection. One man, a great, wheezing, red-faced fellow, stood up—stood up in the middle of our little huddle of Bible-clutching acolytes—and asked, "What if Jesus commands me to enter? What if He sends me in to share the gospel with someone I know is in there?"

"There are no exceptions," the leader said. "We are at all times to avoid such places."

The man who had stood up walked out. And then the leader calmly explained to the rest of us docile pupils that we must always ask ourselves how any act we do will affect our witness. If we went into a bar, even to save a lost soul, do we not think that the very fact of our being in a bar would destroy our witness to that lost sinner?

I believed him then. I no longer do. The question Christ would have us ask is not, "How will this or that act affect my witness?" His question is "What can I do to have effective witness?" There is a vast and fundamental difference between those two questions.

The first question is rooted in the ethic of avoidance. With that question, we're really asking, "How can I keep the status quo? How can I prevent getting close to evil? How can I guard my reputation?"

But the second question is rooted in an ethic of involvement. With that question, we're asking, "How can I change the way things are? How can I shake it up and shape it anew? How can I bring the salt and light of God's truth to bear on this life, this situation, this place? How can I cast out evil and clean up the place where it dwelt?"

The first question teaches us to avoid bars and whores and biker gangs. And Legion. The second challenges us to turn bars into chapels, whores into evangelists, biker gangs into a gathering of saints. And Legion into the one who is told to "return home and tell how much God has done for you" (Luke 8:39).

This is not a quibble over semantics. *"As the Father has sent me,"* Jesus told His first disciples, "I am sending you" (John 20:21). *As.* Whole theologies hinge on the smallest words. John Stott says that the heart of theological language is in the prepositions—in, of, with, to. *As.* Split that word open and out spills an entire philosophy and strategy of missions and ethics. Where do we get our power? To whom are we to go? What should we say? How then shall we live? *As the Father has sent Me, I am sending you.* I don't know how else to understand this except as a call into the world, in all its broken and heartbreaking beauty, in all its seediness and neediness, to be a Christlike presence.

We fear, of course, the risks: that we will not overcome the world, but succumb to it. And the risks are indeed there. I have had to get involved more than once with Christians who fell into sin intending to do good. The couple who, as an act of Christian hospitality, took into their home a female foster child, only to have the husband become entangled in an affair with her. The man who sought to reach out to male prostitutes and ended up using their services. I know a few of these.

But these aren't arguments. Risk attends all our doings: driving cars, drinking tap water, eating beef, snorkeling. And right now, as you read this, thousands of Christians who have scrupulously avoided bars and brothels all their lives are scrolling through pornography on the Internet. *Of the world, but not in it.* If anything, an ethic that sends us out into the world, with all its dangers, toils, and snares, makes us more prayerful and prepared. It makes us more God hungry and God dependent. It makes all the more urgent our need to take seriously the *as* clause. Jesus sends us *as* the Father sent Him. That means more than that we're to go to those to whom Jesus went. It means that we're to go *in the same authority, with the same power, with the same heart after God.* It means we walk by the Spirit and become like Jesus from the inside out.

And if we're going to speak of risks, consider those of not being involved. These can be summed up in a phrase: God becomes less and less real to us. A rumor. An abstraction. A doctrine. An item for coffeehouse debate before we move on to chatting about our favorite web sites. The risks are that we never leave borderland, but sit there caressing our too-safe god who kisses us with comfort until we feel precisely nothing.

In chapter 6 we noticed how Jesus proved His resurrection presence to Thomas. He proved it with His wounds. "Put your finger here; see my hands. Reach out your hand and put it into my side. Stop doubting and believe" (John 20:27). It's those who touch the wounds of Jesus—who reach out their hand—who experience Him in His risen power: "Thomas said to him, 'My Lord and my God!'" (v. 28).

The risk of avoidance is that in the end the one we avoid is Christ Himself.

MARK'S GOSPEL CONTAINS, BACK-TO-BACK, TWO COMMENTS THAT capture perfectly the contrast between the ethic of avoidance and the ethic of involvement. Notice, as you read, one word in particular: *marketplace.* Watch what Jesus does in the marketplaces and what Pharisees do there.

When they had crossed over, they landed at the Gennesaret and anchored there. As soon as they got out of the boat, people recognized Jesus. They ran throughout that whole region and carried the sick on mats to wherever they heard he was. And wherever he went—into villages, towns or countryside—they placed the sick in the *marketplaces*. They begged him to let them touch even the edge of his cloak, and all who touched him were healed.

The Pharisees and some of the teachers of the law who had come from Jerusalem gathered around Jesus and saw some of his disciples eating food with hands that were "unclean," that is, unwashed. (The Pharisees and all the Jews do not eat unless they give their hands a ceremonial washing, holding to the tradition of the elders. When they come from the *marketplace* they do not eat unless they wash. And they observe many other traditions, such as the washing of cups, pitchers and kettles.) (6:53–7:4, emphasis mine)

Jesus uses the marketplace to touch the sick with healing. There He is, Lord of the holy wild, iconoclast of the safe god, striding hugely, robes flying about Him, jostling with the crowds, spreading His hands wide, pressing those hands against flesh scalding with fever or icy with approaching death, letting clutching, disease-soaked hands grab hold of Him. That's Jesus in the marketplace.

Then there are the Pharisees, lords of borderland, charter members of the safe god society. If they go into the marketplace at all, they take great and grave precautions. They avoid even the residue, even the shadow, of the sick people's presence. There they are, prim mannered, mincing their steps, holding themselves tight, picking up items between the pinched ends of two fingers, rushing home to scrub up.

Jesus is about healing the sick. The Pharisees are about avoiding them and making sure, above all, that they themselves don't get sick.

These are two radically different views, as Jesus points out, of what makes us clean. Jesus' approach works. Cleanness is about what's on the inside breaking through to the outside. The Pharisees' method, for all its care and circumspection, doesn't work. Cleanness cannot happen from the outside. It is inside out or nothing.

That's how we're called to live. We're called to live with new eyes, grace-healed eyes, as Arainius called them, seeing every moment, especially those moments when the sick and the sinful throng close about, as an opportunity to do good. And we're called to live with new hearts: to let the cleanness inside us spill out, washing the filth, the evil, the sickness outside us. We're to spend our heart's energy not looking for ways to enter and exit the marketplace with the least amount of involvement, touching, presence; we're to enter the marketplace looking for ways to bring God's kingdom, light, healing into it. We're called off the borderland into the world, into the marketplace, to be Christlike in our speaking and doing.

Earlier in Mark's gospel, he describes *why* Jesus called to Himself the twelve disciples: "Jesus...called to him those he wanted...that they might *be with him* and that he might *send them out* to preach and to have authority to drive out demons" (3:13–14, emphasis mine). Jesus calls us into intimacy with Him, then imitation of Him. The cloister, then the marketplace. Throw off that Pharisee yoke and take on My yoke.

Come! Jesus says. *Come to Me.* And just as we do, He says, *Go! As the Father has sent Me, I'm sending you. Go into the marketplace, the public schools, the prisons, and the hospital ward—go into the world. And don't leave it as you found it.*

Come. Go. Between the two spans the whole new ethic of the holy wild.

Chapter Twelve

LEAVING BORDERLAND

Maybe now you're feeling guilty. Or fearful. Maybe now you're feeling your life is a series of evasions, diversions, aversions. A Jonah-like running, a Jacob-like dodging. A saying *yes* and meaning *no*. You've made your home in borderland. *And maybe you're feeling guilty. Maybe you're feeling fearful.* Guilt and fear have a certain power to them, a binding and loosing power. Who can number the resolves made and oaths sworn in guilt? Who can measure what has been made and unmade, given and withdrawn, sacrificed and forsaken, salvaged and discarded, out of fear? They can move, if not mountains, at least hills.

But the problem is that guilt and fear are just goads. They prompt us to strenuous living as long as the goad is sharp and can bite into the ribs. But they have little sustaining power. They choke or unravel the very things they make. A promise made in guilt or fear either comes undone when the guilt and fear go away or tightens like a noose if they remain.

Fear: as though God were some scowling taskmaster, bristling with cruel caprice, voice raw and raspy with bitter command—*Do it!* Guilt: as though

God were some nagging harridan, sputtering out complaints and jeers, brow-beating us into doing our chores—*You never do it!* Fear and guilt won't carry us very far off borderland. All they can do is warn us that borderland living is no living at all. All they can do is shake our confidence in *life on our own, life as we know it.* But they can't get us to where we need to go.

One of the touchstones of our humanness is to have wrong motives for doing right things. I've caught myself thinking that godly living is a duty, like paying my taxes. I've had moments when I've sifted out my motives and discovered, in my deep self, that sometimes my imitation of God is done for *His* sake, to appease Him, like a child appeases his mother when he makes his bed or puts away his toys. A part of me pursues holiness out of guilt and fear.

How opposite this is from the Bible's call to a holy life:

Therefore, since we are surrounded by such a great crowd of witnesses, let us throw off everything that hinders and the sin that so easily entangles, and let us run with perseverance the race marked out for us. Let us fix our eyes on Jesus, the author and perfecter of our faith, *who for the joy set before him* endured the cross, and sat down at the right hand of the throne of God. (Hebrews 12:1–2, emphasis mine)

Therefore, I urge you, brothers, *in view of God's mercy,* to offer your bodies as living sacrifices, holy and pleasing to God—this is your spiritual act of worship. (Romans 12:1, emphasis mine)

Since we have these promises, dear friends, let us purify ourselves from everything that contaminates body and spirit, perfecting holiness out of reverence for God. (2 Corinthians 7:1, emphasis mine)

Since...you have been raised with Christ, set your hearts on things above, where Christ is seated at the right hand of God. Set your minds on things above, not on earthly things. (Colossians 3:1–2, emphasis mine)

Therefore, as God's chosen people, holy and dearly loved, clothe yourselves with compassion, kindness, humility, gentleness and patience.
(Colossians 3:12, emphasis mine)

Where in all this is the motive of guilt or fear? That figures hardly at all
into the biblical call to holiness. To compel us to live as God's people, the Bible
almost always points out the staggering truth that because of God's love and
mercy, we already *are* His people. He's chosen us, raised us from the dead, put
His Spirit within us, called us by name, called us to His kingdom work.

Since, therefore...this is the language and logic of kingdom life. It's like saying to an heir of a multibillion-dollar bequest, *"Since* you have all this, *therefore* live like it. Stop acting in stinginess and miserliness, in fretfulness and
sullenness. You're rich—act like it!" There's only one thing worse than a rich
man who flaunts his riches: a rich man who behaves like a pauper. So, too,
with the children of God. To flaunt that status is obscene. But to continue to
act like orphans and urchins is even more so.

Holiness is not a bid to be noticed or loved or accepted by God. Holiness,
rather, is acting out and acting upon the truth that God has noticed, loved, and
accepted us long before we did anything to warrant that. It's the discovery that
we're alive when we thought we were, and ought to be, dead. Holiness is simply living into and living out that aliveness.

I have attempted to name the things that hold us to borderland. But this
attempt is modest: The full measure of that which keeps us stuck outnumbers
the sand on the seashore. What John says at the close of his gospel about Jesus'
acts and works, we might say at the close of this section about the excuses and
evasions that keep us borderland-bound: There are "many other things as
well. If every one of them were written down, I suppose that even the whole
world would not have room for the books that would be written" (21:25).

There is no use continuing to name those habits, attitudes, and beliefs that
keep us on borderland. But it's important as we move onto the second half of
this book to be very clear about *what won't move us off it.*

Guilt won't.

❧

I OPENED PART 1 WITH A STORY ABOUT A BORDER CROSSING IN Africa—a double crossing, where between two borders a no-man's-land of dusty earth lies. Borderland. The barren, crowded place, both rule-bound and lawless, where you can spend your days in endless busyness, doubt-ridden and disappointed.

When I was in Africa several years ago, I crossed through that borderland. At first the new land didn't look any different. In Kenya, as in Uganda, I stepped into a town thronged with hawkers and peddlers and taxicab drivers, all shoving and shouting for my business. I went to the bank, a little clapboard booth with thick, rust-scabbed bars in the teller's window, and exchanged a money order for Kenya's currency. Then I negotiated taxi fare to Nairobi, ten hours' drive away, crammed my bags into the cab's shallow trunk, wedged my body between a door and three other passengers in a back seat designed to comfortably accommodate two, and I was off.

We drove through a series of dusty towns that all looked the same. But then, a few miles in, the landscape opened out into sere grassland. Acacia trees stood in gaunt silhouette against the sky, and in the distance I could see giraffes twining their long necks between the limbs. I knew that their agile tongues were plucking leaves off the trees' thorny branches. Huge birds made dark arcs in the white-blue sky. And far behind mountains rose in shades of green, blue, mauve.

In an hour we were in those mountains, climbing the steep, narrow road that ascended in a series of hairpin turns. In places the mountain rose up sheer on one side of the road, its massive height and looming closeness shutting out the sky, and fell straight off on the other, a dizzying vista of empty air spiraling down to valley floor. I held my breath in awe and dread as the driver swooped through turn after turn.

Then we reached the pinnacle, dense with pine forest, and began our long, twisting descent. A cloudburst sent a sudden deluge of rain mixed with hail on us. It hit the windshield with a gray blinding swiftness, and the windshield wipers couldn't push it off fast enough. For several moments we drove blindly. There was only one window crank, and in panic we passed it from driver to passenger to passenger, each struggling to do up the window beside us as the drenching rain swept in. Then, just as suddenly as the cloudburst, a sunburst: The sky, now blinding in its brilliance, scattered a billion tiny rainbows of refracted light and caused white steam to waft from the road's hot pavement.

We were now driving the high, sharp ridge of Kenya's Rift Valley, one of the world's geological wonders—a massive rend in the earth's crust, where a tectonic wrenching has gashed open a quarter continent of rock and left soft, rich deep soil in the scar. This was the southern side of the mountains; here coffee plantations shone a preternatural green in the sun, and workers with baskets held in bright colored slings moved slowly through the plant rows. Far down in another valley, I saw a lake, its shore fringed with pink: Flamingoes, thousands of them, crowded together in the lake's reedy shallows.

We came into Nairobi at nightfall, just as the flowers were releasing their scent into the cooling air, and the taxi drove down a brick driveway lined with orchids to let me off at the steps of my hotel. I stood for a moment, watching in the growing dark as the taxi's ribbon of taillight backed down the driveway. I thought, *that was the most spellbinding trip I'd ever taken—exhilarating, terrifying, and in all, deeply gratifying.*

It was the journey beyond borderland.

Guilt or fear can't move us very far off that land, but trust and hope can. The logic of *since, therefore* can. The conviction that the one who calls us is faithful—that He is drawing us into a world of wonder and danger and goes with us all the way, that He calls us for His glory and for our sake, that His joy might be in us and our joy might be complete—that can.

Love can.

This is the shape of the story we read over and over in the Bible. Paul risks himself through shipwrecks and riots because "Christ's love compels" him (2 Corinthians 5:14), because "the life I live in the body, I live by faith in the Son of God, who loved me and gave himself for me" (Galatians 2:20). Jesus Himself "Who for the joy set before him endured the cross, scorning its shame" (Hebrews 12:2). Even Jonah, petulant and self-pitying beneath his withered vine, may have done God's bidding out of guilt and fear. But what he's angry about and what he refuses to open himself to is God's love. That is what really is behind his story.

I contend this: Scratch the most vigorous, authentic Christian you know, and he or she will bleed love—love for God, love for others, and a deep conviction about God's love for him or her. And the opposite: Scratch the sourest, most sedentary Christian you know, and he or she will bleed guilt. Borderland clots the arteries with it.

Yet here's an irony: The nice god, the safe god, who we've contrived as an antidote to our fear and guilt—that god leaves us stuck on borderland, too. He asks nothing of us. His niceness, his safeness is only cruelty disguised. He lulls all the way to the grave.

The safe god would never act like the true God, who sometimes displays His sternness so that His kindness may break through, who, in Hosea's words, sometimes strips us in order to betroth us (2:3, 19). The true God is "a gracious and compassionate God, slow to anger and abounding in love, who relents from sending calamity" (Jonah 4:2). But because of that, not in spite of it, He *won't leave Nineveh or Jonah alone.* God loves Ninevites and Jonahs—and us—so much that He would sooner chase us with typhoons and leviathans into the holy wild than leave us marooned on borderland. Sometimes Jesus' call to leave borderland seems a sternness close to cruelty. It seems an invitation to hardship and privation. *Come, follow Me.*

But, Jesus, look at all these fish. Things are just turning around here.

It takes faith to believe that the sea and the desert He leads us through comprise the shortest route to a land flowing with milk and honey.

In the movie *The Secret Garden,* the young boy Colin thinks he's an invalid. He can't bear the strong light of day, the clean open air. He believes those things will infect his lungs and snatch his life. He believes he's destined to be everlastingly bedridden or, in the few struggling moments he spends out of bed, bound lifelong to a wheelchair. He believes that because he's been told that. He lives a long time this way, kept in that state by a conspiracy of adults.

Kept in borderland by a god who's too safe.

But then his orphaned cousin, Mary, comes along and sees through the conspiracy. In what looks like sheer defiance, utter brazenness, hard malice, she tears the shutters and blinds off Colin's windows. Bright sunlight pours in through the scrim of dust. Colin shrieks. She throws the windows open, and cool, fresh air swirls through the room. Colin howls. She shoos Colin out of bed. Colin yells. She forces him, sullen and whining, into the outdoors. She scolds and coaxes him from his wheelchair. He stands, filled with self-lament, tottering.

But he's standing. Yes, he's standing. He takes one lurching step, then another. Soon Colin walks. Then runs. Then skips. Then dances.

Mary seems so callous at first. But she is the one who cares most deeply for him. She cares enough to woo Colin to the secret garden; she loves him enough to bring him into wholeness. She knew all along that his bones were sturdy, his lungs deep, his muscles supple and strong. She knew all along he was made for life to the full.

That's a picture of the life Christ calls us into. Christ finds us in our hovel of self-pity, our imagined invalidism, our dreary room on borderland. He seems at first so gruff, stripping off the shutters, throwing open the windows, rousing us from bed, pushing us out to the garden, commanding that we walk. *Come, follow Me.*

But all along it's a gift. He does this, not because we must. It's because *we can.* The musty shadows of the sick room, the pale withered limbs—that's just the devil's conspiracy, the lie we've been told. It takes a God who's not safe, but who's good, to tell us otherwise.

Come, follow Me.

Why would you go back to the sickroom?

Why would you return to borderland?

Part Two

～

LIFE IN THE HOLY WILD

IN THE EIGHTH CENTURY B.C., THE PROPHET MICAH SUMMED up the essence of the Godward life. He cut to the chase and to the quick with the question, "What does the Lord require of you?" First he proposed "natural theology's" solution: "Shall I come before him with burnt offerings...? Will the LORD be pleased with thousands of rams, with ten thousand rivers of oil? Shall I offer my firstborn for my transgressions?" (6:7–8) *Shall I be very religious, God?*

Our instinct is to appease God or impress Him with our stuff and our busyness. Those of us who have tried that—most of us, at some point—discover what is true of the older son, the frugal son, in Jesus' parable: By our very busyness, we cease to dwell in the bounty of the Father's house. By our very religiosity, we get stuck on borderland and become so slow-hearted that we fail to see Christ when He stands beside us, to hear the Father when He asks us to join the celebration. In our arduous efforts to find God, we lose Him.

It is not what God wants. "He has showed you, O man, what is good. And what does the LORD require of you? To act justly and to love mercy and to walk humbly with your God" (Micah 6:8). God asks us to be *like* Him—doing justly, loving mercy. And He asks us to be *with* Him—walking humbly. That is the shape of life in the holy wild.

Perhaps that seems pedestrian. The word *pedestrian* has two meanings: one who walks, and that which is dull, commonplace, boring. The invitation God extends is to walk. "Come, follow me" is Jesus' way of calling us to new life.

We wish for a faster way, easier, more exciting. We wish that the holy wild were an endless escapade. In the Disney movie *Aladdin,* the high point of romance between Aladdin and Princess Jasmine is when they are, in one star-glittering night, whisked away on a magic carpet to survey the world's splendors and wonders. The poor boy forced to cadge and filch his meals, the pampered princess forced into the stifling, boring rigidity of court etiquette—at last they are free, unbound by earth's fetters, dazzled by its beauties. How we wish that the spiritual life resembled that carpet ride.

But there is no other means offered than to walk. As the poet and novelist Annie Dillard says, "How you spend your days is, of course, how you spend your life." This is the secret of living in the holy wild: taking one step at a time, one day at a time.

To walk.

Chapter Thirteen

THE PLACE OF
HOLY HABITS

I would like to delight and inspire you one day with a violin rendition of Johann Sebastian Bach's Concerto in B-flat. "Close your eyes," I'd say. "Sit back and drink it in." When you were relaxed, receptive, listening, I would take the violin, tuck it under my chin, balance it beneath one outstretched arm, and with the other arm draw the bow over the instrument's arched, taut strings.

And I would shatter all your peace. I would wrench from that violin a sound reminiscent of many terrible things: the yowl of a cat whose tail is slammed in a door; the screech of sharp nails raked across a chalkboard; the shriek of rusty nails yanked out of parched planks; the wail of torture victims, their fingernails plucked off with pliers.

I can't play the violin.

But I want to. I think about it. I admire people who do it well. I love music made by violin masters. I'm sincere. And whenever I have the chance to play a violin, I try. I try really hard.

It's laughable. Of course I can't play the violin merely on the basis of my sincerity, my desire, my admiration for those who can play it. I can't play it merely by trying. We all know it takes much more than that. In fact, what would trouble us, myself included, is if I could pick up the violin having never taken a lesson or practiced a note, and I was a virtuoso, making the instrument weep or laugh with the lightest caress of my nimble fingers. That would be uncanny. But thank goodness, no one expects that of me. I don't expect it of myself.

But here is the strangest thing: We do expect that. We expect it of ourselves and we expect it of others all the time. We expect it, not with the violin, not with marathon running, not with mountain climbing. But we expect it in spiritual matters. We honestly think that we ourselves and those around us should be proficient with spiritual power, moving and acting with agility and endurance, wisdom and purity, able to conquer long-established habits of sloth and rebelliousness, *simply on the basis of our desire and effort and sincerity.* Here's a refrain, a stock lament of the average Christian: "I really want to live for Jesus. I really try to live for Jesus. I really admire those who live for Jesus. I'm really sincere about living for Jesus. But I just keep messing up."

I want off borderland, but I keep stumbling back there.

We have to train to run marathons, climb mountains, play violins. That's the most basic idea in the world. It needs no further commentary.

We have to train for the spiritual life. That's the most lost idea to the world, and it requires whole books and sermon series to establish its value, even its validity.

Yet nothing other than that, and nothing less, will get us off borderland.

I was in a friend's guitar shop one day, and he was showing me a song he'd written. One of its chords spanned five frets. I was struggling to play that chord and finally gave up.

"I can't," I said. "I mean, look at these hands. I just can't play chords like that."

Right at that moment, one of the guitar teachers walked past. "Quit your sissy excuses," he said. "Just bloody stretch."

I wanted to call this section of the book "Just Bloody Stretch," but that didn't sound pious enough. However, that really is what I've set for myself as the goal of writing about in these last ten chapters: stretching our stiff, stubby fingers over five frets until that becomes natural, easy, and fluid; until good music flows from it—practicing, note by note, scale by scale, the violin. I've set out to write about that kind of thing in our life with God—the plodding, aching persistence required to learn the practice of the presence of God.

This is about Godward habits. None of them are glamorous or exotic or novel. There is little delight in these practices themselves any more than there is delight in playing violin scales. The delight, rather, comes *through* them. None of them is in keeping with the mood and tone of the age: *Thirty Days to Influence with God. Seven Steps to Spiritual Dynamism. Think Yourself to Holy Power in Only Five Minutes a Day.*

But, as musical practice is the only way to make good music, so Godward habits are the only way off borderland.

Just bloody stretch.

IN THE FIRST PART OF THIS BOOK, WE EXAMINED SOME OF THE subtle slippery ways we evade God and some of the reasons we do that. The borderland stays in business, above all, through bad theology: a steady traffic of invented or distorted or half-baked notions about God. In part 2, I am not, however, intending to give you a doctrine of God. Rather, I intend to help you make the shift, huge and subtle both, by which you become fully present to the God who is, right now, right here, fully present with you.

Practicing the presence of God is what sustains and deepens us in the holy wild. But what sustains and deepens the practice itself? If God is present in the most ordinary moments, events, people, how will we on a growing basis transform the dimness of our eyes and the dullness of our ears into seeing and hearing? What will increasingly sharpen our attentiveness to God in our midst and strengthen our resolve to desire His presence rather than flee it? What will keep us off borderland?

The answer is holy habits, or what are often called spiritual disciplines. I want to call them holy habits because, as with all habits, they are practices that for a while we think about and work at but eventually weave so deeply into the rhythm of our lives that they define us. They become *our ways.* Like violin scales or five-fret chords, they are often awkward for us at first and produce dubious results. But persisted in, they become natural and create beauty.

I want to call them holy habits for another reason: They counter and replace the instinctive habits of slow-heartedness we've looked at. Borderland, after all, is the place we go *habitually*. It's what we're used to. Holy habits train us to be used to something else, something more—to life in the holy wild.

After all, the central obstacle in our relationship with God is not God's aloofness or remoteness, as though God needed chasing down or coaxing out. Holy habits are *not* shrewder techniques for tracking an elusive deity. They are, rather, ways of tracking ourselves down in our elusiveness—of either being still and knowing He is God or making every effort and knowing the same. They are ways of breaking and mending our Jonah hearts. They are ways of fleeing borderland rather than fleeing God.

IN HIS GOSPEL, MARK TELLS A STORY THAT PUTS THIS IN PERSPECTIVE. Jesus has announced to His disciples that some of them standing with Him will not see death until they behold the kingdom come with power. Next thing, Jesus takes Peter, James, and John with Him up a mountain, and they do see it. Jesus is transfigured before them, revealed in all His kingly splendor, and speaks with Moses and Elijah. They hear the voice of God: "This is my son, whom I love. Listen to him." *The kingdom come with power.* This is the real thing. This is not mere window dressing, mere carnival pitch. There is a kingdom, and it is among us, and if we could see it unveiled as it really is, we would be staggered by its grandeur, awe-struck by its dazzling beauty.

Then they come down the mountain. A scuffle and squabble is going on. A father has a son who is demon possessed, thrashing, frothing at the mouth, and Jesus' disciples have no power to cast it out. Despite all their trying and all their sincerity and all their wanting to, they can't budge that demon an inch from that boy. The disciples are embroiled in an argument with the teachers of the law about this. But it's obvious that they're all talk, too. They have no more power than the disciples do.

The passage continues:

> When they came to the other disciples, they saw a large crowd around
> them and the teachers of the law arguing with them. As soon as all the

people saw Jesus, they were overwhelmed with wonder and ran to greet him.

"What are you arguing with them about?" he asked.

A man in the crowd answered, "Teacher, I brought you my son, who is possessed by a spirit that has robbed him of speech. Whenever it seizes him, it throws him to the ground. He foams at the mouth, gnashes his teeth and becomes rigid. I asked your disciples to drive out the spirit, but they could not."

Jesus is frustrated with the whole lot of them. He rebukes them and then impatiently demands, "Bring the boy to me."

So they brought him. When the spirit saw Jesus, it immediately threw the boy into a convulsion. He fell to the ground and rolled around, foaming at the mouth.

Jesus asked the boy's father, "How long has he been like this?"

"From childhood," he answered. "It has often thrown him into fire or water to kill him. But if you can do anything, take pity on us and help us."

"'If you can'?" said Jesus. "Everything is possible for him who believes."

Immediately the boy's father exclaimed, "I do believe; help me overcome my unbelief!"

When Jesus saw that a crowd was running to the scene, he rebuked the evil spirit. "You deaf and mute spirit," he said, "I command you, come out of him and never enter him again."

The spirit shrieked, convulsed him violently and came out. The boy looked so much like a corpse that many said, "He's dead." But Jesus took him by the hand and lifted him to his feet, and he stood up.

After Jesus had gone indoors, his disciples asked him privately, "Why couldn't we drive it out?"

He replied, "This kind can come out only by prayer." (Mark 9:14–29)

Why couldn't we drive it out? Why did we not have power for this? This kind, Jesus says, only comes out with prayer.

The most curious thing about this story is so obvious that we usually miss it: Jesus *doesn't* pray. Not here. Not now. He doesn't excuse Himself for half a day to go off into some austere solitude and soak Himself in invocations and intercessions. He just stands and delivers. He just says the word, and the demon scatters, hell-bent and terrified.

Jesus doesn't pray. My temptation is to say, "Well, it's different for Jesus. He's God incarnate. He doesn't need to pray to cast out demons."

But that's the wrong answer. Jesus became fully human. He emptied Himself, humbled Himself, became a man, a servant (Philippians 2). He was made like us in every way in order that He might completely understand our condition, with all our frailty and temptation and limitation (Hebrews 2:17; 4:15).

No, the correct answer is that Jesus does not need to pray at this moment *because He has already a well-established discipline of prayer.* Mark 1:35 is typical: "Very early in the morning, while it was still dark, Jesus got up, left the house and went off to a solitary place, where he prayed." Or Luke 6:12: "Jesus went out to a mountainside to pray, and spent the night praying to God."

We often lack spiritual power. We're so often helpless, hapless, speechless, bumbling in the face of the world's evil, brokenness, and demon-infested sickness. We have nothing to say to the desperate father whose faith is almost spent, eroded by each doctor or pastor or psychologist that has come along straining with all his might to do something and done nothing. Often, in response to our ineptitude and impotence, we get into arguments with the Pharisees. We squabble and bicker over theological fine points; we coin and bandy about big words like *dispensationalism.* We find fault with the church down the street: They're too liberal or too fundamentalist; they've gotten too preoccupied with the gifts of the Spirit or with the cessation of those gifts; they've reduced the gospel to good works or have forgotten that the gospel sends us out to do good works. Instead of praying, we fight. But secretly, when it's just us and God, we have a different question: "Lord, why can't we, *Your disciples,* do something here?"

He says something to the equivalent of, "Just bloody stretch." You can't play the guitar or the violin; you can't run a marathon; you can't climb a mountain if you don't train. And you can't cast out demons—meeting with authority the world's evil and its brokenness head-on—if you don't pray. This kind only comes out by prayer. If you want to imitate me on the battlefield, imitate me in the boot camp. If you want to stand and deliver when the crisis hits, then get out of bed and pray before the sun gets up.

Practice holy habits.

I have a friend, Boyd, who can stand and deliver. He has a closeness with and a power through Jesus like few I've met. I often entrust him with weighty matters because I know he only acts or speaks out of Christ's authority. Here's what Boyd wrote me when I asked him his "secret":

> Mark, one of the ways that God has taught me to stay alive and focused on Him is through routine: routine in being with Him, routine in taking my medicines, routine in being with and loving my wife, routine in walking my dogs and playing with them, routine in exercise, routine in my routines. I guess that you could substitute the word *discipline* for the word *routine.*

Holy habits are that: *the disciplines, the routines by which we stay alive and focused on Him.* At first we choose them and carry them out; after a while they are part of who we are. And they carry us.

THIS IS NOT ABOUT AN HEROIC STRIVING OF OR AGAINST OUR WILLS. Holy habits, like all habits, obviously involve our wills: a resolve of will, sometimes a breaking of it. But these are not exercises in mere willpower. They assume, in fact, that willpower alone is insufficient to motivate us and sustain us in living in the presence of God.

We have far more won't power than willpower anyhow.

Recently I read Mark Twain's *The Adventures of Tom Sawyer* to my nine-year-old son. Tom is a rabble-rouser, troublemaker, ringleader. His life is a carnival of pranks and escapades, and he gives grief to many. But Tom has a good heart. Many times when his mischief makes too much trouble for himself and those he loves, he firmly resolves with solemn oaths and tearful promises that he's finished forever with his wild way of living. From now on he will lead a wholesome, godly, submissive, productive life—no more tormenting Sid and Mary, no more flouting Aunt Polly's rules and breaking her heart.

But he never keeps his resolves. His won't power is stronger than his willpower. Some new temptation lays hold of him, and off he goes again. His standard defense: "Auntie, I wish I hadn't done it—but I didn't think."[1] Mark Twain makes an amusing story out of that. But for many people, that pattern—forever *intending* to do right, but old ways and fresh temptations always rendering the intention powerless—is the central tragedy of their existence. *I wish I hadn't done it, but I didn't think.* They just can't seem, for all the willpower in the world, to break beyond the habitual, break free the natural.

Spiritual disciplines are not about mere willpower. The best definition I have come across for discipline is John Ortberg's (which is a distillation of Dallas Willard's teaching): *Any activity I do by direct effort that will help me do what I cannot now do by direct effort.*[2] The mountain climber begins with hikes up local hills, clambering up small outcroppings, scaling short cliffs, before he ever takes on Everest. The violin player begins by learning how to tune the violin, then play scales, then rudimentary pieces, before he attempts to master Bach. And the man or woman who chases God? Well, before we cast out demons, we pray. And we pray *not by getting up the first day at 4:00 A.M.* No, first we take on what we can manage: *an activity I can do by direct effort.* We get up, say, fifteen minutes earlier to start. Persisted in, it will *help me do what I cannot now do by direct effort.* This kind only comes out by prayer.

HOLY HABITS ARE NOT LEGALISM. WE ARE NOT TRYING TO EARN anything from God by being disciplined. He doesn't love us more if we practice holy habits or love us less if we don't. They're not about that. They are, rather, about experiencing more and more the kingdom presence and power of Jesus Christ that is available right here, right now.

There is a key confusion in modern Christianity that greatly hinders us. We are overly prone to see legalism lurking behind every exhortation to strive and make an effort to be holy. Every time I say, "Work *out* your salvation," someone will hear me say, "Work *for* your salvation." The two are utterly different things. But our confusion stems from a theological distinction we make that is simply not biblical: We contrast grace with effort. We say, "I live under grace. I don't need to strive. I don't need to make an effort. I reject all that legalistic entrapment and rigmarole, that monkish rubbish."

But grace and effort are not opposites. Grace and *earning* are opposites. *Working for* your salvation is a heresy. *Working out* your salvation is basic Bible. Grace and effort are allies.[3] There are eight New Testament Scriptures that tell us that because God has already given us all things, we therefore must *make every effort* to do what leads to peace and mutual edification; *make every effort* to enter through the narrow door; *make every effort* to keep unity; *make ever effort* to be holy; *make every effort* to be found spotless, blameless, and at peace with Him. Hebrews 4:11 is especially piquant: *Make every effort* to enter rest. Work to rest. The Greek here, I think, is "Just bloody stretch."

The difference between working *out* our salvation—making every effort— and working *for* our salvation can be quickly and easily explained. *You can only work out what you already have.* You already have salvation through Jesus Christ. And with His salvation, we possess every last thing we need to live the full, joyful abundance of that life. But we still have to work it out. We still have to make every effort.

This is how the apostle Peter puts it:

> His divine power has given us *everything we need* for life and godliness through our knowledge of him who called us by his own glory and goodness. Through these he has given us his very great and precious promises, so that through them you may participate in the divine nature and escape the corruption in the world caused by evil desires.

You have everything you need to live a holy life, to know the heights and the depths of God's presence and power, to experience God with you, to live victoriously. Not one thing is lacking. But now look at the next verse:

> *For this very reason, make every effort* to add to your faith goodness; and to goodness, knowledge; and to knowledge, self-control; and to self-control, perseverance; and to perseverance, godliness; and to

godliness, brotherly kindness; and to brotherly kindness, love. For if you possess these qualities in increasing measure, they will keep you from being ineffective and unproductive in your knowledge of our Lord Jesus Christ. (2 Peter 1:3–8, emphasis mine)

Everything you need, you've got. *For this very reason, make every effort.* Add things, bit by bit, step by step. Don't rush at it all at once. Though everything you need for godliness is at hand, you won't actually be acting godly until you've got some more basic things in place. Hike up the local hills first. Later we'll talk about Everest. You want to get to the point where you can actually love your enemies? You want to get to the point where if someone strikes you, your instinct is actually to turn the other cheek rather than to strike back? When somebody curses you, your gut reaction is actually to bless them in return? Where you can cast out the demon from the tormented boy at the pleading of his yet more tormented father? Well, begin here: *Add to your faith, goodness, and then....*

If you live like this—a disciplined life, making every effort, doing by *direct effort that which will help you do what you cannot now do by direct effort*—you will be able to stand and deliver in the moment of crisis. Again, Peter puts it this way: "If you possess these qualities in increasing measure, they will keep you from being ineffective and unproductive in your knowledge of our Lord Jesus Christ." Your knowing God will be no mere head knowledge, some dry theological conceptualization. You will know God from the inside out.

And if you don't make every effort because you can't be bothered with the inconvenience? Peter goes on to describe those who have not been disciplined: "If anyone does not have [these qualities that we make every effort to acquire], he is nearsighted and blind, and has forgotten that he has been cleansed from his past sins" (2 Peter 1:9). The undisciplined live in an amnesiac state, always forgetting the most basic thing: They have been cleansed from their past sin and are not the man or woman they once were. They are a new creation. They are not stuck with the old self, unchangeable, its dead weight of guilt and regret and desire thick in the flesh. But they forget that.

Those who do not make every effort are like the blind man whose sight is restored but who never adjusts to that. He remains in his old ways, tapping his cane on the sidewalk, rattling his cup at the curb, reading by Braille, grop-ing and shuffling, turning light into darkness, day into night.

Stuck on borderland.

ONE LAST MATTER. THE EASIEST THING IN THE WORLD IS TO ENGAGE holy habits for the wrong reasons. To turn them into feats of strength, contests of endurance, displays of self-righteousness. To fast, say, just to prove you can go thirty hours or three days or two weeks without food. Or to fast to lose weight. To pray mainly so that you can feel good about yourself. Always lurk-ing behind our acts of self-denial and self-discipline is the whisper and nudge of self-indulgence: *You will get the glory.*

Jesus warned about this: "When you fast, when you pray, when you give to the poor, do not be like the hypocrites. Be careful not to do your 'acts of righteousness' before men, to be seen by them. If you do, you will have no reward from your Father in heaven" (see Matthew 6:1, 2, 5, 16).

It is important to keep in view the *why* of these habits. Knowing the why helps us avoid two equally destructive tendencies: pride in doing well and weariness in doing good.

So why cultivate and practice holy habits? When Peter lists the virtues that we're to make every effort to add to our faith, the crowning virtue is love. Paul, more poetically, says the same thing in 1 Corinthians 13: "If I can speak in the tongues of men and angels…if I have the gift of prophecy and can fathom all mysteries and all knowledge…if I have faith that can move mountains…. If I give all I possess to the poor and surrender my body to the flames, but have not love…I am nothing…I gain nothing."

The goal of the disciplined life is love: to more and more live in and live out the two greatest commandments. Love the Lord your God with all your heart, strength, mind and soul, and love your neighbor as yourself. The touch-stone of whether you're rightly engaged with any discipline is to ask, "Is my love getting stronger, deeper, richer?" Something is wrong if you find that any discipline or habit you practice is making you arrogant, self-righteous, con-temptuous, judgmental: "Well, I can fast for eight days straight; I get up at 4:00 A.M. every day and pray for two hours. If I ever sin, and I rarely do, I confess it within twenty-four hours. What are you doing for the Lord, sissy boy? You guys are all wimps!"

I took my wife out on a special date last Mother's Day. First, I took her and our children and my wife's mother and father out for Sunday brunch in Cowichan Bay, a little seaside fishing community. Then her parents took our children back to our house, and I took my wife down to Victoria for the evening. I had reserved a hotel room overlooking Victoria's inner harbor, where sleek, white yachts and wide-hulled whalers cut Vs in the glassy water. We walked downtown, past the domed and stately parliament buildings and the ivy-clothed Empress Hotel, and enjoyed a lingering late night dinner together. We walked back along the wide concourse that encircles the harbor, and we looked at all the artists' stalls along there. We returned to our hotel, had a swim in the pool and a soak in the hot tub. In the morning, we had a leisurely breakfast and then went shopping.

There were disciplines involved in having a weekend like that. I had to make the arrangements. I had to come up with the money. I had to carry out the plan. It wasn't just going to happen. I had to make every effort for it to happen. But none of those things were done for their own sake. I wasn't making phone calls, spending money, driving to Victoria just as exercises that had some worth in their own right. The value of each of those things was strictly related to the value of their purpose: intimacy with my wife.

Of course, there's always the danger that I'll do any of those things for the wrong reason. I might have done it so that I could tell you about it in a book, and you would be impressed with me: *My, what an affectionate, attentive husband he is.* I might have done it to try to bribe my wife into letting me get a new something or other, or to oblige her to be more affectionate and attentive to me in the bedroom. I might have done it to get away from my in-laws. I might have done it because I'm thinking about buying shares in the hotel I booked in Victoria and I wanted to check the place out. I might have done it because I'm a spendthrift and I was concocting some extravagance to fill my emptiness.

All bad reasons. This alone is the right one: I did it for love. I wanted to show Cheryl my love for her and to have an intimate and playful evening together to deepen that love. It's that simple.

Why would anyone pray, fast, confess, study? It's death to do these things for their own sake. How dull, how bone wearying, how corrupting. It's death to do them to impress or bribe or oblige someone or to avoid something. The ultimate purpose of discipline is love—that we might actively love God more and more and tangibly love our neighbor more and more. The reason we endure any of these disciplines, cultivate any of these holy habits is for the joy set before us. These things bring us joy because they move us closer to the heart of God and allow us more and more to participate in His very nature.

I HAVE GOOD NEWS: GOD IS HERE, RIGHT HERE. JESUS IS PRESENT now, right now. The Holy Spirit still hovers over the earth, still moves in our midst, still dwells within those Christ has claimed. All you need for life and godliness has already been given.

But, Lord, where? Why don't I see this? Why don't I experience it, notice it, tap into it? Why won't the demons submit to me? Why can't I stand and deliver? And why is my love such a flickering pale thing? Why am I stuck on borderland?

This kind only comes out through holy habits.

Chapter Fourteen

INVOKING HIS
PRESENCE BY YOURS

There is no way to make a single, breathless leap out of borderland. But there is one way to break its gravitational pull: Practice the presence of God.

Where can I go from your Spirit?
    Where can I flee from your presence?
If I go up to the heavens, you are there;
    if I make my bed in the depths, you are there.
If I rise on the wings of the dawn,
    if I settle on the far side of the sea,
even there your hand will guide me,
    your right hand will hold me fast.
(Psalm 139:7–10)

God hovers about us, shadows our every step. Often we speak, glibly I think, about God breaking in on us. We make prayers of invocation at weddings and funerals and worship services calling God down from His heavens, calling God out of His hiding place, calling God to attention and attentiveness. But that sounds as though God is remote, aloof, hanging back in some far reach of heaven and occasionally, at our bidding or as almost a kind of prank, barging in on us.

Psalm 139 banishes such notions. God is always here, around, before, above, beneath. In God we live and move and have our being. But this Psalm also sketches the problem: "Where can I go from your spirit?" the psalmist asks with an urgency beyond rhetoric. "Where can I flee from your presence?... If I say, 'Surely the darkness will hide me and the light become night around me,' even the darkness will not be dark to you" (11–12). The psalmist's declaration of God's here-ness and God's nearness has in it a shadow of ambivalence: Does he think this is a good or a bad thing? Perhaps the heart of exile, the Jonah heart, pounds in his chest, too.

The problem is not that God is distant and needs to be wooed or badgered into coming near; the problem is that God is ever present, ever near, and that some of us seek ways of escape. *Where can I flee from Your presence?* If God is here and here and here, when can I be *myself* and be *by myself?* The cleaving nearness of God becomes claustrophobic, a stifling humidness, a chafing boundedness.

God does not need to be invoked, we do. We need to be called to our senses, to be as present to God as God is to us. To stop running, stand still, breathe in. "Rejoice in the Lord always," Paul says. "I will say it again: Rejoice!...the Lord is near" (Philippians 4:4–5). And then, on the basis of God's nearness, he calls us to pray (v. 6).

But by what prayer do we invoke *ourselves?* The Psalms, again, give guidance: "Why are you so downcast, O my soul? Why so disturbed within me? Put your hope in God" (Psalm 42:5, 11; 43:5). Some days we need this stern soul-talk, this field marshal gruffness with ourselves and with one another. Occasionally when someone comes to my study to recite and rehearse for me all the trouble they're in, I use this approach.

"What are you talking about?" I say. "What are you down about? Aren't you the one Jesus loves? Isn't that you who the gospel speaks about? I thought I read in your biography that the Son of God wanted you so much to be His friend, His brother, His partner, His delight that He gave all He had, even His own life, to make it so. What are you sulking about? You're a rich man telling me how poor you are. Get out of here!"

Oftentimes I have to practice this kind of thing on myself, taking myself in hand, giving myself a good, brisk scolding. Otherwise I can pamper myself into a major funk, all the way back to borderland.

What's better, though, than this occasional pep rally is to cultivate such soul-talk into a habit of life: to practice the presence of God, to train ourselves to hold still, to run toward Him, not away, to have the scales fall from our eyes, and always, everywhere, to behold Him.

We need this practice for another reason. We need it because often there are times when we do want God near; we desperately want Him near, and yet we don't *feel* like He's near—or even *there*. Maybe the chief complaint I hear as a pastor is that, despite people's best efforts at intimacy with God—they read the Bible, pray, study, and worship with other believers—they still experience an unbridgeable gulf, an unbreakable wall between earth and heaven. Such feelings exhaust us and tempt us to give up. I think of John the Baptist in Herod's prison. After he had been such a robust enthusiast for Christ, suddenly he's faced with the prospect of death in the morning, *and Jesus doesn't seem to notice, let alone care.* So John sends his disciples to do a little background check on Jesus. "Are you who we hoped you were, or should we expect someone else?" And Jesus sends back the message that says, in essence, "I'm performing a lot of miracles here, John, but don't think that means one's coming your way. Blessed is he who doesn't fall away on account of me."

Or I think about David. After many long years in exile, skulking among rock crags and border towns, part beggar, part brigand, there comes this day: "And David *thought to himself...the best thing I can do* is to escape to the land of the Philistines" (1 Samuel 27:1, emphasis mine). For a season, David gives up inquiring of God what is best and starts thinking to himself what is best. In his eyes, what's best is a long sojourn in Ziklag, double-dealing with the enemy. What's best is borderland. Well, why not? After all, what has God done for him? Promised him the kingship, then sent him into this hardscrabble, bone-picking life in the badlands. He's king of the marauders, keeper of the hovel, lord of the riffraff. There is no record that David wrote any psalms during this period. Maybe he lost his Godward voice, his heart after God. Or maybe he wrote Psalm 22 at this time: "My God, my God, why have you forsaken me? Why are you so far from my groaning...."

There are seasons, there are sojourns, in which we live so long in exile that God seems exiled. *Deus Absconditus,* the theologians call it: the absconding God, the God who runs away, who hides, who manifests through haunting absence.

That's why we need to *practice* the presence of God: Not just to acknowledge in some philosophical way that God is present, but to rehearse, to repeat, to work and rework our knowledge that even though we don't see Him and sometimes don't feel Him, He is there. He is here. When we practice the presence of God, we train ourselves to *desire* His presence—to resist our temptation to flee Him. We also train ourselves to experience His presence—to resist our temptation to think that He flees us. In other words, the practice of the presence of God helps us to live between the temptations of Jonah bound for Tarshish and John bound in prison. Jonah is the prophet who wants to abandon God. John is the prophet who feels abandoned by God.

When we practice the presence of God, we refuse to live in either sense of abandonment. Instead, we call ourselves to joyful, heedful attention in the presence of the God who is always with us. We teach ourselves to live in that presence and to love living in it.

I am a poor photographer. My brother Adam (my son's namesake) is a superb one. He needs to be because that is what he does for a living. But it is a study in contrasts to watch him and me together on a photographic expedition. Despite having handled cameras all my life, I am forever a raw novice. I bumble and dawdle with the equipment. It takes me dreadfully long to set a photo. Usually by the time I'm ready to shoot, the lighting has changed, or my subject matter has shifted, walked away, taken flight. Even with my best efforts, the photos usually come out blurred, diluted with too much light, or steeped in too many shadows, framed crooked, composed lopsidedly.

My brother is quick and agile with his camera. He can pop lenses off and on with swift, deft motion. He can frame and shoot a photo with sleight of hand speed, and it comes out saturated with rich color, mesmerizing in its exquisiteness, composed so well he may as well have designed it.

What is the difference between us? I believe that I could, if I really desired, be as good a photographer as he is, or close to it. I don't think there is a fundamental difference in ability, capacity, and sensitivity. My mediocrity is more self-induced than inborn.

The difference is in the practice.

He has, through slow and grueling apprenticeship, worked and worked at his craft. He has risen early and bedded late, has slogged through mud fields and waded rivers, has driven long, dreary distances and sat still for uneventful hours, waiting to exhale so that he might perfect his art. He is practiced.

And so photography for him is second nature. His cameras hang tight to him as shadows—or closer, like skin. Yes, skin: the organ through which he touches and absorbs his surroundings. He sees everything in terms of its photographic potential, is ever attentive to the subtlety and intricacy of earth's infinite textures. Because he is practiced, and every bone and every muscle has been trained in obedience and quick responsiveness to his craft, taking a picture—a good picture—is as natural for him as sleeping and sweating.

That is how it is for the person who is practiced. And that's how it is with those who practice the presence of God. Too often we are, in our relationship with God, like me and photography: Our knowing Him is sporadic and sparse and not much worth the effort if we consider the results. My thoughts rarely turn to consider how a scene, an event, a face might be photographed. That's just not under my skin or in my bones. I'm not practiced. That's no tragedy. It only means my photographs are not much worth seeing. But this is tragic: when my thoughts rarely turn to consider and encounter the God who is there and here.

The secret remedy for almost all our slowheartedness is to practice the presence of God. This one thing has the power to break borderland's gravitational hold. Jesus walks the road to Emmaus with those disciples, if only they noticed. Jesus is in the midst of our days and our events, our weeks and our weaknesses, our rising up and our lying down. If only we noticed.

Because my brother is a practiced photographer, you get the sense, walking with him and talking with him, that there is no moment, no setting, no place, no person, who would fail to be of photographic interest. When we practice the presence of God, we will come to a point in our relationship with

Him at which we walk in continual expectancy. Each moment brims with the possibility of encounter and discovery. We become conscious that each breath is given by Him, each word is spoken in His hearing.

We drive down the street, stand at the sink, pluck weeds from the garden, hammer nails into planks, hang clothes on a line, write a poem on a napkin. We preach, we pray, we sing, we weep. In all these things, God is present. Whether we notice Him or not is a matter of vision, attentiveness, alertness—practice.

The phrase "practicing the presence of God" is not my own. It comes from the title of a little gem of a book, *The Practice of the Presence of God*, by a monk named Brother Lawrence. The book is slender, written with a childlike directness and simplicity. It is structured as a conversation between Brother Lawrence and an anonymous person who reports what the gentle monk has answered in response to his questions.

> Brother Lawrence insisted that it is necessary to always be aware of God's presence by talking with Him through the day. To think that you must abandon conversation with Him in order to deal with the world is erroneous. *Instead, as we nourish our souls by seeing God in His exaltation, we will derive a great joy at being His.*[1]

Devotion to God, the gathering up and the giving over of ourselves to God, needs to be pounded into us. It needs to be fixed down with rope and nails. If such devotion is ever to become second nature—and something we actually want where we "derive a great joy at being His"—we can't rely on it happening by nature. It comes about by design, by our willing it even when we don't want it.

I don't know why, but I know that virtue has weak, straggling roots, and vice has wild, racing ones. Virtue withers as quickly as plucked grass, spreads as slowly as lichen. But vice—ah, vice flourishes like the weeds.

I know that the most captivating, staggering, extravagant fact in all time and space—that God came down, became one of us, died by us and died for us, did it to make us His children and bride, and now walks every moment with us in love and companionship—that this amazing truth I can treat as no more important than, and forget as easily as, my yearly car insurance renewal. It can become dull routine, one more thing to know, do, worry about. One more thing to try to remember.

Such a God doing such a thing surpasses all things in greatness and marvel. Nothing even remotely, even vaguely, compares with it. Yet the Sunday flyers, with yet another 40 percent off sale on kitchenware at Wal-Mart, or the pages with reviews of the latest batch of books or movies, can distract me from it. A simple backache can ruin my joy in it. An unexpected car expense can steal away my thankfulness for it.

I need a steady vigilance in holy things.

SUCH VIGILANCE IS MOSTLY EMBODIED IN ORDINARY DISCIPLINES, and later we'll look more closely at that. But here I want to talk about praying without ceasing, about our entire life being an act of worship. There was a time, prior to the Enlightenment, when Western society was saturated with Christian conscience and consciousness. We often hold this time in scorn because of its religious wars and dissensions, its inquisitions, its witch-hunts and heretic burnings. But at least this can be said: Those things happened because people took their faith seriously. What one believed really mattered. They had a wrong-headed faith in many instances, but at least a living one, brimful of energy, feisty and sinewy and down to the bone. Life, all of it— plowing and reaping, sleeping and eating, spinning and cutting cloth, being young and growing old—was laden with religious meaning and woven with holy purpose. Life was danced out in rhythm to God's own play and work, His coming and going.

The writings of almost anyone from that time—monk, ploughman, statesman, clothier—show this quality of attentiveness to God. What stands out is how unconscious the people were of their consciousness of God. Thinking of God wasn't a contrived thing, a studied art. They didn't have to work themselves up to it or into it. It was just how they lived and breathed. God skulked near, mixing earth and heaven. All of this could lead to bouts of superstition, to seeing devils in jackdaws, omens in comet tails, portents in hail storms. But is this any worse or any more harmful than some of the fallout of the cult of science—our poll-mongering, our body-freezing, our technological insatiability and arrogance, our awe of a man, any man, in a white coat and glasses?

Theology was once queen of the sciences. It ruled over and gathered into it all disciplines. Cardinal Newman, though writing after the Enlightenment, still viewed religion as the condition, the foundation, of all knowledge, not just *part* of knowledge.

But we live in the ruins of such a world. A wedge has been driven between the things of God and the things of man, between the sacred and the secular, church and society, faith and physics, the invisible and the visible. So if we're sick, we go to the doctor. We don't call the elders, or if we do it's against not just our common sense, but very often our intuition, our deepest sense of what's right. Prayer in such moments is more a talisman, a way of hedging the bet. A last resort. We all buy insurance and have pensions. We plan our journeys before we start them. We plan our lives before we live them. This is the way it should be, isn't it? It's stupid and irresponsible to think otherwise.

This is the world where talk of God has become a quaint diction, a whispered language, a lexicon arcane, and rare as an alchemist's potions. Nietzsche was wrong. We haven't killed God; we've just domesticated Him. We've made Him too safe, soft, fastidious. In our moments of sentimentality, we allow that He might dwell in hushed cathedrals, musty cloisters, tranquil forests, the laughter of children, the soft petals of roses, blah blah blah. But not, surely not, in the jostling, brawling world of our doings and undoings. Man makes history; God keeps heaven. In boardrooms and bedchambers, in lecture halls and marketplaces, God is hardly seen as a player let alone the author, the one who holds in His hand each king's heart and directs it like a watercourse (Proverbs 21:1).

This is our habit of thinking, our way of seeing. *Ours.* Do you doubt it, claim exemption from it? But look: We take courses on American literature; we read books on landscaping; we water ski and house build and make love and rarely, if ever, consider that we're engaging in religious exercises. This is secular work, secular pastime. If we call it sacred, we don't mean *sacred.* We mean *special*, important *to me.* We mean *sacred* in a trivial, ironic way: *My computer is sacred. My car is sacred. My day off is sacred.*

Our day-to-day life is over here, and God is over there. End of story.

Here's a problem: The Bible doesn't know about this distinction. Read the Old Testament or read the New: The Bible makes no room for the idea of the secular. In biblical worldview, there is only the sacred and the profane, and the profane is just the sacred abused, unkempt, trampled down, trivialized, turned inside out. It is just the holy treated in an unholy way. Paul writing to the Colossians captures the extent of God's involvement with the world and in the world:

> For by [Christ] all things were created: things in heaven and on earth, visible and invisible, whether thrones or powers or rulers or authorities; all things were created by him and for him. He is before all things, and in him all things hold together. (Colossians 1:16–17)

There goes the distinction.

"The world is mine," declares the Lord, "and all that is in it" (Psalm 50:12).

There goes the distinction.

"For in [God]," Paul tells the Athenian intelligentsia, quoting one of their own poets, "we live and move and have our being" (Acts 17:28).

There goes the distinction.

Do you see what it means? God is as present now as He was then, here as He was there. God dwells in barrooms and brothels, in judgment, in anger, in heartbreak, and sometimes maybe in blessing. He dwells in churches, and in all those ways just mentioned. He dwells even on borderland.

Nowhere, as Psalm 139 testifies, can we flee from His presence.

But there is something deeper still. When we remove the false distinction between sacred and secular, see all things existing by Him, for Him, and through Him, we are then free to redeem many so-called secular activities for the kingdom of God.

I have met Christians who have felt guilty for reading Shakespeare or taking a course in philosophy or spending an evening talking—just talking—with friends, because they feel that this was time they could have spent praying, evangelizing, or reading their Bible.

I am aware of the subtlety and insidiousness of idolatry. "Man is surely stark raving mad," Montaigne said. "He can't make a worm, but he makes gods by the dozen." For some people Shakespeare is idolatry, an excluding and consuming love, a venture in god making. That can happen with anything: cars, sports, stamps, hydrangeas, church. Anything can stop becoming that which we offer up in worship and instead become that which we worship.

But there is another way to live. Why shouldn't Shakespeare's plays and courses in philosophy and long midnight chats enrich rather than diminish our life before God? God owns these things, too, and can bend them to His purpose. His light shines on them, too.

This thinking can be carried too far. That's obvious. I once read about a male stripper who was a Christian and who stripped, he said, for Jesus' sake. It conjures an impossible image. In truth, some things can't be redeemed. Paganism, perversion, pettiness—none of this can be pressed into the service of Christ. Some of our life, like plague clothes, can't be salvaged, only burned.

But only some. The vast majority of our life, instead, needs not burning but baptizing. Why can't we read a book, build a house, cobble a shoe for Jesus' sake? Why can't we gather our whole lives into the divine embrace? Why have we such a ready impulse to see pastoring as a *vocation* and plumbing as a *job?* Why can't we practice a different way of seeing, where God is honored as much in the well-spliced pipe as the well-spoken sermon?

Brother Lawrence says it well: "Our sanctification does not depend as much on *changing* our activities as it does on doing them for God rather than for ourselves."

Beyond those things that we need to forsake or repent of, there is a vast inventory that needs only to be consecrated. "Whatever you do," Paul says, "work at it with all your heart, as working for the Lord, not for men" (Colossians 3:23). This is Paul's counsel to Christian slaves. *Whatever you do? But Paul, you don't know what I do, what they make me do. You don't know the shadowy, slippery, reeking undersides of things they make me scour, the dirty work and heavy work and lonely work I toil at.* But Paul won't let up: *whatever* you do. Turn your slave work into worship, he says. Make it a gift to God. This is gospel alchemy, taking pewter and making it gold, mixing elixir out of any old puddle of water.

And it's true. It works. I had a job once that I resented as bitterly as slavery. I worked in a bakery. It was actually a good job, well paying, good hours, pleasant staff, fine working conditions. But I had lost sight of all that. I had become a university student, and my vision for who I wanted to be sat increasingly out of kilter with my work there. I had a self-image that the bakery stifled. At the time, I would have told you I wasn't "called" to this kind of work. I would have told you I was stuck. Looking back, I can see I was merely stuck-up. At any rate, my work became a heavy, dreary business, a yoke of slavery.

Then I read this very passage from Colossians, and God spoke. The Spirit convicted. I made a resolve before God that I would offer my work to Him. My work became worship. I sliced and bagged bread, arranged frozen croissant dough on char-darkened pans, boxed and sold tarts and cakes, replenished shelves with bags of breadcrumbs and sourdough rolls. Before, I'd done all this in sullen weariness. But now I gave it all to God. I did it with a keen sense that God Himself watched. The work was for Him. He inspected, applauded or reprimanded it, held it in His hands.

This is what happened: I went from being a sour, grudging worker to a joyful, grateful one. The manager noticed, with thankfulness. The other employees noticed, and my joy in the work began to leaven their attitudes. But this mattered most: My Father in heaven noticed, and that increased my joy even more.

Our world is full of gimcrack and gimmicks, haste and hustle. God has become merely another appointment in a crammed Day-timer. When is there time for God? There's so much work to do. Oh yes, how we'd love to take a year off, live in a monastery, study at a seminary, hole up in a hermitage with just our Bible. But do and do, rule on rule, a little here, a little there: It eclipses worship.[2]

How different our lives could be if we instead made work into worship: *as working for the Lord, not for man.* And what if we did this, too, with our play, our leisure, our family time, our garden chores?

Imagine.

We need amidst all this to learn once again the sheer nonutilitarian delight of stopping all work and gathering simply to worship God. But the flatness and dullness or the hype and hysteria of much of our

Sunday gatherings is probably owing as much to our poor practice as anything. If Sunday for one hour is the only time we worship, no wonder we do
it sloppily, haltingly, hastily, and leave as hungry as we came. If we only ate one
day a week, and on that day only one meal, we would die soon enough. And
man does not live on bread alone. Robust worshipers worship in spirit and in
truth. They don't need a temple. The kitchen will do.

We are all in the habit of asking the Spirit to open our minds before we
read Scripture or hear a sermon. But rarely if ever do we ask the Spirit to reveal
to us more of God when we study a leaf, rock, bird, child, painting, carving,
or poem. As the child's prayer puts it,

God be in my head,
and in my understanding;
God be in my eyes,
and in my looking;
God be in my mouth,
and in my speaking;
God be in my heart,
and in my feeling;
God be at my death,
and at my departing.

"Our life," the duke says in Shakespeare's *As You Like It,* "finds tongues in
trees, books in running brooks, sermons in stones, and good in everything."[3]
This is not animism, not pantheism. This, rather, is the recognition, a biblically shaped and grounded recognition, that God's ways of speaking, His
methods of disclosure, are wide and varied. As such, we need to walk open
eyed and with ears pricked.

Our lives should be lived with expectancy. Not necessarily with expectation, because expectation tends to dictate terms. The Pharisees lived with
expectation and rejected Christ when He did not fit the rigid narrowness of
their expectations. Often I wonder if we, waiting for Christ's return, do it more
with expectation than expectancy. Expectancy is the belief that God will do
something. Expectation insists He do it in *just this way.* Sometimes expectation

blinds us more to the God who is here right now than outright disbelief does. The Pharisees couldn't see Jesus *for looking*. Or those two disciples on the road to Emmaus: There they are, bemoaning the absence of the very one who's present with them. What made them deaf and blind? Expectations: "We had hoped that he was the one who was going to redeem Israel" (Luke 24:21). But that "hope" took a form that shut out surprises, like crosses and resurrection and a deeper redemption.

But imagine a life buoyed by expectancy, by the conviction that the Lord will show Himself. How, where, when—we don't know that. We don't dictate the terms. We have, of course, certain touchstones, certain ways of sifting out the good from the bad, the real from the fake: fruit, truth, the exaltation of Jesus. We don't want to become spiritual rubes, open to the mountebank's bluff, too easily dazzled. But by living with biblically girded expectancy, our lives stir to vibrant wakefulness. Elizabeth Barrett Browning writes,

> *Earth is crammed with heaven*
> *and every common bush afire with God;*
> *but only he who sees takes off his shoes.*
> *The rest sit around it and*
> *pluck blackberries.*[4]

We are talking here about a tectonic shift in the way we see the world. We are talking about eyes that see glints of heaven flickering in earth's shadows; ears that hear angelsong counterpointed with the barking of dogs and the wailing of sirens.

When our first child, Adam, was born, I had such a moment. There were complications at the birth. The cord was cinched, nooselike, around his neck, and my wife Cheryl's pushing tightened it. Cheryl had been in labor thirty hours, hard labor for ten, and both she and our son were exhausted. It was a bad moment for surgery, for the intrusive violence of Cesarean, but my son would die without it, and possibly my wife as well. So off they went in the middle of the night, the nurses rolling my wife down to the O.R. in that brisk, stern-mannered way medical people get when they're trying to contain panic. I asked if I could go in the operating room—Cheryl had an epidural and would be awake through the surgery. But this was an emergency surgery; the head nurse didn't want me in the room. I insisted. They relented. They told me to scrub up and get into a gown. They'd call me when they were ready.

I sat in an anteroom, waiting to be called. How terrible anterooms are. How much like borderlands: in-between places, situated precariously between the what was and the what will be. Yet anterooms can be places we discover ourselves, touch down to the roots. They are places where, if there's a still small voice, we hear it. If there's a whirlwind passing, we see it. Minutes swell hugely there. The air gathers to a crushing weight. All the anxiety of the world is distilled in anterooms. They are places where you can be broken or made.

I usually don't do well in them.

But that night, I spoke to God with psalmlike directness. *God, show Yourself,* I asked. *Show Your glory in the midst of these sallow yellow walls. Spread Your fragrance amongst the sharpness of this antiseptic smell. Speak into this silence.*

And God did. Not audibly, not visibly, not even tangibly, but God genuinely visited me in that anteroom. He made the drabness brilliant. He made the heaviness light, the slowness of time swift. His still, small voice spoke, and I heard. And I heard this: *No matter what, all is well and all manner of things are well. No matter what.*

I knew something in that moment. I knew something that now, ten years later, I still know. Oh, I have lapses. I have bouts of amnesia, where I become oblivious to the truth I knew then with such piercing clarity, a truth that took hold of me and demanded I take hold of it. But it's not difficult for me to recover that truth and to know it again: That if God is present in anterooms, then He's present in borderland; that if Christ is on the road to Emmaus, then He's on every road; that if Christ was *there,* then He is *here* now.

He doesn't need to be invoked. I do.

They called me, *Come.* I came. The operation began. I saw blood, blood everywhere, Cheryl and Adam's blood, mingled, surging, spilling. I saw the hurried working of the doctors and nurses, heard their edginess. I saw the screen, the jittering jagged line monitoring my son's heart. I saw his heartbeat plunge way down and hover low, sluggish to come back up. I saw the doctor reach inside the wound in my wife and scoop out our son, his skin porcelain blue from breathlessness. I saw the doctor deftly untangle the umbilical cord that was wrapped tightly around his neck. I listened for his cry: silence. Terrible vast silence. But then a sputtering and then wailing. And then color suffused his flesh. *Adam. Red earth.*

I should have been a wreck.

I was, I think, the calmest person in that room.

God had come to be with me.

Actually, no. I had come to be with Him.

Chapter Fifteen

THE WOUNDS
WE SHARE

In chapter 9, we looked at how pride is often broken through brokenness. That is the gift of wounds—Jacob's limp that at last sets him steady on his feet. It's many times the broken who break free of borderland. A heartache or hardship ruptures the earth beneath them, and they leave that place for the holy wild, to pursue and embrace the God who isn't safe, but who's good.

But there is also danger here. Brokenness can destroy us. Wounds can cure, but they can also kill. Too much trouble can shackle us to borderland, bury us there.

This is especially true when the wound is in the heart. A friend betrays us. Another deserts us. A colleague undermines us. A spouse is unfaithful to us. A child makes foolish decisions.

Sometimes these wounds are inflicted to spite us, at other times in spite of us. Some are acts of vengeance, but some are acts of indifference, done without us in mind at all. My own deepest heart wounds have been inflicted by people who never set out to hurt me. It was worse. At some point they stopped even caring that what they did would hurt me. I became beside the point. My existence ceased to matter. The importance I believed I occupied in the heart of the other, the place of cherishing I thought was reserved for me, turned out to be a myth.

Either way—the wounds inflicted to spite us, the wounds inflicted in spite of us—they are killing wounds. They are septic things, riddled with infection. They are gashes that rend, raglike, the tissue. They lack the sterile precision of the surgeon's cut. They lack, too, the sense of impersonal randomness of the madman's wounds. These are *personal wounds, against us, a canceling out of who we are.* They are the wounds David knew:

> If an enemy were insulting me,
>   I could endure it;
> if a foe were raising himself against me,
>   I could hide from him.
> But it is you, a man like myself,
>   my companion, my close friend,
> with whom I once enjoyed sweet fellowship
>   as we walked with the throng at the house of God.
> (Psalm 55:12–14)

They are the wounds Karen knows. Karen lived in Germany and was married to a physician, Eduard, whom she supported for the first five years of marriage as he went through medical school. He was considerate, handsome, intelligent—"an extraordinarily kind, gentle, and loving husband and father," Karen says of him. "I had friends who would complain about their husbands. I used to walk away, shaking my head. I didn't have a single complaint about my husband. He was perfect."

Just after Eduard graduated from medical school and became a specialist in radiology, Karen became pregnant. Identical twins. Soon, Karen and Eduard were overjoyed to welcome into their lives two beautiful blond girls, intensely curious, fiercely intelligent. Then after two miscarriages, Karen became pregnant again and had Joel, a feisty little fireball. They decided to buy Karen's grandmother's house. They began laying plans for extensive renovations to it. Life was beautiful. Could it get any better?

Yes. Karen was a Christian, and a year after Joel was born, God gave her assurance that Eduard would soon come to know Christ personally. In two weeks he did and immediately became an enthusiastic witness among friends and colleagues. Seven months later he was baptized, and a few months after that they were ready to begin their planned renovations on the house. Eduard decided that Karen should take the children to Canada for three months to visit her parents in Victoria while the renovations took place. This made sense. The house was going to be gutted, the roof removed and raised. It would be unlivable.

So in March 1994, Karen and her three children—the twins now five, Joel a year and a half—kissed their weeping husband and father good-bye, boarded a plane, and flew to Canada. Eduard told them—he told this to many people—that he had no idea how he was going to live without them for three months. He asked Christian friends to pray for him for strength.

Eduard phoned them every day in Canada, told them he missed them and he loved them.

After a week he phoned Karen and told her something else. He told her he had been having an affair for several months with a twenty-six-year-old radiology technician. He didn't want Karen or his children to come back. He wanted a divorce. When Karen asked him how this had happened, why it had happened, all he gave for an explanation was that he had watched the movie *Mrs. Doubtfire,* and that it had been a sign from God.

Karen's life was shattered. For three years she wept every day. Her heart was sometimes swollen with rage, other times withered in grief. She struggled with weariness, bitterness, hopelessness. She clung to God, pleaded with Him to come near, feared that she would somehow slip away, go spiraling endlessly down into cold, black nothingness. She begged God to give her life, and at times she wanted to take her life. And every day she had to pull herself together to dress her children, feed them, bathe them, be their mother. Their single mother.

Eduard, newly married now and with another family on the way, moved into a posh suburb and renovated a house exactly to the specifications that he and Karen had worked out. He started a practice of his own, which is flourishing.

If an enemy were insulting me, I could endure it; if a foe were raising himself against me, I could hide from him. But it is you...my companion, my close friend, with whom I once enjoyed sweet fellowship as we walked with the throng at the house of God.

These wounds are deep.

CAN THEY CURE US, SUCH WOUNDS? I'M NOT ASKING, *CAN WE BE cured of them?* I'm asking something harder: Can they—these messy, dirty, poisoned wounds—can they themselves cure us? Is it possible ever to find that the wound inflicted, knowingly or unknowingly, to kill us, the *personal wound,* actually gives life?

I say yes. Yes, but not easily.

I was asked once, as a pastor, to speak to a group of people who were beginning a Twelve-Step program. The program was generic. It was for people struggling with a whole range of things, from eating obsessions to control, from sexual addictions to obsessive fear. I was to go in and address the group as *One Who Knew the Way.* I was to tell them that if they got stuck somewhere—for those twelve steps are walked through treacherous land or sometimes are just a maze way through borderland, giving us the illusion of progress without actually making any—they could make an appointment with me, and I would get them unstuck.

I came in, sat down, was introduced. The leader had everyone around the room say their name and what they were looking for in a support group. As the people began to speak, I really saw them. I thought of Jesus' question to the smug Pharisee Simon, who is looking with disdain at a woman weeping at Jesus' feet. "Simon," Jesus said, "do you see this woman?" And the answer is no; Simon doesn't see her. He sees a woman of ill repute, a woman who has invaded the quarantine of his sanctimony. Simon sees a slut, a whore, a tramp. But no, he doesn't see *this woman.*

I had come in that night and, looking around at first, I didn't really see anyone. I saw only addicts. I saw only people who had made stupid choices and were now living with the mess and grief of them. But as they spoke their names one by one, I really saw them. I saw their hurt. I saw that they inflicted wounds and received wounds. I saw that the wounds were very dark, purplish, half-scabbed things, hastily bandaged. I saw they tried to get on with life—working jobs, driving children to school, visiting relatives, watching movies—and spent a great amount of energy trying to ignore the wounds. But the wounds kept bleeding through, kept waking them and hounding them with the ache. And I saw that, more than anything, they wanted to know: *Can these wounds be healed?*

And what came to me—I didn't speak it then, I pondered it in my heart—was that not only could the wounds be healed, but the wounds might themselves be a source of their healing.

I read to them the story of the two disciples on the road to Emmaus. I had planned to make some "pastoral" remarks about it. But I stopped. God, I believed, wanted me to speak more personally, from the heart. So I swallowed and began.

"My father was an alcoholic," I said. "My mother was going to divorce him because of it. One Christmas, he got hired to play Santa Claus for the party of a corporate oil company in Calgary. He got so drunk that he never came home. My mother had been fearing this, that one night he just wouldn't show up. She had been watching the clock and the door every evening, hoping it wouldn't happen, knowing with dreadful certainty that eventually it would. That night she bundled up and went looking for him. She found him crumpled up in a snowbank, his Santa suit soiled and reeking with his own vomit. She managed to get him home. But soon after that, while he slept off yet another hangover, she got up early and rode the bus into downtown Calgary to see a lawyer, to seek a divorce.

"While she was gone, a fuller brush salesman came by, waking my father who was sleeping off his hangover. My dad told the man that his wife was gone, come back later. The man could see my dad's condition and said, "I better come in for a coffee." My dad was too weak to protest. The man was a member of AA and had walked all the steps. That day, my father started walking them as well. He never turned back."

I paused. This story was famous with my mother. I was only a toddler when it happened, so I had no living memory of it. But my mother told and retold this story, and for me it was vivid as touching fire. Over the years I had grown dull to it. That night, though, as *I* told it, it gathered on me with fresh power. The wonder of it, the providential wonder, swept in on me and nearly broke me open with thankfulness, with an ancient unnamable longing. I could barely get through it.

"The twelve steps," I continued, "were steps out of sickness for him, and for my mother, and for his children. For me. They're the reason I had a father growing up at all—the reason he didn't die on some frozen winter night, collapsed in a snow bank with no one to fetch him this time, or spend his days in some dreary flop house, sodden, rotting, alone."

I looked at the people in that room. I *saw* them.

"I don't have any more wisdom in our courage for this journey than you do. Maybe less. But if you could use a traveling companion, I would come along. I would be only like one of those two men on the road to Emmaus, mostly confused myself, with a slow heart that burned within. Maybe together we would be able to discern Christ on the road beside us."

They thanked me. We said good night. I went home

But the question lingered: *Can wounds themselves be a source of healing?*

Not long after that, I went with my wife and some other pastors to a pastors' conference in Banff. One of the speakers was Maxine Hancock, a lively, funny, feisty little lady. She spoke on the second morning of the conference, and she spoke about healing. She used the prophecy of Zechariah, the promise of God's anointed one who will open a fountain to cleanse people from sin and impurity. This is what she read:

> And I will pour out...a spirit of grace and supplication. They will look on me, the one they have pierced, and they will mourn for him as one mourns for an only child.... If someone asks him, "What are these wounds on your body?" he will answer, "The wounds I was given at the house of my friends." (12:10; 13:6)

And I had my answer. The wounds we inflict and the wounds inflicted on us ultimately find their mark, literally *find their mark*, in Christ: "See the marks in my hands. Put your hand there." These wounds we give and receive are gathered into the wounds He took.

"By his wounds," Isaiah says, "we are healed." *By His wounds*. We gave those wounds. We lunged the spear, brandished the hammer, lashed the whip, pressed down the thorns. We did it. By the very wounds we inflicted, we are healed.

And I realized also that the wounds we take are wounds He shares in and gives ultimate meaning to. In our woundedness, we "fill up in [our] flesh what is still lacking in regard to Christ's afflictions" (Colossians 1:24). In our woundedness, "the sufferings of Christ flow over into our lives, so also through Christ our comfort overflows" (2 Corinthians 1:5). In our woundedness, "we always carry around in our body the death of Jesus, so that the life of Jesus may also be revealed in our body," and though "outwardly we are wasting away, yet inwardly we are being renewed day by day" (2 Corinthians 4:10, 16). These wounds are a way of knowing the one who was "despised and rejected by men, a man of sorrows and familiar with suffering" (Isaiah 53:3).

Wounds are one of God's deepest forms of intimacy. The weight of the world's sickness and sin was braided into a whip and brought down on Jesus' back. It was woven into a thorny crown and pushed on His head. It was shaped into rough wood and pressed hard on His thin body. It was forged into cold metal and driven through the soft spot on His hands.

The early Christians understood their own suffering, or were exhorted to, not as a random, accidental thing, not as punishment, not even as the retaliatory evil inflicted by a wicked generation—no, they understood their suffering as this communion with the Christ who, for the joy set before Him, endured the cross. "I want to know Christ," Paul declares, "and the power of his resurrection." To which we all say, "Amen!" But Paul doesn't stop there: "And the fellowship of sharing in his sufferings, becoming like him in his death, and so, somehow, to attain to the resurrection from the dead." *The fellowship of sharing in His suffering, becoming like Him in His death* (Philippians 3:10). To which we want to reply, "Is there another route—a detour and, hopefully, a shortcut—to resurrection power?"

There isn't.

Here is the hard but healing truth: Wounds are, in Christ's economy, a means of God's wooing. It is the strange kiss of God, the reverse of the Judas kiss—a kiss to restore us and not to betray us. The pain becomes a narrow passage that leads down into a unique intimacy with the suffering servant.

There is a dark and odd comedy film called *Being John Malkovich*. A man discovers a secret passageway—lightless, cramped, dirty, cold—that whisks those who clamber in into the mind of the actor John Malkovich. Those who go through find themselves seeing the world as Malkovich sees it, experiencing what he experiences, feeling his sensations, his responses, his thoughts.

The gospel promise is if we belong to Christ, we can have the mind of Christ. But here is what we each discover at some point: Wounds are one of the main passageways into that mind—the tight, frightening tunnel that ushers us into a fresh way of seeing, where we begin to perceive and respond to the world as Jesus does.

Karen found that. She found the wounds inflicted on her became not just healed wounds—in some ways they remain unhealed, perhaps until heaven—but rather *healing* wounds. They have taken her deeper into the fellowship of sharing in Christ's suffering. There were times, many, when all strength was gone from her. She was hollowed out, swallowed up. She was deathly weary and weary for death. Yet she kept discovering in the places of deepest aloneness and emptiness the God who was with her, for her. She discovered Christ's presence from the inside out, seeing what He sees as He sees it.

She now has a sense of what the world looks like from a cross. She knows the darkness of the inside of a grave.

And she knows, more and more, the brightness of a new day when the world is glimpsed as from a tomb, its stone rolled away.

SO WOUNDS GIVE US CHRISTLIKE VISION. BUT I THINK THEY OPEN up all our senses. Wounds I've given and received have helped me to hear the Word of God. When I first became a Christian, I read the Bible many times. It was an exciting book to me, and some things came at me with great force. But most of it was in monotone—a flat, drab voice, like someone reading the minutes from an old meeting. But wounding and being wounded, the grief and pain that comes with that and finally the intimacy of being with Christ in that, has transposed the Word of God out of that flat key. It's given more and more of the Bible a tonal richness. I can increasingly hear the *voice* of God in the Word of God, hear the inflections of anger, heartache, joy. It has become intensely personal, and at the same time more universal: a word to me, about me, for me. But not just to me. It has become a word whispered in my ear that I must shout from the rooftop.

Marshall Shelley, in an editorial in *Leadership,* tells of meeting the actor Bruce Marchiano, who plays Jesus in a film version of Matthew. Bruce told him about playing the scene where Jesus denounces and calls curses down on unrepentant cities: "Woe to you, Korazin! Woe to you, Bethsaida! If the miracles performed in you had been performed in Tyre or Sidon, they would have repented long ago.... But I tell you, it will be more bearable for Tyre and Sidon on the day of judgment than for you." Only the actor couldn't get the voice right. How does the Messiah, the only begotten Son, God incarnate—how does He speak words of doom and damnation? Marchiano tells what happened:

> I was standing in front of five hundred people—cast members, Moroccan extras, sound and lighting crews—and suddenly, in a fraction of a second, something happened. I'm not a mystical person, but what happened was so horrible that my heart broke. I saw people living their lives in ways that God didn't plan.
>
> The closest I can come to describing it would be what parents might feel if they look out the window and see their toddler walking into the street and a truck approaching. They scream for the child to come back, but the little one keeps going into the street...."[1]

Marchiano broke and wept for an hour. And then he did the scene, "Woe to you, Korazin!"

This time he got the voice right.

I believe that through our wounds, the ones we give and the ones we take, God helps us get the voice right. He helps us to hear His voice in His Word. And He allows us, when we speak His Word, to speak it with the right tone—with the anger of the beloved's heartache or the urgency of the parent's warning or the tender whisper of the father who wants his child home, any time of day or night, dressed any way he chooses.

Wounds allow us to *see* the crowd, the woman, the twelve-step group, and speak to each as He would speak—"Woe to you," "Go in peace," "Come to me"—and to discover that, indeed, the *voice* is the same, the very same: always the voice of love.

⤬

I DON'T THINK THAT GOD, THIS SIDE OF THE JORDAN, EVER completely removes our wounds. I have at times wished He would. I wish He would obliterate the past and remake it. *Take this cup away from me. Spare me the wounds, and if not, spare me the scars from them, the deep ache in the flesh and the memory.*

But God has set this limit on His power. Not even He can remove the past. And the past comes bearing its wounds.

What God does is better. He redeems the past and its wounds. I have not given or taken a single wound that has not made me wiser—slower to judge, more discerning, more forgiving, more open to forgiveness, more shrewd and yet more trusting. In fact, I have not given or taken a single wound through which I did not come to know Christ better and even, this is the amazing thing, become more like Him.

The one way we recognize the risen Christ is by His scars. He wears them like medals of honor.

And so they are.

Chapter Sixteen

THE GOOD
CONFESSION

I have a confession: I used to hate confessing.

Former President George Bush once became suddenly, violently ill at a state dinner. He retched on the Japanese prime minister. The media caught it all: the president's slow-motion blur of groveling, writhing humiliation; the Japanese prime minister's serene smile being replaced by a twisted look of anguish and revulsion; the president's bodyguards panicking, scrambling, rushing about, diving in. The Japanese prime minister no doubt moments before felt honored to be sitting beside the president of the United States. But in the next moment, the U.S. president was throwing up on his lap, and his spontaneous reaction was disgust.

That was the default picture I had when I thought about confessing: groveling on my knees, reeking stuff spewing from my mouth, the person receiving it pulling back in revulsion, those appointed to protect me panic-stricken, and the paparazzi capturing the moment for all to see and forever remember.

Confession, I thought, was wrecking the dinner party.

I hated confessing. But the image, I discovered, is wrong. Confession is not like that at all. It is, for sure, uncomfortable and awkward to begin—as most holy habits are. But running, swimming, skipping, skiing, riding a bike, climbing a mountain—all are uncomfortable and awkward to begin. We think at first we're going to kill ourselves doing this, locking two long, thin boards onto big clunky boots and flinging ourselves headlong down a snowy, icy slope. But after a while, it's exhilarating. It makes us feel alive.

At first we'd rather die than open up our inner life, its secrets and doubts and hurts and fears and wrongs, to someone else.

But after a while it makes us feel alive.

I have often wondered if Adam and Eve would have fared much differently had they confessed their sin. God gave them opportunity for it: "Have you eaten from the tree that I commanded you not to eat from?" (Genesis 3:11). God is not seeking information since He knows full well what they've done. He's seeking confession. He wants them—interesting phrase, this—to *come clean.* But instead of confessing, they blame. Adam, in a brilliant ploy of victimhood, blames both God and Eve (*"This woman you* gave me" is at fault). Eve, inventing the original version of "the devil made me do it," blames the serpent. Avoidance, accusation, and excuse making crowd out confession. These things are, after all, easier, more *habitual,* more natural.

This is the shape of life in the borderland. It is maintained by a giant game of masquerade, concealment, finger pointing, blame shifting. No one is owning up to anything there, coming clean with anyone.

Yet confession is a first and necessary step back to the Garden, back to the place where we can be "naked and feel no shame" (Genesis 2:25). Confession is the ground clearing before the building goes up. Confession is stripping down all the extra weight before running. Confession is cleaning out all the black sludge and dead leaves in the eaves' troughs so the rainwater can wash them clean. Confession is a portal out of borderland. "If I had cherished sin in my heart," the psalmist writes, "the Lord would not have listened" (Psalm 66:18).

Confession is the first move we make in salvation. We confess, and God forgives. But it is also for Christians an ongoing discipline that helps us practice the presence of God. It's to become a holy habit, not because we lose our salvation if we fail to do it, but because apart from it we often lose the joy of our salvation (Psalm 51:12). Jesus says that if we come to the altar and there discover that our brother has something against us—in other words, we have sinned and need to confess—that we're to leave the altar and go and be reconciled. Our forward, Godward motion is stymied and sidetracked if we do not replace the habits—old as Adam, fresh as this morning's trouble in your workplace—of hiding, covering, accusing, excusing with the holy habit of confessing.

But it needs some definition. It needs to be distinguished from the picture of retching at the dinner party. Historically the practice of confession has suffered abuse and needs rehabilitating. On one side the Roman Catholic church instituted confession as a sacrament that the faithful were expected to resort to regularly. This began as a good thing but in many ways deteriorated into mere mechanism and manipulation.[1] Frank McCourt in his memoir *Angela's Ashes* gives a vivid portrait of this. Recounting his Irish Catholic upbringing, he tells how he went from church to church in his city of Limerick until he found an old doddering half-deaf priest who would mostly sleep through his confession. That way he could confess, be "in a state of grace just for going to confession," and then carry on as usual.[2] Confession became a loophole for sin, not a cleansing of it.

I lived in a small town in the interior of British Columbia for several years, and the town council had a problem. A few years before, they installed parking meters along the downtown streets, but the townspeople, offended by or indifferent to the meters, continued to park where they wanted for as long as they wanted and simply discarded the tickets tucked under their car's windshield wiper. The council didn't want to get into all the messy, unpopular business of towing and impounding cars, so they came up with an innovative way to motivate people to pay their parking meter tickets. They installed locked metal boxes with a slot in their sides on every block. The meter cop left you an envelope with your parking ticket. You could pay your fine by putting money, with a stub torn off the ticket, in the envelope and depositing it in one of the metal boxes. And here was the incentive: If you did that within twelve hours, the fine was half price.

It worked, sort of. More people, indeed, began to pay their fines at half price. But the cost of half a fine was considerably cheaper than a day in the paid-parking garage. It was the equivalent of about four hours metered parking. So people would park all day on the curbside, pay their half-price ticket before driving away, and gain a savings over every other form of paid parking in the downtown area.

That's the danger when confession becomes institutionalized: Some see it as a cheaper way to do what you planned to do anyhow. Sin boldly, then confess. And you can avoid for a long time, maybe a lifetime, the real issue of spiritual growth, of actually changing on the inside.

On the other hand, Protestants became so scornful of the Roman Catholic practice of confession that we dropped it altogether and ended up creating churches of smiling, laughing, savvy people who are dying on the inside and too afraid to let anyone know. First Church of the Whitewashed Tombs. This, too, bypasses the real issue of spiritual growth. Rather than bear fruit, we've tended to paint it on and hope nobody notices that we have no real roots or sap to grow fruit anyhow.

To add to our confusion, the culture at large suffers from a glut of confession. Television and radio talk show hosts have become international celebrities, and wealthy to boot, getting complete strangers to disclose to other complete strangers—millions of them—the most randy, sordid, intimate details of their private thoughts and lives. This kind of confession only increases the burden we carry, the filth inside, rather than relieving the burden, washing the filth. It is being naked, not without shame, but shamelessly.

So what is confession? I have my own definition. It's not based on a minute dissection of the Greek, a cross survey of the Homeric and Platonic literature, a fine sifting of Syrian papyri fragments. It's just my own homemade definition: *Confession is presenting our real self to God.* It's bringing before God not the person we hope to be, but the person we actually are. The parable of the Pharisee and the tax collector illustrates the principle crisply. Two men go up to the temple to pray, a Pharisee and a tax collector. The Pharisee boasts to God about all he is and all he does: "God, I thank you that I am not like other men—robbers, evildoers, adulterers—or even like this tax collector over there. I fast twice a week and give a tenth of all I get." But the tax collector can't even look up. He beats his breast and says, "Have mercy on me, a sinner." He presents his real self to God—not who he wants to be or wants others to think he is, but who he really is. And Jesus says he's the one God deals with in mercy, the one God justifies, the one God exalts (Luke 18:9–14).

Confession is when we quit all the deal making, the sidestepping, the mask wearing, the pretense and preening, and we get bone-deep honest before God: I am the man!

There is nothing startling or controversial about that. Everyone can, I think, agree with that definition of confession. But now here's a subclause: *In order to present our real selves to God, we need to be honest with ourselves about ourselves, and honest about ourselves to at least one other trusted and godly person.*

It's that last part that gets us: *honest about ourselves to at least one other trusted and godly person.*

Let me be clear about what I am *not* saying. I am not saying that if you don't confess to another person, God doesn't cleanse you from sin. I am saying, though, that we often do not *experience* the reality of God's cleansing apart from an honest confession to another person. In a few pages we'll look at what the person who hears our confession should be like. Confession is not getting on the Oprah show and exposing our secrets to a zillion viewers. That's striptease, not confession.

But is this kind of confession to another person necessary? Richard Foster writes:

The person who has known forgiveness and release from persistent, nagging habits of sin through private confession [that is, to God alone] should rejoice greatly in this evidence of God's mercy. But there are others for whom this has not happened. Let me describe what it is like. We have prayed, even begged, for forgiveness, and though we hope we have been forgiven, we sense no release. We doubt our forgiveness and despair at our confession. We fear that perhaps we have made confession only to ourselves and not to God. The haunting sorrows and hurts of the past have not been healed. We try to convince ourselves that God forgives only the sin; he does not heal the memory. But deep within...we know there must be something more. People have told us to take our forgiveness by faith and not call God a liar. Not wanting to call God a liar, we do our best to take it by faith. But because misery and bitterness remain in our lives, we again despair. Eventually we begin to believe either that forgiveness is only a ticket to heaven and not to affect our lives now, or that we are unworthy of the forgiving grace of God.[3]

That, I submit, is a description of life in the borderland.

A friend of mine was a key leader on a parachurch ministry to young people. It was thriving, and he was the visionary, the driving force, the fire-maker. He led the band and could draw people into passionate worship. He did the speaking and could convict, console, edify. He recruited and rallied the workers. He inspired the fund-raising.

And then, secretly, he fell into sin. He was single, good-looking, and highly gifted. And he was lonely. Many women found him attractive and wanted to take away his loneliness, have him take away theirs. With one of these women, he gave way.

She got pregnant. They were stricken, ashamed, overwhelmed. But then, together, they came up with a flawless plan. Why let this interrupt this man's active, vibrant, fruitful ministry? The woman had a job offer overseas. Their relationship was not going well anyhow. She would take the job, have the baby, give the child up for adoption.

No one had to know.

But it didn't work. It couldn't. It was flawed, not in logistics, but in logic. My friend imagined himself getting up to exhort young people about purity and integrity, his sense of hypocrisy scalding his insides. He pictured himself speaking about the need for transparency, but doing it cloaked, masked, wearing fig leaves, pointing fingers, crouching behind bushes. He could see himself meeting with donors and potential donors to inspire them with the vision for the ministry. "We're making radical disciples for Jesus," he'd tell them. But always he'd want to tell them: "The vision is to help these kids not become like me. I am the counterexample."

Neither he nor the woman felt like their plan was anything other than a cop-out, a cover-up, a ruse. Confession to God alone wasn't enough. Both of them were weary with guilt. It was like the psalmist wrote: "When I kept silent, my bones wasted away" (32:3).

So they confessed to another person. And then they walked through the consequences of what they did. He resigned from the ministry. She kept the child. After years of sorting out their relationship, they married. God restored him to ministry. His authority and humility in ministry is now great indeed. "Confess your sins to each other," James says, "so that you may be healed" (James 5:16).

The apostle Peter, in his first letter, explains something that helps make clear the importance of confession *to another*. Peter distinguishes between a *cover-up* for sin and a *covering over* of sin. "Live as free men," Peter says, "but do not use your freedom as a cover-up for sin" (1 Peter 2:16). My freedom—including my right to privacy and to keep my sin strictly as a secret matter between me and my God—that freedom can end as a cover-up, a smoke screen, a camouflage. Never having to tell another person, only God, about my sin threatens to keep me trapped either in the repetition of the sin or beneath the guilt-ridden weight of it. It wasn't until King David confessed—was forced by the prophet Nathan to confess—his adultery with Bathsheba and his murder of her husband, Uriah, that healing began for him. Psalms 32 and 51 record the shape and depth of that healing. Part of what David discovered is that surely God desires "truth in our inner parts" (Psalm 51:6). In other words, God wants truth to soak our insides and spill out. There's to be no cover-up.

What did David think about in that year—that's how long it took—between adultery and murder and confessing it to another? Did he never, not once, confess to God? Did he never get on his knees, broken and repentant, and implore God to forgive? David was a man after God's own heart. I think he probably confessed and confessed to God. He would probably get up from his confession and say, "Well, there. That's enough. It's done. I've said it. God knows I'm sorry."

But the weight wasn't gone. It didn't feel real. Like my friend with his logistically flawless, logically flawed plan, confession to God alone was not enough. David was still trapped. He lived that year, I think, in borderland, practicing not the presence of God, but the avoidance of Him.

Do not use your freedom, Peter says, *as a cover-up for sin*. But then Peter, a little later, says this: "Above all, love each other deeply, because love *covers over* a multitude of sins" (1 Peter 4:8, emphasis mine).

Let me state my thesis in the simplest possible terms: *Love can't cover over the sins we cover up.* If I am to love another as Pete: says I should love—*above all,* above my shock, my heartache, even my disgust—I'm going to have to know what that sin is. *Love can't cover over what pride or shame covers up.* "He who conceals his sins does not prosper, but whoever confesses and renounces them finds mercy" (Proverbs 28:13).

If anyone is going to love you, and if you are going to love anyone the way Scripture exhorts and commands, you're going to have to show someone the real you. The real you will have to stand up. You'll need to confess.

And what if you don't? What if you cover up? What if you never let anyone into your real life, never confess? There are consequences that come with that. I can think of two obvious ones.

The first is that Christian fellowship becomes a masquerade—a game of hide-and-seek, of pretense and jargon, with no real life and no real depth. We end up investing so much in the *appearance* of holiness that we miss the substance of it. We end up so preoccupied with saving face that we fail to live in God's saving grace. We walk around with insecurity and fear: *If you really knew me, you wouldn't like me. The only reason you like me is you don't really know me.*

It's true that some believers are immature and will use the knowledge of your sin to blackmail, blackball, demean, scorn, or gossip about you. As a general rule, *don't* confess to *that* person. To confess is to entrust to another the deepest part of yourself—don't do that lightly.

But confession and true fellowship are deeply joined. John in his first letter makes that explicit. He writes, "If we claim to be without sin, we deceive ourselves and the truth is not in us. If we confess our sins, he is faithful and just and will forgive us our sins and purify us from all unrighteousness" (1 John 1:8–9). But here's the verse that comes just before that: "If we...walk in the darkness, we lie and do not live in the truth. *But if we walk in the light, as he is in the light, we have fellowship with one another,* and the blood of Jesus, his Son, purifies us from all sin. If we claim to be without sin, we deceive ourselves and the truth is not in us" (1:6–8, emphasis mine).

Walking in truth requires admitting our sin. It means coming out of the darkness and into the light, the light that both exposes and heals. When we walk in the truth and in the light, we have real fellowship. In other words, real fellowship takes place not among perfect people, but honest ones, people willing to deal with their imperfections. Otherwise we have a country club, not a church. Otherwise we have borderland. Someone might protest again that John means we are to confess to God. But that's not how James, the brother of Jesus, understood it: "Confess your sins *to each other,*" he counseled, "and pray for each other so that you may be healed" (James 5:16).

That's one consequence of a people without the holy habit of confession: Our fellowship becomes a shallow, gaudy, fickle thing, a nonfellowship, an exercise in faking it.

The other consequence is our bones waste away—what we might call "osteoporosis of the soul." Again, David after his sin of adultery and murder wrote Psalm 32 (this is the likely context for this psalm). He begins, "Blessed is he whose transgressions are forgiven, whose sins are covered." There's that language of *covering over* once again. But then David describes what it was like when he merely *covered up* his sin: "When I kept silent, my bones wasted away through my groaning all day long.... My strength was sapped.... Then I acknowledged my sin to you and did not *cover up* my iniquity. I said, 'I will confess'" (Psalm 32:1, 3–5).

If you want God and others to cover over your sin, stop covering it up. (As a side note, David says here his confession is "to the Lord"; also, in Psalm 51, he says to God, "Against you, you only, have I sinned." So it seems that David treats his sin as a private matter. Yet are not these Psalms themselves public confession?)

Unconfessed sin rots the bones. It withers and scalds our insides. Or worse, it hardens us up. To live with the pain or shame of hidden sin, you have only two choices: to groan all day long or to sheath your heart in boilerplate. This is what I believe Nathan meant when he told David that his sin and his cover-up were, in effect, an act of despising the word of the Lord (2 Samuel 12:9). A cover-up is a sure path to despising God's Word, because I can only carry on the pretense on the basis that God's Word doesn't apply to me. *What God said about anger or immorality or anything—that's for you. I'm above all that.*

Hide your sin and your bones waste or harden. Both are misery. But here's the good news: The opposite is also true. To confess is to discover again the joy of our salvation, to find that the bones that once seemed crushed or wasted are now sturdy, supple, ready for dancing (Psalm 51:8).

LET ME GIVE A FEW PRACTICAL SUGGESTIONS ABOUT CONFESSING and about finding a confessor. First, a few things to be careful about. Be aware of the too-little or too-much syndrome. Confession should be neither vague— "Forgive me, I've done some bad things"—nor overly graphic, the minute and infinitely detailed inventory of every last thought and deed. Instead, it should be specific: *I have lied to so-and-so about money. I have stolen from this store these things.* It's important that you avoid saying too little or too much. Say too little, and your confession is generic, and generic confession usually only produces generic forgiveness. If you want the covering over of your sin to be specific, make the uncovering of it specific.

But when you say too much, you court other dangers. You might, in yourself or the one to whom you confess, so imprint things on the heart and mind that you plant the seeds of more sin. Or you might end up turning confession into a kind of covert boasting. Or you might end up confessing a lot of other people's sin beside or instead of your own.

Also watch that you don't just end up spilling your rubber guts: inventing, embellishing, faking anguish and heart-strickenness. These kinds of confessions are usually made to anyone, everyone, anywhere, any time. It's not real confession. It's grandstanding, soap opera, melodrama. (In the next chapter I write about the counterbalancing disciplines to confession: silence, secrecy, and solitude. Some people are in need of those holy habits more than confession.)

And be wary of mistaking confession for repentance. Again, Proverbs 28:13: "Whoever confesses *and renounces* [their sins] finds mercy." Confession in itself is only a beginning. It is lifeless if it's not followed by renouncing sin— without repentance. Without that we might end up being the tax collector who, after beating his breast, thanks God he's not like those Pharisees. *I don't tithe; I don't give alms; I don't fast—and look how holy I am, being earthy and vulnerable enough to admit it.* Let me repeat: Confession is ground clearing, getting the garbage and debris out of the way so that we can build something there. It has zero value unless you actually get on with building.

Last, beware the trap of regretting your confession, of feeling not released but more condemned because you told someone. Confession is based on the truth that Jesus already, always, in all ways loves you. Confession is not some desperate bid to get Jesus to love you: It is done in the full confidence that He already does. Besides, Jesus completely understands. Hebrews refers to Jesus as a high priest who goes before us into the presence of God to intercede on our behalf when we sin. It reads: "We do not have a high priest who is unable to sympathize with our weaknesses, but we have one who has been tempted in every way, just as we are—yet was without sin." It continues: "Let us then approach the throne of grace with confidence" (Hebrews 4:15–16).

In 1993, two ten-year-old boys committed a horrific crime. They led two-year-old James Bulger by the hand out of a London mall and threw him to his death in front of a moving train. Initially the two boys pleaded innocent. But tough interrogation exposed the flimsiness of their testimonies. They were trapped in a makeshift house of lies collapsing about them. The father of one of the boys asked for a moment to speak with his son. The father assured his boy that, no matter what, he loved him. He always would. The boy went back to his interrogators. In a soft voice, he said, "I killed James Bulger."[4]

Jesus loves us, no matter what. Confession doesn't earn that love. Confession, rather, is done in the full confidence that we have irrevocably received that love. Only, the cover-up is killing us, wasting our bones.

Confession is coming clean and experiencing anew love's covering over.

BUT TO WHOM SHOULD YOU CONFESS?

Eventually, if possible, to those whom your wrongdoing has harmed. If your sin has harmed your family, your church, the nation, then your confession should reflect that. Don't confess a sin that's only hurt two people to the entire church. And don't confess to only two people a sin that's hurt the entire church.

But it is often good to begin with confessing to one person who has not been affected by your sin. This person should be wise, mature in the faith, aware of her own frailty, honest about her own sin and weakness. She should be earthy, able to laugh. She needs to weep with those who weep and rejoice with those who rejoice. She needs to be someone who is not shocked by sin but is frequently grieved by it, in herself as much as in others. She needs to be trustworthy, not given to gossip. She needs to be truly pursuing God. She needs, above all and in all, to love. She can know the worst about you, and she'll use that knowledge to pray for you and help you and not hurt you. Her love should cover over a multitude of sins.

Oh, and this: If you're a man, change all the pronouns above to "he" and "him." Confession is intimacy. It is nakedness. It is exposing our inmost self. And so it is not old-fashioned prudery but time-honored wisdom that confession should be man-to-man or woman-to-woman.

THERE IS A STORY ABOUT FREDERICK THE GREAT, KING OF PRUSSIA. He was inspecting the Berlin prison. As he walked through the hordes of shackled men, they fell pleading at his feet, protesting their innocence. They claimed to be falsely accused, models of virtuous living, completely innocent of all crime. Only one man didn't do this. Frederick called to him, "Prisoner, why are you here?"

"I robbed a man, Your Majesty."

"And are you guilty?"

"Yes, Your Majesty."

Frederick called the guard over. Pointing at the man who confessed, he said, "Release this man immediately. I will not have this scoundrel thief kept here where he might corrupt all these other fine, virtuous, and innocent men."[5]

That's the lovely irony of confession: The one who actually confesses gets out of prison—or off of borderland—and gets to go free.

Chapter Seventeen

LEAVE YOURSELF ALONE

Dead space. That's entertainment jargon, the nomenclature of Hollywood and Broadway and Madison Avenue. It means any time when nothing happens—no sound, no motion, no image.

In the entertainment world, dead space is death. It is the primal void. It is a voodoo curse. It is anathema, and to be avoided always.

One day, I was meeting with some people I work with in leading worship at church on Sunday mornings. I was critiquing the Sunday past, and the sharp edge of my criticism came down on a worship leader who had taken about thirty seconds—thirty seconds!—to end one song and begin another. In my scolding and warning, I spoke that word: dead space. That was dead space. We don't want dead space. Eliminate dead space.

No one objected—no prophet stood up and thundered grim admonishment. No priest recoiled in horror. No one even muttered. Everyone nodded. I smiled, triumphant: The great consensus-maker wins again.

It was not until months later that I realized I had uttered a word deeply, tragically amiss. It was not until then that I saw, stark and sudden, that with that one phrase I had bought into the claptrap and clatter of the culture of commotion, the cult of noise. I had become a destroyer of stillness, an enemy of silence. I had learned to call the living places, the breathing room, dead space.

But here's the truth: the loss of dead space is killing us, inch by noisy inch.

How easy, how natural it is to get caught up in the busyness and noisiness of life: work life, home life, leisure life (for we're the culture that works at playing), and of course church life. And in the midst of all that, we often lose Jesus: We lose any sense of His presence, His power, His love, His comfort, His conviction. How very easy. Then, in our panic and despair, we go looking for quick cures: *If I go to a conference or have an ecstatic religious experience or have so-and-so pray for me, maybe I'll find Jesus and never lose sight of Him again.*

One thought rarely occurs to us: Maybe killing dead space is killing me. Maybe I've been duped into calling dead space what is in truth holy ground, a place brimful of life, a large tract of holy wild.

I WANT TO LOOK AT THREE CLOSELY RELATED HOLY HABITS— solitude, silence, and secrecy. If I had to give a general definition of these three disciplines, I would say that they are holy habits for rediscovering that our culture's so-called dead space is really holy ground.

Or this: They are holy habits through which, to use John the Baptist's language, Jesus becomes greater, I become less. When John's disciples came to him complaining that Jesus was stealing the limelight, stealing the thunder, John replied that that's how it ought to be—he was only a groomsman, not the bridegroom, and that Jesus must increase, he must decrease. All three of these practices—solitude, silence, and secrecy—help us to do that. They are holy habits by which we train ourselves to be still, humble, watchful. And so they help us break our addiction to self-absorption and self-avoidance. Consequently, they help us to stop missing Jesus in our midst.

We're obsessed with ourselves and afraid of ourselves. And part of that fear and that obsession—both the key symptom and the main drug that feeds it— is our need for approval. Me, I'm an addict. I can scrounge and scavenge approval in all kinds of ways, and when I don't get it, I know how to act like it doesn't matter anyhow. But that's the addiction: the need for Mark to be approved, applauded, sought after, highly regarded. One of the reasons it's so easy for me—and maybe for you—to lose Jesus is that I rarely go looking for Him anyhow. I go chasing approval and fleeing rebuke. I'm on a great commission to exalt myself and, at one and the same time, avoid myself.

Consider the energy we expend trying to get credit for things we've done right, or trying to avoid blame for things we've done wrong. Consider, when we retell our involvement in some matter, how often we, according to how it serves our interests, either embellish details or downplay them. *Oh, I wasn't really paying attention to what they were doing. I just thought they were playing with the dog. If I had any idea that they were torturing it, I would have stopped it right away.... Well, when I heard her complain one more time, I stood right up, and I said in no uncertain terms.... Actually, the only reason I'm eating this chocolate sundae is I didn't eat all day. Only some toast this morning, dry, and a peach. Oh, and a banana at lunch and a small, very small, handful of potato chips. But basically I haven't eaten a bite all day. They did have other things on the menu, but I thought, what can I get for under five dollars that has all the basic food groups, more or less, and provides the calories I need after a day without food?*

It's so important that you think right thoughts about me. I mean—oh my!—what if for a moment you thought I was lazy, gluttonous, gossipy, cowardly, stupid, inept? I have to stay very busy ensuring that you see me in the most heroic, humble, dignified, competent light I can cast on myself.

But sometimes I get tired of living like that—addicted to approval and, consequently, losing Jesus just about everywhere. Don't you? If you still enjoy that way of living, then by all means, hold the course. Do not veer to the right or to the left. Stay in borderland. But if there is even a tiny part of you that's weary and wondering if there's a better way to live, then let's talk holy habits. Let's talk about learning to leave yourself alone.

Solitude, silence, secrecy. He must become greater, I must become less. These three practices are, as I said, closely related. But let's look at each in turn.

SOLITUDE. JESUS OFTEN SOUGHT SOLITUDE, WHAT THE BIBLE describes as lonely and solitary places. Mark 1:35 is typical: "Very early in the morning, while it was still dark, Jesus got up, left the house and went off to a

solitary place, where he prayed." Or Mark 6:32: "They went away by themselves in a boat to a solitary place." One of the most convicting things I have
recently come to realize about Jesus is that He was never, not once, in a hurry.
He never insisted He had too much to do—too many lepers to heal, too many
disciples to teach, too many dead people to raise, too many Pharisees to
rebuke—to take time for rest and solitude. And then, rather than rushing out
of that solitude, panicky about catching up with all the work He left undone,
He emerges clearheaded *and slow.*

Jesus was slow. *Jesus, Jesus, Jesus, come quick, come now! Lazarus is dying;
demons are wreaking havoc; people are hungry! Jesus, do something, and do it now!*
But Jesus just strolls along, talking to this blind beggar, showing kindness to
that prostitute, taking a nap, eating a meal. As Philip Yancey says, the one person who never suffered from a Messiah Complex—an anxiety about having to
fix the world—was the Messiah. Jesus took time and took His time.

What is solitude? It is, first, a space we make for listening. But solitude is
also—and here we strike its richest irony—a cure for loneliness. In 1950, sociologist David Riesman wrote a book that defined the failure of the American
way of life. The book was called *The Lonely Crowd.* All our bravado, all our
bright and gaudy celebrations, our malls and our dance halls, our clubs and
our playgrounds, our condominiums and our suburbs—all of it had the net
effect of further isolating and alienating us.[1]

When I was in my early twenties, I went through a time of terrible loneliness. I felt abandoned, marooned. I didn't understand myself and felt there
was no one else who did either. I tried to cure my loneliness with crowds. I
would go endlessly to parties. I might be barely invited, maybe only heard
rumors that a party was going on, maybe only had a distant acquaintance who
had been invited—but wherever two or three gathered together, there I was
also. But the crowds deepened my loneliness. In fact, I never felt so alone as
when I was surrounded by dozens, maybe hundreds of people.

Solitude is the cure for loneliness. It's the cure because we discover that
solitude is not *aloneness.* It is, rather, the place where the one who knows and
loves us always, in all ways, the one who does understand us—that one comes
to meet us.

Back in chapter 7, we looked at the story of Jacob. Jacob was the party boy, the popular one, always getting his way. He was the one voted most likely to succeed and who would swindle anyone—from his brother to his father to his father-in-law—to self-fulfill the prophecy. He was the poster boy of the self-absorbed and the self-avoiding.

But a moment of crisis comes for Jacob when, after fifteen years of making it on his own, he returns home to face his angry brother Esau on whose back Jacob climbed to success. Jacob does what he's always done—he plots and schemes how he will bribe and flatter his way out of this one. But this is what happens:

> That night Jacob got up and took his two wives, his two maidservants and his eleven sons and crossed the ford of the Jabbok. After he had sent them across the stream, he sent over all his possessions. So Jacob was left alone, and a man wrestled with him till daybreak. When the man saw that he could not overpower him, he touched the socket of Jacob's hip so that his hip was wrenched as he wrestled with the man.
>
> Then the man said, "Let me go, for it is daybreak."
>
> But Jacob replied, "I will not let you go unless you bless me."
>
> The man asked him, "What is your name?"
>
> "Jacob," he answered.
>
> Then the man said, "Your name will no longer be Jacob, but Israel, because you have struggled with God and with men and have overcome."
>
> Jacob said, "Please tell me your name."
>
> But he replied, "Why do you ask my name?" Then he blessed him there.
>
> So Jacob called the place Peniel, saying, "It is because I saw God face to face, and yet my life was spared." (Genesis 32:22–30)

And Jacob was left alone. That aloneness, that austere and vast solitude, is the place of discovering he's not alone. He discovers that the one who is passionately interested in him, in knowing his name, in giving him a new name, in wrestling him and wounding him and blessing him—that one meets him in the solitary place. Jacob has been losing Jesus all his life. But in this place of solitude, he comes face-to-face.

Robert Benson writes:

If we take…no time to be apart and listen for the Voice, give God some directives and pointers and call it prayer, and do none of the things that the faithful who traveled this road before us would remind us to do, then we are likely to talk to God and never hear a response.[2]

We'll just keep losing Jesus.

Solitude's other gift is that it takes us outside the rush and crush of time, and in doing so reorients us to eternity. I believe one of the reasons Jesus moved so slowly was that He was so keenly aware of eternity. Maybe that doesn't make sense at first. We might think that those who are aware of eternity should have a greater sense of urgency and emergency about the fleeting moment allotted to us, this brief span and spasm of time, and fret about all the important things we must do *while there is time*. But, in fact, the opposite always proves true in practice: Those whose minds are set on eternity are far more focused, far less pulled hither and thither by every crisis and whim and new-fangled idea, than all the great time managers lumped together. I know that the more time I take—away from the tyranny of clock and calendar, away from the hounding demands and heavy pressures of my life—the more my mind opens to the eternal. And when I return to my normal workaday life, I go slower and somehow do more.

Solitude, the act of being alone, is a holy habit to break our sense of loneliness and urgency.

SILENCE. IN THE LAST CHAPTER WE LOOKED AT CONFESSION AS A necessary discipline to breaking borderland's hold—we called it a ground clearing. But the next two practices, silence and secrecy, balance confession. We are most tempted to stay silent when we ought to speak out—to proclaim or defend the innocent or confess our sins. And we are most tempted to speak out when we ought to remain silent—when we want to boast or scold or gossip.

Here is a typical move in the life of Jesus:

A man with leprosy came to him and begged him on his knees, "If you are willing, you can make me clean." Filled with compassion, Jesus reached out his hand and touched the man. "I am willing," he said. "Be clean!" Immediately the leprosy left him and he was cured. Jesus sent him away at once with a strong warning: "See that you don't tell this to anyone." (Mark 1:40–44)

See that you don't tell this to anyone.
Now watch this:

The chief priests and the whole Sanhedrin were looking for false evidence against Jesus so that they could put him to death. But they did not find any, though many false witnesses came forward.

Finally two came forward and declared, "This fellow said, 'I am able to destroy the temple of God and rebuild it in three days.'"

Then the high priest stood up and said to Jesus, "Are you not going to answer? What is this testimony that these men are bringing against you?" But Jesus remained silent.

The high priest said to him, "I charge you under oath by the living God: Tell us if you are the Christ, the Son of God."

"Yes, it is as you say," Jesus replied. "But I say to all of you: In the future you will see the Son of Man sitting at the right hand of the Mighty One and coming on the clouds of heaven."

Then the high priest tore his clothes and said, "He has spoken blasphemy! Why do we need any more witnesses? Look, now you have heard the blasphemy. What do you think?"

"He is worthy of death," they answered. (Matthew 26:59–66)

Jesus is silent and He commands silence when speaking would gain the most attention, applause, financial support, adulation, self-protection. But He speaks when it costs Him the most.

Compare Jesus' manner of silence and speaking with the apostle Peter. Peter is the first to speak up if it makes him look good. When he's in church, with all the faithful listening, he gives the loudest, longest testimonies about his undying loyalty and commitment to Christ. But when he's in the work-place or before the palace guards where that kind of talk might get him in trouble, he clams up.

I derive a principle from that: In general, it's best to speak when tempted *for selfish reasons* to be silent, and it's best to be silent when tempted *for selfish reasons* to speak. That's the holy habit. When you are tempted to justify, explain, excuse, exalt, gossip, or scold—it's a good signal to button up. And when you are tempted to just lay low, let things sort themselves out, don't rock the boat, don't say anything that might cause trouble—that's a good signal to speak out. Both speaking and silence should be costly, and at their heart should be self-giving.

Are we always going to get it right? No. Is it a new law to be rigidly adhered to? No. Are there never exceptions to it—where I do defend myself or tell of something I've accomplished or hold my tongue when doing so might be to my own advantage? Yes. There are many exceptions.

It's not a law; it's a discipline. It's a holy habit, one that ensures Jesus becomes greater and I become less.

There's something else. Silence is for listening to God and to others. A man at my church, Graden, told me about a millwright at his workplace. He's the best millwright Graden's ever seen. He is unerring in his ability to home in on the exact trouble spot in a machine, and then he's swift and sure in repairing it.

Graden noticed for a long time that this man always left the lunchroom ten minutes before everyone else. Graden thought at first that he was going to check over the machinery. But then he followed him out one day and discovered the millwright never looked at a single machine. He just stood in the middle of the room, eyes closed, listening. In the silence, in the absence of workers working and talking, he could tune his ears to catch the most subtle pitch and timber, cadence and inflection of those machines. He could hear what was working well, what wasn't. And he could locate the problem.

Our lives swarm with noise, and in the din we have no place for listening. We know there's a problem. Things keep breaking down all the time, but we have no idea how to remedy it.

Silence is for listening. I think many of us don't listen well. My own pray-ing can easily descend into mindless chatter, where I get so busy talking to

God that I talk past Him. And I never hear anything He's saying. Many years ago, President Franklin Roosevelt grew weary of all the trivia and preening, the empty talk and the smooth talk, at White House receptions. Everyone listened to themselves but not to one another. So Roosevelt tried something. As he met the guests at a social gathering, he would flash his huge smile, extend his firm and confident handshake, and say, "I murdered my grandmother this morning." With a single exception, people smiled back and responded with comments like, "You're doing a fine job," or, "Oh, how lovely." The exception was a foreign diplomat. Without missing a beat he responded, "I'm sure she had it coming to her."[3]

Apart from the discipline of silence, prayer deteriorates into White House reception chatter.

In chapter 14 I said that the practice of the presence of God is rooted in the biblical teaching about God's omnipresence—the reality that God is here now, always and everywhere. And I pointed to Psalm 139 as a primary text: "Where can I go from your Spirit? Where can I flee from your presence?" The psalmist answers emphatically and poetically: nowhere. In all places, at all times, there is God. That psalm opens with a declaration: "O LORD, you have searched me, and you know me." Yet it closes with an invitation: "Search me, O God, and know my heart.... See if there is any offensive way in me, and lead me in the way everlasting."

Silence is the room we create for the searching of God, where we hear His voice and follow.

LAST, SECRECY. SECRECY IS NOT THE SAME AS SECRETIVENESS. Secretiveness is hiding what we should disclose. Secretiveness is Adam and Eve hiding from one another behind fig leaves, hiding from God behind bushes. Secretiveness is hiding something out of shame, out of humiliation, out of selfishness. But secrecy, as a holy habit, is hiding something out of humility. Another way to look at this and to fix a general principle in our minds is to view secretiveness and secrecy through the lens of pride. When I subject my motives to honest scrutiny, I almost always find that I keep secrets and I tell them for exactly the same reason: pride. If revealing something shows me in a good light or maybe shows you in a bad light, I want to tell for pride's sake. But if revealing something shows me in a bad light or maybe shows you in too good a light, I want to keep it under wraps for pride's sake.

Jesus says in Matthew 6:1, "Be careful not to do your acts of righteousness before men, *to be seen by them.*" He goes on to give three examples—giving, praying, and fasting—where we should do these things in secret so that our Father, who sees, will reward us. *So be careful not to do your acts of righteousness before men, to be seen by them.* It's that last part that we need to emphasize: *to be seen by them.* It's not that we never let anyone see us doing good deeds. Just a chapter earlier in Matthew, Jesus tells us to "let your light shine before men, that they may see your good deeds and praise your Father in heaven" (Matthew 5:16). It all comes down to motive, and the options are stark: Either we do good things in order *to be seen* by others, or we do them in order to bring praise to God.

Secrecy is one of the most profound theological statements we can make. It is *acting on* the belief that the reward of God matters more than the reward of man. It is trusting in the trustworthiness of God. If I don't believe that God sees the good I do when no one else notices—or if I resent that when others do notice it, God, not me, gets the glory—then I'll forever be fishing for compliments, finding subtle and not-so-subtle ways of getting applause, flaunting my so-called wisdom, boasting about my self-styled heroism. *The other day when I was distributing blankets to homeless people under the bridge, I happened to say.... When I was praying this morning at four o'clock, after about, oh, an hour of intercession for the lost, a thought came to me....*

Our lives are ultimately cosmic dramas lived out in full view of God, His angels, and for that matter, the devil and his angels. Consider Job's suffering. What was that about? His friends didn't have a clue. In fact, they got it all wrong. They were convinced Job had this coming to him. What was it about? It was cosmic drama. God and Satan had a bet on the line: Would this man stay faithful no matter what? The main audience, those who had most at stake in the outcome of Job's life, were not Job's friends, not Job's family, not even Job. It was God and the devil.

In the end, it matters not at all what others think about you and say about you. Your life is cosmic drama.

The practice of secrecy is simply taking that seriously.

LEAVE YOURSELF ALONE. ENTER SOLITUDE. BE SILENT. DO YOUR good deeds in secret. Make dead space into holy ground.

You will become less, it's true. But you will also become more: you will discover your true self and meet more often, lose less often, the Lord of the holy wild. For out of empty tombs and dead spaces comes the living Christ. Be still and know that He is God. Behold, the Lamb of God: See how He becomes greater.

Chapter Eighteen

GO FAST AND LIVE

There was recently an antispeeding ad campaign in British Columbia, Canada. The centerpieces of the campaign were huge billboards, placed in prominent spots along the province's major roadways, showing black-and-white photos of car wrecks—gashed and mangled metal, clouds of steam and smoke, all illumined under the luridness of fire, flares, search lights, siren lights. The caption beneath the ads was as stark and grim as the photos: "Speed is killing us. Slow down and live."

If this book were a multimedia presentation, I would flash up a picture of our lives—our mindless preoccupations, our ranting over not getting our way, our insatiable need for more and more and more, our boredom and blaming. And beneath I would put the caption: "Consumption is killing us. Go fast and live."

YOU CAN'T READ THE BIBLE VERY FAR IN ANY DIRECTION WITHOUT realizing that fasting was simply a part of the natural rhythm of life for the people of God. They expected and planned to fast as naturally as they expected and planned to eat. To them, fasting was woven into the rhythm of life, like day and night, summer and winter, sowing and reaping, waking and sleeping. There were times you ate, and there were times you fasted. Doesn't everybody live like that? Richard Foster writes:

> The list of biblical personages who fasted reads like a "Who's Who" of Scripture: Moses the lawgiver, David the king, Elijah the prophet, Esther the queen, Daniel the seer, Anna the prophetess, Paul the apostle, Jesus Christ the incarnate Son.[1]

He goes on to name some of the great men and women throughout history who made fasting a discipline. John Wesley, in fact, refused to ordain anyone to the Methodist ministry who did not fast twice a week.[2] Jesus Himself, though He stood against the Pharisee's rigid, self-promoting, judgmental practice of fasting, expects us to fast: "When you fast," He says in Matthew 6:16. *When* you fast—not *if*.

Jesus began His ministry with an intense and prolonged fast: forty days without food or companionship. It was a Spirit-led experience. Mark says that the Spirit drove Jesus out into the desert, where He fasted. And at the end of those forty days, the devil came to tempt Him. I have always thought that the devil came to Jesus at His weakest moment, when He was gaunt, wild-eyed, ready to scavenge any moldy crust of bread, scrape any meat shreds off a lamb's bone. Even pork looked good. The devil's first temptation was to offer Jesus food: *Turn these stones into bread.* I always saw that as attacking Jesus at His lowest, most vulnerable point, tempting Him with the very thing He craved most.

But I'm not so sure anymore.[3] The more I personally learn from fasting, the more I see that Jesus actually stood at His strongest when His belly was empty. The forty days without food, far from weakening Him at the moment of encounter with the devil, actually strengthened Him for it. Jesus was in peak condition, a fighter who had been training hard for forty days straight. And when He stepped into the ring, His opponent didn't stand a chance. Jesus' swift and unflinching rebuttal to the devil was to quote from Deuteronomy 8:3: "Man does not live on bread alone but on every word that comes from the mouth of the LORD." How does anyone get to know, inside out, that this indeed is so?

One thing is almost certain: It's a truth that's hard, maybe impossible, to learn between fistfuls and mouthfuls of food.

The serpent came to Adam in a garden—Adam surrounded by an abundance of delicious food freely given to him, Adam with his belly full—and tempted him and Eve with food: "Here's something you haven't tried. Want some?" And they licked their lips, reached out grasping hands, took, ate. But the devil came to Jesus in a desert, Jesus surrounded by stones and scorpions and snakes, Jesus with His empty belly, and tempted Him with food: "Wouldn't you like just a slice of bread?" And Jesus flicked him away like a fly.

So now the quiz: Who understands—*really* understands—that we don't live by bread alone but by every word that comes from the mouth of God? Who not only understands, but withstands because of it, overcomes on the basis of it? The man with his belly full? Or the man with his belly empty?

Let me be blunt: If you never fast, then the whole concept of being wholly nourished and sustained by God's Word alone will likely be only a nice, sweet, and totally irrelevant idea to you. You may pay the idea lip service, but you'll be too busy licking sauce off your lips to do any more. And worse: If you never fast, when the day of testing and temptation comes, you may not stand.

Consumption is killing us. Go fast and live.

JESUS' RETORT TO THE DEVIL—*MAN DOES NOT LIVE ON BREAD ALONE but on every word that comes from the mouth of the LORD*—is a good place to begin:

> Be careful to follow every command I am giving you today, so that you may live and increase and enter and possess the land that the LORD promised on oath to your forefathers. Remember how the LORD your God led you all the way in the desert these forty years, to humble you and to test you in order to know what was in your heart, whether or not you would keep his commands. He humbled you, causing you to

hunger and then feeding you with manna, which neither you nor
your fathers had known, to teach you that man does not live on bread
alone but on every word that comes from the mouth of the LORD....
Know then in your heart that as a man disciplines his son, so the LORD
your God disciplines you. (Deuteronomy 8:1–3, 5)

Remember how the LORD your God led you all the way in the desert....
And the Spirit drove Jesus out into the desert.
Your God led.... The Spirit drove.
Fasting is a God-led, Spirit-driven activity. It is not just your own idea. It
is not a legalistic requirement. It is not a work we perform. It is not a weight-
loss technique. It is not a hunger strike. No, it is a God and Spirit work, a
response to the leading and the driving of the Godhead. In fact, fasting begins
with a hunger for more of God's direction in your life. Fasting is born of an
appetite for more of God's presence, wanting God to lead, wanting the Spirit
to drive. And what He often leads us and drives us into is a fast.

Deuteronomy 8 indicates that there are three main purposes behind a God-
led and Spirit-driven experience of hunger. God orchestrates and engineers
hunger to humble His people, to test them and to teach them. That, then, is the
structure for the rest of this chapter: *A fast is a God-led or Spirit-driven hunger*
whose purpose is to humble us, to test us, and to teach us.

FASTING HUMBLES US BECAUSE IT QUICKLY SHOWS US OUR LIMITS
and our frailty. It shows us our utter dependency—ultimately upon God but
also upon one another. If farmers don't grow crops, if mills don't grind grain,
if truckers don't bring it close to hand, if bakers don't make it into bread, if
stores don't stock it fresh and sell it cheap—then I don't eat. I once talked to
a man who spent some time in the Ukraine. He was a tenured university professor, well-respected and highly paid. But when he lived in the Ukraine, he
had to stand in food lines like everybody else and wait two or three hours for
bread. It humbled him. He realized that all his education and affluence meant
nothing in a country where bread was scarce.

It's so arrogant for you and me to sit around our well-laden tables and talk about the poor—how, if they would only get motivated, get focused, *be more like us,* they would be fine. Hunger humbles us. It opens our eyes to our own stark-naked neediness, our own daily dependence: Unless God in His mercy provides manna for this day, we're in trouble. Look at us. We start coming apart after only twelve hours of not eating. We get depressed, cranky, weary. Now tell me again about how poor people should be more like us: strong, dependable, independent. Hunger humbles us.

That's why Jesus rebukes the Pharisees' manner of fasting: "When you fast, do not look somber as the hypocrites do, for they disfigure their faces to show men they are fasting" (Matthew 6:16). In other words, the very thing that God intends for humility they use for self-adulation. The very thing meant to break their indulgence is used to feed it. Rather than an experience of humility, fasting has become an experience of pride. Let me say it again and say it clearly: Fasting is meant to humble us, to make us understand how small and frail and needy we really are. It should increase our sense of dependency, not become a way of lauding our spiritual superiority. It is not a demonstration of superhuman strength. It is exactly the opposite: a demonstration of very human weakness. If fasting—or any other spiritual discipline—is not producing in us genuine humility, if it only proves breeding ground for self, it's gone awry.

So it's good that we feel hungry, weary, weak when we fast. When I first began fasting on a regular basis, I tried all sorts of things to avoid the sting and the weight of it. But after a while I came to realize that the discomfort of fasting was God's primary means of humbling me. I can run on my own strength for long stretches. I can forget my limits and become self-reliant, cocky, swaggering, thinking that apart from me Jesus can do nothing, but that He can do all things through me who gives Him strength. I can act the big man in borderland.

I need a holy habit to prove to myself that the opposite is true—to move me from self-imposed worship to real worship, to move me from false humility to genuine humility, to move me from some self-glorifying treatment of my body to a recognition of my frailty.

Fasting humbles us.

⤳

AND FASTING TESTS US TO SEE WHAT IS IN OUR HEARTS. FASTING brings to the surface that which is deep down, that which we mask from ourselves and others with large doses of corn chips and Barq's root beer. Fasting churns that stuff up from the depths. Is there anger in me? I can usually control that with a hamburger and fries. Am I resentful, irritated, overly ambitious, fearful? I can smother that with a pizza. Am I depressed or embittered, suffering from a sense of life's unfairness? I can artificially perk myself up with a Mars bar.

But hunger strips away the disguise. Hunger, like Solomon calling for the baby to be cut in two, usually forces out the real issue. It tests me and makes me face honestly what is in my heart. Part of what I'm learning to pray about during a fast are the dark things hidden inside me which fasting brings to light. There's all manner of junk down there that, apart from fasting, I had no idea existed. *Search me, O God, and know my heart…see if there be any wicked way in me.* Fasting is one of God's surest means of searching out the wicked ways.

I'm confessing that one of the wicked practices God brought to awareness in me was this: Food itself had become an idol. I don't just like food; I love food. And our culture loves food. I am a man of stuffed lips, and I live among a people of stuffed lips.

C. S. Lewis in *Mere Christianity* has a chapter on the Christian view of sex and sexuality. One line floored me. Lewis said that sex is, in one sense, an appetite. And like all appetites it should be fed in healthy ways, but not titillated, indulged, or gorged. Then Lewis says that one sign that our sexual appetites are totally out of bounds is the growing phenomenon—he was writing in the 1940s—of striptease shows. Here is the line that floored me: "Now suppose you came to a country where you could fill a theatre by simply bringing a covered plate onto the stage and then slowly lifting the cover so as to let every one see…that it contained a mutton chop or bit of bacon, would not you think that in that country something had gone wrong in the appetite for food?"[4] I read those words in the mideighties, when one of the advertisements frequently aired on television was an item of food—I don't remember what—that was unveiled to an audience in exactly the manner Lewis describes.

Would you not think in that country something had gone wrong in the appetite for food? Our preoccupation with food has entered the realm of the absurd. For example, look at any magazine—page after page of succulent, sauce-laden, sparkling, glistening food. It's a kind of culinary pornography. McDonalds' golden arches and Coca-Cola's logo are likely more widely recognized symbols worldwide, and certainly more widely accepted, than the cross of Christ. Our world's most prevalent iconography depicts food.

Fasting tests the food obsession, sees if this absurd, soul-withering, body-swelling fetish is in our hearts. When I first started practicing this discipline on a regular basis—and this is still sometimes true—the smell of my neighbor's barbecue on a day I was fasting could almost make me insane. I would fantasize about food. I would picture myself building a hamburger, layer by layer, and then settling down, opening wide, the juiciness of it squirting out, the mayonnaise and mustard mixing together and dribbling down my hand. Then I would get angry at my neighbor: What sort of hedonistic man is barbecuing on a day like today?

There is a simple, theological name for this: idolatry.

One way our culture has turned food into idolatry is by overemphasizing the pleasure of eating and downplaying the nutritional value. That's obvious in what I called culinary pornography. It's not that food is good for you, but does it look good and taste good? What that has formed in us habitually is that we eat not to fill up real hunger, but to satisfy craving. We eat not out of a need for the food itself, but out of a desire for *eating* itself. When the serpent tempts Adam and Eve with forbidden food, what convinces Eve to indulge it is that "it was pleasing to the eye, and also desirable for gaining wisdom" (Genesis 3:6). What really matters here is the look good, feel good value of the food.

I know this. I might be stuffed to the gills, barely able to roll off the couch, but I'll manage if there's food that's pleasing to the eye and tempting to the palate. *I don't care if it's sweet or rich or salty. I just need some in my mouth. Oh, I know it will harden my arteries, thicken and soften my flesh, clog my heart, rot my teeth. I may have to unbutton my pants just to make room for it. And I'm not eating because I'm hungry. I'm not eating for nourishment. I'm eating because that food looks good and tastes good.*

Did I tell you that we have a simple, theological name for that? Idolatry.

And that gets to the rub: God uses hunger to test what is in our hearts—what we've really given our hearts to—*to see whether or not we will keep His commands*. Fasting is a test of obedience. Are we God's men, God's women, or not?

Is there a test for this? Some cardiogram where we can run stress monitors on the heart and see what shape it's really in? See what truly is in there—obedience? Disobedience?

There is a test. It's called fasting.

FASTING TEACHES US. IT TEACHES US THAT WE DO NOT LIVE ON bread alone but by every word that comes from the mouth of the Lord. Deuteronomy 8, as it continues, makes clear that our dependency upon the Lord is jeopardized by an abundance of and indulgence in food. Gluttony is companion to amnesia:

> Observe the commands of the LORD your God, walking in his ways and revering him. For the LORD your God is bringing you into a good land...a land with wheat and barley, vines and fig trees, pomegranates, olive oil and honey; a land where bread will not be scarce and you will lack nothing....
>
> When you have eaten and are satisfied, praise the LORD your God for the good land he has given you. Be careful that you do not forget the LORD your God, failing to observe his commands, his laws and his decrees that I am giving you this day. Otherwise, when you eat and are satisfied...then your heart will become proud and you will forget the LORD your God.... You may say to yourself, "My power and the strength of my hands have produced this wealth for me." (6–12, 14, 17)

It's the man with his belly full who is most likely to forget from whom all blessings flow.

Hunger makes stark and raw our humanness, our neediness and frailty. Hunger makes me understand my own poverty—my poverty of soul, poverty of spirit, poverty of ends. Blessed are those, Jesus said, who hunger for righteousness. Admittedly, I don't get around to hungering much after righteousness, apart from the experience of physical hunger. As Cornelius Plantinga observes, gluttony is an appetite suppressant for the things of God.[5] But as I go into the place of hunger and all the junk starts to surface in my heart, I realize that there is only one sure way to deal with that: by reading the Word of God. My opinion will not cut it. My feelings are not adequate. The only thing big enough, tough enough, true enough to speak to the power of the flesh, the world, and the devil is the Word of God. Fasting makes me hungry for every word that comes from the mouth of the Lord.

More and more people in our churches are food gluttons and biblical anorexics. Even our intake of Scripture has been reduced to a kind of fast-food drive-through, nibbling the crumbs tossed from the pulpit on Sunday. "I left that church. They just weren't feeding me."

When my son was eight, we taught him a discipline in keeping with his age. He would come home from school or some activity, flop on the couch, and yell, "I'm starving!" The discipline was to show him that there are certain foods he can help himself to—foods that are good for him, not just tasty—and *that he was fully capable of getting them himself.*

"I'm starving—this church isn't feeding me." Maybe that's a legitimate complaint from a three-year-old. From a grown-up, it's a self-indictment.

Physical hunger is meant to deepen in us hunger for the Word of God and motivate us to get our own food.

Physical hunger also teaches us to feast on Jesus. In John 6, after Christ feeds the five thousand, He has an instant megachurch. But in what seems like a case of extreme self-sabotage, He chases all but the most committed away with a few stern words:

> I tell you the truth, you are looking for me, not because you saw miraculous signs but because you ate the loaves and had your fill. Do not work for food that spoils, but for food that endures to eternal life, which the Son of Man will give you.... I tell you the truth, it is not Moses who has given you the bread from heaven, but it is my Father who gives you the true bread from heaven. For the bread of God is he

who comes down from heaven and gives life to the world.... I am the bread of life.... Whoever eats my flesh and drinks my blood has eternal life.... For my flesh is real food and my blood is real drink. (vv. 26–27, 32–33, 35, 54–55)

As I said, most everyone clears out at these words. Then Jesus turns to the twelve and asks,

"You do not want to leave too, do you?"...Simon Peter answered him, "Lord, to whom shall we go? You have the words of eternal life. We believe and know that you are the Holy One of God." (vv. 67–69)

When our bellies are full, we are in danger of following Jesus for all the wrong reasons. As long as you keep the bread coming, keep serving my appetites, keep meeting my felt needs and not my real needs, I'm part of Your church, Lord. True, Christ in His deep compassion does want to feed us real bread. But He wants more for us than that: He wants to give us Himself. He has the words of eternal life. He is the Holy One of God. He is the bread of life that came down from heaven. The deepest need we have is to eat Christ's flesh and drink His blood.

Ultimately, and perhaps paradoxically, fasting also teaches us to be like God. Isaiah 58, the Bible's most extensive passage on fasting, is explicit about this. It is God's rebuke to Israel because of the way they fast: They have missed the one thing needed. Fasting does not change their exploitative habits, their bullying and grasping. "Is this the kind of fast I have chosen?" God roars. And then He describes what He has chosen:

Is not this the kind of fasting I have chosen:
to loose the chains of injustice
    and untie the cords of the yoke,
to set the oppressed free
    and break every yoke?
Is it not to share your food with the hungry
    and to provide the poor wanderer with shelter—

when you see the naked, to clothe him,
     and not to turn away
from your own flesh and blood?
(vv. 6–7)

THE FAST GOD CHOOSES TEACHES US TO HAVE HIS HEART FOR THE
hungry, the oppressed, the naked, the homeless. It's to motivate us to do good
works, God-works—what Isaiah calls repairing broken walls. When we taste
a little brokenness ourselves, we have a greater sense of urgency to repair for
others what is broken. Fasting *is meant* to scour our gut. It is God's intent that
we would feel the pangs of hunger, the gnawing emptiness, the dizziness and
weariness. That's how a third of the world *lives*. And if we never live that way
even briefly, how will we learn to care for the least of these? Without hunger,
our consumption will lead us deeper and deeper into acts of oblivious or
intentional neglect, abuse, exploitation of those who are hungry. Fasting gives
us a small *taste* of what their world is like, a taste we will never get if we do
not for a time forsake the taste of food.

I have a friend who organized a dinner at his church to raise money for
famine relief in the Sudan. About eighty people signed up to come. He had
tables set for various sized groups—as small as six, as large as fifteen. People
came in and took seats at random. Then the servers came out. The smallest
tables were served first. They received an abundance of rich, sauce-laden food,
hot, tender, tasty. The servers were polite, attentive, quick to bring more food
at the slightest indication that it was running low. They were quick to do the
guests' bidding and usually anticipated this before the need was spoken.

Next, some of the larger tables were served. Theirs was a sparse, messy,
bland meal. The few dishes were brought out in no particular order. The
servers were curt and hurried. There were no seconds.

Two of the largest tables were served second to last—after the few guests
at the first tables had already had all they could eat and their dinner plates,
piled with uneaten food, were whisked away and replaced with rich desserts
and coffee. At the large tables, the servers plunked down, with rude haste, one
bowl of rice in the middle of each table. No one got a plate or bowl. There

were no utensils for serving or eating. The waiters never came back.

The very largest table was served last of all. They got a bucket of water. There was barely enough to go around. The water was brown and lukewarm. If you wanted some, you had to drink it from a wooden ladle, passed from hand to hand. Most people didn't bother.

At first the people at the largest tables, the last ones served, complained. Several people got up and spoke to the servers. The servers ignored them. Some went to my friend, the organizer. He ignored them. He and the servers only paid attention to—in fact, lavished attention on—the guests who sat at the smallest tables and who had received the most. The servers would come around often to those tables, ask if everything was pleasing and agreeable, and did they need anything else? There was much laughter, banter, politeness.

After a while it became obvious to everyone what was happening, though it took the few who were served first and served the most the longest to notice. The church was being given a taste of how the world works—its lopsidedness, its patchy rhythm of squandering and emptiness, of affluence and desolation. Some were able to experience, and all to witness, the hunger of the forsaken.

The offering for famine relief was good that night.

That's part of God's purpose in fasting, the kind of fast He has chosen: to teach us to care for the oppressed, the homeless, the ones with empty bellies, to allow the gnawing in our stomachs to cause the breaking of our hearts, and the breaking of our hearts to make us the breakers of yokes and the repairers of walls.

Consumption is killing us. Go fast and live.

Chapter Nineteen

THE HONEYSUCKLE BIBLE

You are what you eat. And in mind and heart, what you eat is what you study. Martin Luther, Martin Luther King Jr., Malcolm X, Adolf Hitler, Billy Graham, Genghis Kahn, Abraham Lincoln, the apostle Paul—they all were students. Each made a serious and dedicated study of a certain philosophy, a system of thought and action. As a monk, Luther studied St. Augustine as well as a philosophy known as nominalism, but he was transformed by a penetrating and painstaking read of Paul's letter to the Romans, and then by a careful reread of the entire Bible. Malcolm X began reading widely while in prison for larceny, but fell especially under the spell of the Black Muslim leader Elijah Mohammed. Adolf Hitler, a sulking and awkward teenager stung twice by rejection from Vienna's elite art school, came under the tutelage of Frederick Nietszche's will to power philosophy and Richard Wagner's bombastic, anti-Semitic, rabidly nationalist music that paid homage to the pagan gods of Nordic and Teutonic legend.

And so it goes. Each was shaped by the books he read and reread, by the art they surrounded themselves with, by the music they soaked themselves in, by the teachers they bowed to. In mind and heart, they were what they ate.

Study is the ingesting and digesting, the chewing and swallowing and being filled with ideas, images, thoughts, and attitudes. To browse an idea, to skim it and dabble in it—that's like getting a whiff of food, maybe a faint taste on the tongue. But to study: To really plunge into the depth of a thing, to interrogate it and allow it to interrogate you, to probe it and be probed by it—that is study. That is eating.

The Bible often uses the image of eating as a metaphor for study. Jeremiah says that when God's Word came to him, he ate it (15:16). When the apostle John meets with an angel who holds a scroll of God's Word, he is commanded to eat it before he is sent out to preach (Revelation 10:10). The prophet Ezekiel is similarly commissioned to proclaim God's truth, but is first told he must eat God's words (Ezekiel 2:8, 3:3).

The Ethiopian emperor Menelik II took this literally. Whenever he fell ill, he'd eat actual pages from the Bible in the belief that this would cure him. He died in 1913 after ingesting the entire book of 2 Kings.[1] I want to scoff at his superstition, except that a sliver of warning pricks my skin: I have seen many people—myself included—writhe in soul sickness by a *refusal* to eat the Word of God. Borderland is a virtual colony of biblical anorexics and bulimics, where appetites rage for everything but Truth.

I WORKED IN MY FINAL YEAR AT REGENT COLLEGE FOR DR. KLAUS Bockmuehl, a man of towering intellect and, though short of physique, commanding stature. The air seemed to churn with violent energy from his mere presence. He was one of the most humble and godly men I've ever known. He was German and had a German manner: Words flew from him like hot flak, blunt like stones. His motions were brusque, taut, gestures more akin to wood chopping, rabbit punching, stick whittling, fish scaling. The passion of his convictions often worked his face into scowls and grimaces. There was a hint of wildness about him, as though he might suddenly break forth like a whole mountain collapsing in landslide.

But he loved God. He loved God with a complicated and yet a simple love, a love like the ancient saints had. His love for God was mixed, paradoxical:

warriorlike and childlike, brash and meek, pious and scholarly, ascetic and extravagant. He was the man I aspired to be.[2]

Before each class he would take ten minutes or so and give a devotional based on his Scripture reading that morning. In imitation of the trappist monks, he had often read only one verse and then meditated on it throughout the day.

I don't think there was a single student under him who did not marvel at the richness and penetration of his insights into Scripture, the moving eloquence with which he shared those insights. Dr. Bockmuehl's devotionals were a seminar unto themselves.

One morning he came to class and instead of his devotional, he read to us a portion of a letter he had received from a former student. It went something like this:

Dear Dr. Bockmuehl:

I wanted to write to thank you for all those devotionals you gave before your lectures. When I think back on my days at Regent, I see that those devotionals kept my faith alive. The other studies somehow depleted me. Only your times of sharing filled me. In some ways, your devotionals saved my faith.

Many teachers would have been flattered by such a tribute. I think I would have. Dr. Bockmuehl, though, was rigid with anger. He put the letter down with a curt, sharp motion. He looked at us: His mouth was tight; his eyes were wild.

"Why," he asked, "is it possible for a student to be in danger of losing his faith at a Christian college? Why did he depend on my devotionals to feed him, and not his own? Why did he need to eat from my hand? Why didn't he gather food with his own hands?"

Good question. Why didn't he?

Curious times, these. There is simultaneously a glut of the Word of God and a famine of it, a drought and deluge. We have every translation of the Bible you can imagine—the NIV, the NEV, the KJV, the NKJV, the NASV, the NRSAV, the Preacher's Bible, the Worshiper's Bible, the Spirit-Filled Believer's Bible, the left-handed bald gypsy fiddler's Bible, with versions for the nearsighted and the farsighted. (That last was made up.)

You can have it in hardback, paper, leather, cloth, in pink, blue, red, oxblood, turtleshell, iridescent orange, psychedelic paisley, with maps and charts and indices and appendices and concordances and holograms of the Temple in the back, and a little sleeve with a CD-ROM that takes you on a guided tour of the Holy Land.

The food is out there—and it's a banqueting table. We're just picky eaters. Oh, we're buying Bibles. And sometimes we're even reading them. But there's not much evidence that we're studying them. We're nibbling, not devouring.

And you are what you eat.

Our reality is dwindling because of it.

The playwright David Lodge tells a story about a day—November 22, 1963, to be exact—when he was in a playhouse, watching one of his own creations being performed. There was a scene in the middle of the play where a character, according to the script and the demands of the plot, turns on a transistor radio and tunes in to a local station. On this day, the theater was full. The actors were caught up in the drama of their performance, the scripted lines and choreographed movements and contrived emotions. The audience was spellbound, pulled into the world powerfully conjured up before them. And along comes this scene. The character takes the radio, flicks it on: a crackle and hiss of static. He dials the tuner: a jumble of noise, voices surge and fade, music blares and then sputters. And then, stark and urgent, a voice breaks through: "Today in Dallas, Texas, President John F. Kennedy was shot and killed...."

The actor quickly switched off the radio. But it was too late. The reality of the real world had, with just a few plain words, burst in upon the closeted, self-created world of a play being staged. And the play was over.[3]

There is only one reality big enough to burst in on all the little plays we script and stage and act out with dramatic intensity or watch with absorbed interest in borderland. Only one thing can really break in and break us out of that. The Word of God.

THE BIBLE IS NOT A BOOK OF PHILOSOPHY—DEEP THOUGHTS TO ponder. It is more like a manual. You don't read a book on kayaking technique simply to ponder the idea. You read it to learn how to kayak.

The Bible is clear that there is no freedom, no blessedness in just knowing Scripture. In one of the clearest descriptions of the authority and integrity of God's Word—2 Timothy 3:16—the emphasis is not on knowing Scripture but on living it:

> All Scripture is God-breathed *and is useful* for teaching, rebuking, correcting and training in righteousness, *so that the man of God may be thoroughly equipped* for every good work. (emphasis mine)

The book—God-breathed, every word of it—is *useful*. Useful for what? For propping up overheads? No. For studying the ancient languages and customs and cultures of the Middle East? Well, maybe. But that's not what Paul had in mind. How about for devising and defending certain theological systems? Again, we're wandering off the mark. The Bible is *useful* for this: shaping and training you to be the kind of person who walks in righteousness and is ready to do good works, God's works, in a fallen world.

If you are not using the Word of God for that, you're misusing it.

Paul goes on in 2 Timothy to paint a vivid picture of the fallenness—the selfishness and godlessness—of our world. Here's how he describes it:

> There will be terrible times in the last days. People will be lovers of themselves, lovers of money, boastful, proud, abusive, disobedient to their parents, ungrateful, unholy, without love, unforgiving, slanderous, without self-control, brutal, not lovers of the good, treacherous, rash, conceited, lovers of pleasure rather than lovers of God—having a form of godliness but denying its power....
>
> They are the kind who worm their way into homes and gain control over weak-willed women, who are loaded down with sins and are swayed by all kinds of evil desires, always learning but never able to acknowledge the truth....
>
> The time will come when men will not put up with sound doctrine. Instead, to suit their own desires, they will gather around them a great number of teachers to say what their itching ears want to hear.

They will turn their ears away from the truth and turn aside to myths. (3:1–7; 4:3–4)

The situation is grim. What ought we to do? Appoint commissions to investigate? Bring on a panel of experts in psychology and sociology, in demonology and demographics? Send forth an army of social workers? What?

Paul's counsel to Timothy is simple: *Study* "to present yourself as one approved, a workman who…correctly handles the word of truth.… Preach the Word…in season and out" (2:15; 4:2).

BUT DR. BOCKMUEHL'S QUESTION STILL HAUNTS: *WHY DIDN'T HE gather food with his own hands?* Why are so many of us with the Bible like the proverbial sloth of Proverbs: "The sluggard buries his hand in the dish; he is too lazy to bring it back to his mouth" (Proverbs 26:15)?

Perhaps it is because the God we meet in Scripture—if we take it all in— is often strange, enigmatic, fearsome, *unsafe.* All these messy stories and earthy details and clay-footed saints.

There's so much in the Bible that bores us—those Levitical laws on mold and goats, the endless genealogies in 2 Chronicles; there's so much that puzzles us—God ambushing Moses, bent on murder until Zipporah circumcises her son and touches the bloody foreskin to Moses' feet; there's so much that frightens us—all those brutal wars, God ordering the death of women and children, or making the earth open wide to swallow families whole. And what about this God who hardens Pharaoh's heart and then punishes him for it, who anoints Saul king and then repents of it? Who loves David, and then goes on to describe, in almost more detail than we can digest, his maimings, his murders, his wife-stealing? A friend of mine was once asked while in prayer group if he wanted to confess having read anything in the past month that in some way undermined his faith.

"Yes," he said. "The Bible."

Why didn't he gather food with his own hands? Maybe it's what we spoke about at the beginning of this book, what I called the secret agenda of most pulpit committees: "When the people saw the thunder and lightening and heard the trumpet and saw the mountain in smoke, they stayed at a distance and said to Moses, 'Speak to us yourself and we will listen. But do not have God speak to us or we will die'" (Exodus 20:18–19).

Maybe we like our Bibles softened, sharpened, explained, embellished, tidied up, boiled down. Both distilled and diluted. David ruddy-cheeked and virtuous, groomed for Sunday school, a portrait of Middle American vigor and piety. Ezekiel 23, the prophet's shockingly graphic depiction of Judah and Israel as two adulterous sisters, censored out. Judges' concubine cut into twelve pieces and mailed to the tribes bowdlerized. Narratives and parables whittled down to principles. Stark commands dressed up as funny anecdotes.

Speak to us yourself and we will listen. But do not have God speak to us.

I HAVE A PROPOSAL: THAT WE START TAKING OUR BIBLE RAW AND uncut. And I suggest—this is a radically evangelical concept that may sound liberal—that we stop trying so hard to explain the inexplicable parts and clean up the unmentionable bits. I propose, rather, that we eat the entire thing, stringy bits, gristle, bones, and all. I propose we practice the holy habit of reading the Holy Bible whole. We are, after all, purportedly the people of the book. And the whole book is God-breathed and useful. If this stuff gets in you, down in your guts, it is going to shape you in ways beyond your asking or imagining. "For the word of God is living and active. Sharper than any double-edged sword, it penetrates even to dividing soul and spirit, joints and marrow; it judges the thoughts and attitudes of the heart" (Hebrews 4:12). We don't probe and hairsplit and dissect the Bible; *it does that to us.*

The holy habit of study means we let the reality of Scripture break in on the closed safeness of our sometimes tightly scripted piety. Enter fully into it— or better, let it enter fully into you, uncooked, uncensored, startling news from the outside. "Take it and eat it," the angel told John, offering him the scroll upon which was written the words of God's speaking. "It will turn your stomach sour, but in your mouth it will be sweet as honey" (Revelation 10:9). *Take it and eat it.* Let this word get down in your guts, where as often as not it gives you a stomachache. Let it disrupt you. Let it shock you, offend you, confuse you. Let it bore you, even. And by all means, let it teach and nourish and comfort you. Taste its sweetness. Then let the useful word train you. Let the double-edged sword cut you. "Humbly accept the word planted in you, which can save you" (James 1:21).

We hear the statistics over and over: the staggering numbers of North Americans who claim to believe in God, even to be born again. The surprisingly high percentage of North Americans who attend church regularly. But with all of that there's the empirical reality: the lack of a robust, turn-the-world-on-its-head faith among us. Faith has become, in Stephen Carter's biting term, a hobby. It has become, as Canadian sociologist Reginald Bibby puts it, à la carte: a smorgasbord we pick and choose from, according to taste and appetite.

And you've got to wonder: Does it not have something to do with our obsession with Bible study reduced to devotional delicacies? The God of Scripture is wooing, tender, forgiving, slow to anger, abounding with love. But He's also prickly, dangerous, wild, demanding. I think the whole drift in our culture is toward eating only those parts of the Bible that show the one face of God and not the other. We lick the honeycomb—*in your mouth it will be sweet as* honey—but avoid swallowing.

Proverbs warns, "If you find honey, eat just enough—too much of it, and you will vomit.... He who is full loathes honey, but to the hungry even what is bitter tastes sweet" (Proverbs 25:16; 27:7). A Bible that is reduced to its sweetest parts after a time becomes merely cloying. Barbara Kingsolver's novel *The Poisonwood Bible* is considered by many evangelicals a diatribe against Christian imperialism and fundamentalism. Her title is based on an unintentional pun which the main character, African missionary Nathan Price, keeps making: He bungles the Congolese language for "Jesus is Lord," and instead announces, "Jesus is poisonwood"—a prickly, stinging, rash-inducing plant. Kingsolver has angered many Christians with her mockery and audacity.

I think she's off the mark. I'm tempted to write a counternovel about North American Christianity and call it *The Honeysuckle Bible*. By unintentionally bungling the language, what comes from many is the proclamation, "Jesus is sugar and spice, and everything nice."

Haven't we yet noticed that no one takes *that* Jesus seriously? *That* Jesus only exists to propel me toward personal fulfillment, when I've got time and inclination. *That* Jesus I accept on my terms.

This is not the Lord of Scripture.

The irony here stings. It was the whole liberal impulse to make God intellectually palatable. The wild and primitive God of the Old Testament who smote entire villages and made His demands had to be either explained away or sent away. The dangerous Lord of the New Testament, who insists we carry crosses when we want to wield swords and who returns bloodstained and warring when we want him wearing kid gloves, had to be lost beneath a flurry of academic preening and doublespeak. But as I touched on in chapter 5, evangelicals have taken over the liberal program by default: instead of demythologizing God Bultmannlike, we've simply ignored much of who He is and what He does. To prevent anyone from thinking we subscribe to a poisonwood Bible, we've substituted a honeysuckle Bible. Both approaches—the liberal one by design, the evangelical one by default—have attempted to make God more attractive.

And this is where the irony comes in: He has, in fact, become less so.

My argument here is that our selective reading of the Bible—our pickiness, our sweet tooth—is in large part the culprit. We're not meeting God as He really is. In our aversion to the *unholy* parts of the Holy Bible—the boring stuff, the violent stuff, the puzzling stuff—we've sated ourselves with honey and starved ourselves of the very sustenance that in fact can make us holy. We are what we eat.

All Scripture is God-breathed and is useful for teaching, rebuking, correcting, *and training in righteousness, so that the man of God might be thoroughly equipped for every good work.*

IN 2 KINGS 22 AND 23, A STORY TELLS OF A BIG BUILDING CAMPAIGN underway. The temple is being renovated. People are busy choosing carpet colors and light fixtures, wall plates, decor. And in the midst of it all, a remarkable discovery is made: They find a Bible. *A Bible. In the temple.* It's astounding, but they haven't had a Bible around for a long time.

King Josiah has the Bible read, and he comes undone. He weeps, he tears his robes, he repents. And then he starts the *real* cleanup in the temple and throughout the land. The place is overrun with pagan idols. Josiah has them torn down and burned up. Then he has *the book*—the Bible, the Word of God—read. And everyone resolves that this is the book they will live by.

The real world broke in on their little stage play of idols and religious busyness—they got a glimpse of the holy wild beyond borderland—and the play abruptly ended. And reality, the real thing, took hold.

That's ancient history. We have plenty of Bibles around. We don't have to discover it under the rubble of our idols, in the midst of our religious busyness, to rediscover it buried somewhere in our churches.

Or do we?

Chapter Twenty

THE FIVE HUNDRED CHRISTS OF TZOUHALEM

In 1964 in Ypsilanti, Michigan, there was not just one Jesus Christ. There weren't two.

In 1964 in Ypsilanti, Michigan, there were no fewer than three Jesus Christs. All three were residents at the psychiatric ward of the local hospital. Their real names were Leon, Joseph, and Clyde. All three suffered from psychotic delusional disorder. All three claimed to be Jesus. All three were patients of psychologist Milton Rokeach, who wrote *The Three Christs of Ypsilanti* about his experience with these would-be messiahs.

Rokeach labored for two years with these men, trying to break reality in on their delusions. It was a tough go, almost barren of progress. Finally, Rokeach decided to try a risky experiment: He put Leon, Joseph, and Clyde together. They slept, beds side by side, in the same room. They ate meals at the same time and at the same table. They were assigned shared tasks. And every day they met together for group therapy.

In the end the experiment failed. Leon, Joseph, and Clyde were each so convinced that they were the messiah, so affronted by the others' claims to that status, so terrified by the prospect of themselves being merely ordinary, that no amount of contrary evidence, no amount of airtight reasoning, no amount of impassioned pleading could dislodge their delusions. There were some minor breakthroughs. Leon, who had claimed he was married to the Virgin Mary, finally admitted the woman was only his sister-in-law. But the breakthroughs didn't amount to much and didn't last long. What endured was the messiah complex. In one group discussion one of the men announced, "I'm the messiah, the Son of God. I am on a mission. I was sent here to save the earth."

"How do you know?" Rokeach asked.

"God told me."

One of the other men shot back, "I never told you any such thing."[1]

IT'S FUNNY. IT'S SAD. AND WORST OF ALL, IT'S FAMILIAR. LEON, Joseph, and Clyde—their messiah complex was a noisy, gaudy affair, all grandstand play. Me, I'm more subtle than that. Up to this point, I've been able to manage my messianic delusion with tact and dignity, been able to conceal it beneath a veil of humility.

Haven't you?

Let's confess. You have *those* moments, don't you? You know what I mean: It *all* depends on you. You're the only one who *really* gets the big picture, who *really* knows what the score is, who *really* has what it takes. In your mind, in your hands is *the answer.* If only these other lunkheads would acknowledge it. If only they would see you for who you are. But they're too insecure for that.

I am a pastor of a church of about five hundred people. All of us, to varying degrees, suffer the messiah complex. Most of our arguments are rooted in that condition:

How do you know we're to build a new Sunday school wing?

God told me.

I never told you any such thing.

The road where our church building is located has a funny name: Tzouhalem (pronounced ZOO-hail-um). I fear someone one day will write a book: *The Five Hundred Christs of Tzouhalem.*

But here's a surprise: God wants us to have a messiah complex. It's no delusion. "Be imitators of God," Paul says, "...and live a life of love, *just as* Christ loved us and gave himself up for us as a fragrant offering and sacrifice to God" (Ephesians 5:1–2). "Husbands, love your wives," Paul says again, a bit further on, "*just as* Christ loved the church and gave himself up for her" (5:25). "I have given them the glory that you gave me," Jesus prayed about His disciples, "that they may be one as we are one" (John 17:22). "As the Father has sent me," Jesus said to His followers, "I am sending you" (John 20:21).

Sounds like a messiah complex to me.

Do you have it? And how would you know? What are the hallmarks, the touchstones, of a true messiah complex? Who among us most resembles the lord of the cosmos? Who among us is the greatest in the kingdom of God? Who among us is closest to showing what Jesus is really like?

Philip Yancey tells a story about the pastor of a church he attended while he lived in Chicago. "Who is the greatest in the kingdom of God?" the pastor asked. "Who is the greatest at LaSalle Street church?" He named a number of high-profile and influential people in the church, including Yancey. All of them winced with embarrassment.

Then the pastor walked to the back of the sanctuary and took a newborn from the arms of a young mother. "Here," he said. "Here is the greatest."

It's a paradox: We imitate the all-powerful, all-knowing, everywhere-at-once God, not trying to be all-powerful and all-knowing and everywhere at once. Rather, we imitate Him most and best by receiving little children and becoming like little children. We imitate Him not by wielding power, but by becoming weak; not by being served, but by being servants.

God wants you and me to have a messiah complex. But it's not the delusion of grandeur: *I'm here to show the world.* It's the reality of servanthood: *I'm here to serve the least of these.* It's not acting big, but becoming small. It's not played out in gestures of defiance and demand, of swaggering and bullying, of heroics and histrionics. It's worked out in acts of love and kindness, giving cups of cold water to the thirsty, clothes to the naked. We emulate the Messiah by becoming like little children and welcoming little children in His name.

The apostle Paul spells out the messiah complex that Jesus' followers should have:

Do nothing out of selfish ambition or vain conceit, but in humility consider others better than yourselves. Each of you should look not only to your own interests, but also to the interests of others.
Your attitude should be the same as that of Christ Jesus:
Who, being in very nature God,
    did not consider equality with God something to be grasped,
but made himself nothing,
    taking the very nature of a servant,
    being made in human likeness.
And being found in appearance as a man,
    he humbled himself
    and became obedient to death—even death on a cross!
(Philippians 2:3–8)

But made Himself nothing, taking the very nature of a servant.... That's the Messiah's messiah complex. God wants to infect us with it.

OUR TRUE AIM SHOULD NOT BE THE HOLY HABIT OF SERVICE, BUT the Christlike attitude of *servanthood*. Anyone can do acts of service. We can give blankets to homeless people, food to the hungry, water to the thirsty, and all of that might deepen rather than break our delusional messiah complex. It might be done only to exalt self, to become something, to be a star.

But it's another thing to make yourself nothing, to become humble, to be a servant. That's the only messianic complex the Bible invites us into.

In borderland if we have any religious impulse at all, it's the impulse to be great for its own sake. So we want to be either heroes or martyrs. Our acts of service tend to rise from the yearning to be one or the other. We want to be either carried on the crowd's shoulders or trampled beneath the mob's feet. Put upon me the laurel wreath of triumph or put upon me the thorny crown of suffering; emblazon my name on the marquee or set me ablaze at the stake; hail me victor or hail me with stones; shower me with accolades or bludgeon me with curses; celebrate me or crucify me. Make me a hero or make me a martyr. That's the delusional messiah complex.

God's messiah complex looks very different. God invites us, Christlike, to become servants. That means we'll do many of our acts of service in secret. We'll do them regardless of whether we're thanked or applauded. We'll do them not seeking persecution, but not avoiding it either. We'll do them when we feel like it and when we don't. We'll do them despite their inconvenience. We'll do them because we're servants, and servants serve.

ACTUALLY SERVANTHOOD IS ONE DISCIPLINE THAT IS UNIVERSALLY attractive. Its attraction is not uniquely Christian. Most of the holy habits—studying and meditating on Scripture, praying, fasting, confessing—have a uniquely Christian appeal. People on the street are generally not intrigued by or drawn to someone who is well practiced in Bible study or worship. But everyone admires and appreciates those who demonstrate servanthood. When we meet a famous person, what impresses us most is if we find him or her humble. We don't meet Julia Roberts and say, "It was so cool. She was totally stuck-up. She hardly talked to me, and when she did she kept saying, 'Who are you again, and why are you bothering me?' She would just snap her fingers, and the waiters jumped to attention, and she said, 'What is this garbage? It's tasteless and cold. Take it away, airhead scum.'"

No. What impresses us is when we can report back, "Julia's just an ordinary person. She asked me to help her pick earrings. Can you believe it? I chose the dangly ones, and she bought them and wore them. And she bought me a pair, too. See? And she kept asking me questions about me—where was I from, what was my job, was I married? She seemed genuinely interested *in me*. When I told her my grandmother was sick, she really seemed to care. And then—this blew me away—she *made me* lunch. She insisted I sit down, and she waited on me. Can you believe that? Julia Roberts."

Servanthood is just plain attractive.

But only if you do it.

Lorne Sanny, the founder of Navigators, was once asked how you could tell if you really were a servant. "By how you act," he said, "when you're treated like one." If I'm going to be your servant, the last thing I want is for you really to think *I'm a servant*. No, I want to impress you with how very humble I am.

I want you to say, "Look. Isn't that the pastor stacking chairs? He's, he's…he's just like Jesus."

And I think, *It's nothing, really. I just saw those chairs needed to be stacked, and hey, I thought, I know how to do that.*

I don't actually want you to treat me like a servant. "Hey, you. After you're done with the chairs, can you give the toilets a quick scrub?"

"There's no brush."

"You'll just have to use your hands."

Servanthood is a noble idea—for you. Me, I'm out to get as much as I can as fast as I can and keep it for as long as I can. I'll do an act of service here and there, especially if it's noticed and advances my reputation. But never, ever treat me as a servant.

Leonard Bernstein, the conductor, was once asked, "What is the hardest instrument to play?" Without a twinge of hesitation, he replied, "Second fiddle. I can always get plenty of first violinists. But to find one who plays second violin with as much enthusiasm, or second French horn, or second flute, now that's a problem. And yet if no one plays second, we have no harmony."[2]

So how about you play second fiddle, okay? Then we'll have harmony.

If I am to be a servant, your servant, I need some deeper source to inspire and sustain me than simply admiring servanthood in others.

What I need is a true messiah complex.

SERVANTHOOD HAS A THEOLOGICAL TAPROOT. IN FACT, THE MAIN discipline for becoming a servant is not an act at all. I will not become a servant simply by admiring servants or even by serving. Rather, at the heart of servanthood is an idea—in fact, three ideas. If you meditate on these three ideas and knit them to your bones, servanthood will flow out of them.

The first idea: Jesus loves you.

That's it. Jesus loves you—loves you totally. He's holding nothing back. He couldn't love you any more than He already does. He'll never love you any less. His love for you does not depend on the good you do; it is not threatened by the bad you do. Yes, you can delight His heart when you're good. Yes, you can break His heart when you're bad. But one thing you can never do: You can't make Him not love you. His heart will never grow cold toward you. Nothing can separate you from His love. Never will He leave you; never will He forsake you.

That's the idea.

The times I struggle to be a servant, I know precisely what's lacking: security. Real servanthood can't exist with insecurity. I'll be driven by a quest for self-protection and self-promotion if I'm haunted by the questions, *Do I matter? Am I important? Am I noticed? Am I valued? Am I loved?* In the absence of knowing I'm loved, I've got to look out for me and mine. I need others to acknowledge my greatness. I need somehow to convince myself that others are less talented, less educated, less worthy, less godly, less attractive than I am. I play—in sophisticated ways, of course—endless variations on pig in the middle and king of the castle. Borderland is a carnival of one-upmanship, a gauntlet of me first.

When writer and pastor Eugene Peterson was a seminary student in New York, he worked part-time at a large church. The janitor at the church was a fellow named Willi Ossa. Willi cleaned the church to make money, but his real passion was painting. Willi asked Eugene if he could paint his portrait. Eugene agreed, partly for the honor of having his portrait done, but partly to try to establish a friendship with Willi. He had detected in Willi a hostility, even a hatred, toward Christians. So for days and weeks, Eugene came and sat for his portrait. Whenever Eugene would ask if he could see the work in progress, Willi would adamantly refuse. He would not allow him to even glimpse it until it was complete.

One day, Willi's wife walked in while Eugene was sitting. She looked at the picture and shouted *"Krank! Krank!"*—German for "Sick! Sick!"—"You paint him to look like a corpse."

Ossa was angry with her. *"Nicht krank, aber keine Gnade."* He said: "He's not sick. That is the way he will look when the compassion is gone, when the mercy gets squeezed out of him."

As the story unfolded, Peterson discovered that Willi felt deeply betrayed by Christians. He had grown up in Germany during the war and watched the state church fail—the church Jesus had called to be His hands and feet and voice in the world. In cowardice and hypocrisy, it had succumbed to acts of self-preservation: It was sick, corpselike, because the compassion had been squeezed out of it. It had failed to be a servant.[3]

In the moment of reckoning, when we have to choose whether we will be true servants or just self-servers, what tips the balance? Where does compassion for the least of these, for our enemies even, come from? Where does the courage to be servants even when it costs us something, maybe everything—where does that come from?

It comes from knowing the love of God. And the more secure I am in God's love, the more free I am to be your servant.

Jesus loves me and gave Himself up for me. "How great is the love the Father has lavished on us," the apostle John says, "that we should be called children of God! And that is what we are!" (1 John 3:1).

Am I important? Infinitely. *Do I matter?* Ultimately. *Am I loved?* Completely. So you know what? I don't have to sweat and fret about having a bigger slice of pie than you, a shinier nameplate on my door, more feathers in my cap, more notches in my gun stock, more letters after my name. I don't need anyone to pat me on the back and tell me how great I am.

God's done all that and more. Now I'm free—to be your servant.

THE SECOND IDEA THAT WILL BRING FORTH TRUE SERVANTHOOD IN us is this: Serving others is the best way to love Christ. Jesus says that as we love others, we love Him. "This command I give to you," He says. "Love each other.... If you love me, you will obey what I command" (John 14:15; 15:12).

There is a Hassidic legend about a community of Jewish monks that had descended into factionalism, rivalry, gossip, suspicion. A wise man visited the abbey, and the abbot told him about the deplorable condition of the monks. "It is so bad," he said, "that I do not believe we will survive as a community."

"I am so surprised," the other man said. "For it is widely rumored the Messiah is in your midst."

The abbot went back and reported to the monks the conversation. It entirely transformed the place. Each treated all the others with deep love and high regard—this one might be the Messiah.[4]

It is widely rumored the Messiah is in your midst. For I came to you thirsty. I came to you naked. I was a stranger. I was sick.

⤸

THE THIRD IDEA IS THAT SERVANTHOOD IS THE BEST WAY TO LOVE like Jesus. "Having loved his own who were in the world," John writes about Jesus, "he now showed them the full extent of his love."

He now showed them the full extent of His love.

The devil had already prompted Judas Iscariot...to betray Jesus.

He now showed them the full extent of His love.

Jesus *knew* that the Father had put all things under His power.

He now showed them the full extent of His love.

Jesus *knew* He had come from God and was returning to God.

He now showed them the full extent of His love.

"He got up...took off his outer clothing...wrapped a towel around his waist.... He poured water into a basin and began to wash his disciples' feet" (John 13:4–5).

He now showed them the full extent of His love.

He became our servant. Let the same attitude that is in Christ Jesus also be in you.

IN THE CITY OF VICTORIA, NOT FAR FROM WHERE I LIVE, IS THE Museum of British Columbia. It is a showcase of spectacle, a shrine of the grandiose: room-sized sculptures, wall-sized paintings, life-sized recreations of historical epochs. There is also an IMAX theater three stories high, which shows adventure-nature movies so vivid and fast paced your stomach swoops and flutters watching them.

The whole thing is history and nature, art and archaeology, on the grand scale. It is meant to overwhelm the visitor, and it does.

But my favorite room is a small, quiet one filled with glass cases. In the cases are ordinary items, the commonplace stuff that once defined an era—gramophones and iceboxes of a hundred years ago, turntables and platform shoes of thirty years past. In the fifties case is a poodle skirt, a varsity sweater, a tube of Brillcream, a tapered black comb. In the seventies case is a man's red satin bell-bottomed jumpsuit, a Commodore 64 computer, a *Partridge Family* LP.

If heaven keeps a museum, I don't think it will be a grand theater of Christendom's triumphs—a 3-D movie of Satan writhing in inflamed agony, or mock-ups of the mighty empires, from Caesar's to Stalin's, that the man from Galilee smote to rubble, or Constantine's decree to make Christianity a state religion.

I think it will be a small, quiet room filled with ordinary things: a cup of cold water given to a refugee. A laundry basket of clothes washed and ironed for teenagers who never say thank-you. A stack of dishes, rinsed and soaked and cleaned, left dirty by people who never stay around to help. A meal cooked for a sick neighbor. A hundred dollars given to an unemployed man whose giver could hardly afford it. A Samaritan's donkey. A widow's mite. A towel, still damp from wiping feet.

They will be souvenirs of the Messiah's messiah complex and the mementos of all those who let the same attitude—the heart of servanthood—also be in them.

Chapter Twenty-One

PERFUME AND BOMBS

There's a rocky island where I go most summers to fish. I do more than fish. I comb the beach, watch for eagles, go for walks, make repairs on the aging beachside cabin I stay in. I whittle sticks, split wood, dig for clams, swim in the bracing water. I grow my beard out to a cutting, itching stubble. Mostly, though, I fish.

I use a small boat. Sometimes the water surges up to its gunnels, and the boat teeters on the waves. At other times the water is dead calm. It stretches taut and darkly gleaming, unmarked except for the rod lines on its smooth surface that pucker like the pressure of a needle on skin not yet pierced.

The sea is like that, benign or bullying at its own choosing. Sometimes it's cold in the boat. The hands go numb, the ears sting. A chill shivers beneath the skin. Other times it's hot. The air presses the flesh like fired metal. The sweat almost scalds.

Fishing is about waiting. Waiting for the wind to die or shift, or the tide to rise. And always waiting for the fish: the shiver of the rod, the way it curves down sharply and shrills as the fish plunges, leaps, races. On occasion the fish are abundant and voracious. They almost leap into the boat. I can hardly spool out my line the full length before the next one, bigger than the last one, hits. But those times are rare. They are strange windfalls, almost omens. They are as foreboding as they are exhilarating, hinting that something in the inner structure of things has tripped out or gone haywire, that some mutation has occurred. It's a feeling you'd get if you entered an alleyway ankle deep in hundred-dollar bills: thrilled, but disturbed. *Something's wrong here.* You know it's plundered goods. Gathering it, your conscience rankles.

No, fishing is really about waiting.

Fishing is as good a metaphor as anything for the life of prayer. The unpredictability of the element, its tempestuousness at times, its windless calm at others. And its depth, its vastness—the feeling that we're just skimming surfaces, that the mystery and marvel folds down into unfathomable and often unreachable darkness. The thrill when something, anything, takes the line, and the disappointment and often the mess when it's not what you hoped for.

And always the waiting.

I KNOW A WOMAN WHO'S BEEN WAITING A LONG TIME FOR GOD. She's been praying, sometimes in numbness, sometimes in anger, sometimes in sorrow, sometimes in fainting hope. She was once vigorous, vivacious. She spent her weekdays teaching a classroom of small children, her weekends kayaking and mountaineering with her husband, making beautiful things with her hands, worshiping with a community of people. Now she can do none of that. Now she spends her days and most of her nights staring at a ceiling. Something has afflicted her, something the doctors haven't a clear name for, and now she lacks the energy to stand. She's everlastingly tired. And yet she can't sleep. Something raging inside her, a sorrow and a terror, keeps her from it.

She waits. Her husband waits. Her friends wait. They wait and they pray. The waiting is long, dreary, heavy. At times their faith is huge, robust, militant: They defy, they command, they harangue. Other times they pray falteringly. Even begging has gone out of them. They pray, not in faith, but out of faithfulness, out of loyalty to a God they haven't seen or heard from in a long, lonely time.

When I think about her, I have only a single argument as to why she or anyone should keep praying. It's this: Prayer and waiting are intrinsically linked, joined at the hip. Prayer makes no sense apart from waiting. Prayer is about being made in the likeness of Christ. Conformed, reformed, transformed. If prayer was only about getting things—getting even, getting rich, getting well, getting justice—then we would call it something else. We have lots of names to describe the quest and method for getting those things: magic, medicine, capitalism, lobbying.

But prayer is not about bartering and bargaining with God, haggling for the best deal: a pound of piety for a remission of sickness. Prayer, at its heart, is about becoming like the crucified and risen Christ. And that is a work like wind carving stone. It is a slow, painful, toiling work, rarely swift or easy. It is riddled with wrenching setbacks, and its breakthroughs are more serendipitous than calculated. There are disciplines for prayer, to be sure, but no mechanisms. Gimmicks and panaceas—like glittery gimcrack lures for fishermen—are widely available and equally useless. There is simply no substitute for becoming like Christ other than being with Christ, and especially with Him in solitude and suffering and sorrow. And so prayer, like fishing, is about waiting. Prayer is the poetry of waiting. It is the language of those who know that what is now is not what should be and not what will be, if we wait.

The apostle Paul was, I think, an impatient man, loath to wait. I picture his walk, his gestures, his speech—brisk, brusque, clipped. He writes in tumbling, sprawling language. It has an urgent feel to it, like a man giving directions in a firestorm. He wants things, difficult things like spiritual conversion and sanctification, to happen quickly, without falter or compromise.

And yet he learned to wait. He learned to pray, which means he learned to wait. Moses, Samuel, Nehemiah—I think they also hated waiting. They were unflinching men of daring decision and sure, swift action. Nothing done in half measures. God used their gruff, storming impatience to get done what otherwise would never have been done. The tasks God called them to required an unapologetic urgency, a hard-edged vigor, a quicksilver boldness.

"The Kingdom of God violently advances," the King James Version renders Jesus' words in Matthew 11:12, "and the violent take it by force." These men—Moses, Samuel, Nehemiah, Paul—were among those violent men who, while others hesitated in timidity or apathy, seized hold with both fists and ran with all their might.

Still, they had to wait. They had to wait for people—stubborn people, lazy people, rebellious people, cowardly people.

But mostly they had to wait for God. God, who had made known to them His purposes but was in no apparent hurry to accomplish them. God, who could wait for one Pharaoh to die and another one to succeed him. God, who promised a land flowing with milk and honey but could hold up the journey for forty years in a land parched of water and with only one thing on the menu in order to work out some character issues in the people. God, who could depose King Saul and anoint David, but could then watch for the next dozen or more years as Saul clung to this throne and crown and hounded David into beggarliness and vagabondage.

WE NEED TO TALK ABOUT THE HOLY HABIT OF PRAYER IN THIS context. In my experience, personally and pastorally, few things in the Godward life puzzle and aggravate us more than prayer. Much of what we explored in the early part of this book—our borderland habits of doubt, disappointment, wonderlessness—can in one way or another be traced back to times in our Christian life when we ached and begged for God to speak, to move, to reveal His will, and *nothing happened.* In some ways borderland habits are the encrustation of too many unanswered prayers: the thickness of indifference that scab over our hearts to protect themselves after our longings have too often gone unrequited.

So it is vital—not merely an academic concern, but a burning one—that we grasp the logic of divine delay. "But do not forget this one thing, dear friends," Peter writes. What one thing? What is the essential matter, Peter, the urgent thing, the one insight you take pains that we don't miss and never forget? This: "With the Lord a day is like a thousand years, and a thousand years are like a day." And then this: "The Lord is not slow in keeping his promise, as some understand slowness" (2 Peter 3:8–9).

There is a scene recorded in John 9 where Jesus and His disciples see a man born blind. "Rabbi," the disciples ask, "who sinned, this man or his parents, that he was born blind?"

"Neither this man nor his parents sinned," said Jesus. "But this happened so that the work of God might be displayed in his life" (vv. 1–3). Then Jesus heals the man, restores his sight.

This has happened so that the work of God might be displayed in his life. We never learn the man's age other than that "he is of age": He was at least thirteen but probably much older, at least in his twenties. And he was born blind. His blindness *has happened so that the work of God might be displayed in his life.* That's a long time to wait for the purpose of God to be displayed. All those years of feeling walls, clutching rails. All those years of wandering in a blackness of empty space and jumbled obstacles. Simple things—bread and fire, stones and beetles—are reduced to their starkest, most elementary form: tasty, hot, hard, ticklish, sharp. You hear laughter, the scuffling of children; you hear the clatter of ox cart, the haggling of vendors, the clanging of swords, but these things only exist as disembodied noise, a vast shapeless shifting soundscape.

And why? For what good, for what purpose? *So that the work of God might be displayed in his life.*

Do not forget this one thing, dear friends: With the Lord a day is like a thousand years, and a thousand years are like a day.

God doesn't mind waiting.

THERE ARE TWO IMAGES THAT JOHN USES IN REVELATION TO describe prayer. In Revelation 5, John describes the worship of heaven, the ever-widening circles of adoration and proclamation that surround the Lamb's throne. In the inner circle, closest to the throne, are twenty-four elders, also seated on thrones, and four living creatures. The Lamb, the worthy one, takes the seven-sealed scroll. And the elders, all twenty-four along with the four living creatures, fall together in reverence before Him, amazed at His worthiness and willingness to consummate history and inaugurate eternity. This is what John sees:

> The four living creatures and the twenty-four elders fell down
> before the Lamb. Each one had a harp and they were holding

golden bowls full of incense, *which are the prayers of the saints.* (v 8 emphasis mine)

It is a stunning image: prayer as incense. I find it deeply consoling, knowing that our prayers are gathered as fragrance in the presence of God, that my prayer this morning for my wife and my children, my church, my neighbors, mingles now with the purity and intensity of heaven's worship. As the magi brought incense as part of their gifts to the Christ child, now we, by the ministrations of the twenty-four elders, bring incense as gifts to the risen Christ. My prayers, your prayers, the prayers of our brothers and sisters in Uganda and Korea and Sri Lanka and Alaska, the prayers of the afflicted, the comforted, the lonely, the reunited, the dying, the rejoicing—they blossom, redolent, in the throne room of God. Incense. Its thickly sweet perfume soaks God's robes; its bluish languid smoke entwines the room, hovers and swirls in diaphanous sheets over the prone bodies of heaven's company.

But it also troubles me, this image of prayer as incense. It too easily conjures before me, confirms for me, my greatest fear about prayer: That it is mere smoke and scent, an aromatic vapor devoid of substance and can do no more to heal a broken world than a splash of aftershave can do to revive a corpse. The image of prayer as incense distills my own frustrations with prayer. Honestly? I pray to move God's hand. I pray to watch those hands bend and break things, make and shape things, remove things, implant things.

I don't pray to make some otherworldly fragrance.

Mothers are dying down here, Lord. Children are starving. Death breeds, destruction stalks, evil gloats. There is trouble everywhere. We are praying fervently, feverishly for You to do something about it. Don't just smell our prayers—answer them.

Down the street from where I live, new houses are being built. This is always a revelation to me, a house being built. Their sudden appearance startles me: one day a stony, muddy weedy lot; the next week a skeleton of white spruce; the next week a house, its fresh-tiled roof like a dark fin against the sky. In five to six weeks, it's all there—doors and windows, siding, silver pipes emerging from the roof, and black cables draping to the earth, a flower basket hanging at the eaves' edge and an excited, exhausted family unpacking boxes from the garage. A child runs across turf so fresh the seams show through, geometric and offset like a hopscotch game.

I want prayer to work that way, like a house going up. I want it to work quickly, tangibly, noticeably. I want prayer to transform, from bedrock to sky-line, the very order and appearance of things, to raise up unmistakably and for all eyes to see a new thing in our midst.

Too often I've experienced prayer as akin to the weather that passes over those building lots. It follows its own mysterious patterns. It changes the quality of the air temporarily. It sometimes alters the wetness or dryness of the ground, shifts the mood, fluctuates the temperature. But otherwise it changes very little. It leaves things virtually unchanged.

Incense. Perfume. Prayer sometimes just seems to make a nice fragrance when what's needed is to move the earth.

WHY PRAY? THIS, I THINK, IS THE QUESTION THAT DWELLS BEHIND all our struggles *to* pray. If prayer worked more tangibly—if it was like house building—we might find it difficult work. But we wouldn't doubt its useful-ness, the difference it made. Day after day, week after week, we'd witness its progress.

One day, Jesus' first disciples asked Him, "Lord, teach us to pray." Had I been among them, I might have made a different request: "Lord, teach me not *what* to pray or *how* to pray—no, Lord, teach me *why* I should pray. Teach me, when I'm standing with a family holding a desperately sick child awaiting surgery, and I say, "Let's pray"—Lord, teach me not to be haunted by doubt and despair, to be able to dispel the voice inside saying, *Why bother? What good will it do? We all know that this depends on the ability of machines and medicine, doctors and diagnoses."*

In chapter 13 I mentioned the story of the boy with the evil spirit that tries to kill him by tripping him into water, hurling him into fire. A squabble breaks out between Jesus' disciples and the teachers of the law over their inability to do anything. When Jesus arrives on the scene, the father explains that Jesus' impo-tent, incompetent, shouting-match followers have failed to help.

"But if You can do anything," he says, "take pity on us and help us."

"'If you can'?" Jesus says. Perhaps in His voice there is, like a bristle of splinters at a board's edge, some jaggedness of offense or annoyance: "What do you mean, 'If you can'?" Or maybe He says it with a wry laugh tickling up beneath the surface of sternness: "'If You can'? That's a good one. Of course I can!" Or maybe He says it as a brother who, being tempted in all the ways we are, is able to sympathize with this man's weakness: "'If You can'? Let me assure you, I can. I really can."

"Everything is possible for him who believes," Jesus tells him.

And the man blurts out: "I do believe; help me overcome my unbelief" (Mark 9:14–29).

That is deeply poignant. The boy has been like this for a long time, since childhood. For years his father has watched his little son, his limbs thin as saplings, his chest a pale washboard of bones, fight a power he's no match for. No father would stand and simply watch a thug thrash his little boy. But this father's been forced to do that. Day after day, in angry desperate helplessness, he's been forced to stand and witness a demon—merciless, gloating, grue-some—pummel his child, bent on destruction.

It would wither a man's insides. He would have tried everything by now. Every doctor. Every frothing greenish potion and quack cure. Every purported miracle worker. Every rumored holy man. Every concoction of prayer, incan-tation, imprecation. He would have reached the point where the smudgy ads on the cluttered back pages of tabloids, touting the miracle powers of magnets or holy water or irisology, would prick his heart with a mix of black despair and faint hope. Then one day Jesus' disciples come to town. They have had some proven success in these matters: "Even the demons submit to us in your name!" they once exclaimed to Jesus. So now, the father thinks, is the day of redemption.

But they can do nothing.

And for that man, it is just one more failure in a long miserable string of them. *But if You can do anything, take pity on us and help us. I do believe; help me to overcome my unbelief.* How else could he put it? He's been to too many charismatic healing services that sent him away empty-handed. He's been to Catherine Culman when she was in town, and he's sent money to several television evangelists who promised to pray for the boy in response to a cash gift (the prayer of a righteous man is powerful and effective, they quoted). Nothing. He prays himself, every day. Sometimes he's bold in his praying, the five-star commanding general. Sometimes he's afraid, the ragged beggar imploring. Sometimes he's empty, and he just weeps. And sometimes he can't do even that. He has read all the books about this, ransacked the Internet, consulted with Christian radio gurus. It's all added up to nothing.

But if You can do anything...

...help me overcome my unbelief.

How could he say otherwise? How could his faith be any more daring, swaggering, robust than that? He is a man for whom long and futile waiting has staggered hope, almost crushed it. Who would blame him if he'd made his home in borderland?

Because all prayer seems like mere vapor, a wisp of scent borne away on a swift wind. And if he was told, *Take heart! Your prayers and all the prayers on behalf of your boy are a sweet fragrance, incense before God*—well, the man might have thrown off what few tatters of faith still clung to him. He might have spit that pious bromide out like a bug that flew into his open mouth.

But suddenly, after all these years of hoping and despairing, his prayers are answered. Jesus *can* help. Jesus commands the demon; it flees, and the boy is healed.

"Why couldn't we drive it out?" His disciples ask Him later.

"This kind can come out only by prayer," Jesus says.

Which seems, as it so often does with Jesus, not an answer at all, but an enigma, a way of making the mystery of faith and faithfulness deeper yet.

THIS KIND ONLY CAN COME OUT BY PRAYER. REVELATION PORTRAYS the fullness of prayer with a second image, intrinsically related to the first. It is in Revelation 8. After the Lamb has opened the seventh seal, there is silence. And then John witnesses this:

> Another angel, who had a golden censer, came and stood at the altar.
> He was given much incense to offer, with the prayers of all the saints,
> on the golden altar before the throne. The smoke of the incense,

together with the prayers of the saints, went up before God from the angel's hand. Then the angel took the censer, filled it with fire from the altar, and hurled it on the earth; and there came peals of thunder, rumblings, flashes of lightning and an earthquake. (vv. 3–5)

The perfume becomes bombs. The long wait is finally interrupted, and everything is altered. At a point beyond our choosing, beyond our ability to predict or control or delay or hasten, the sweet but inert fragrance of all the prayers we've sent heavenward is ignited with holy fire, and sent hurtling back to earth. The *status quo* is forever shaken, split open, reordered. The demons flee. The blind see. The dead arise.

As He did with Elijah, the God who is not safe answers with fire from heaven, and Baal loses. A famous quote from Annie Dillard:

Does anyone have the foggiest idea what sort of power we so blithely invoke? Or, as I suspect, does no one believe a word of it? The churches are children playing on the floor with their chemistry sets, mixing up a batch of TNT to kill a Sunday morning. It is madness to wear ladies' straw hats and velvet hats to church; we should all be wearing crash helmets. Ushers should issue life preservers and signal flares; they should lash us to our pews.

AND YET, THE PRIMARY DISCIPLINE OF PRAYER IS WAITING. THAT IS the holy habit—living out the conviction that *the Lord is not slow in keeping His promise, as some understand slowness.* What we expect may take almost forever—a thousand years, anyhow—can happen in a day. More often, what we wish would happen in a day may take a thousand years. The holy habit is getting used to the reality that with the Lord one is like the other.

We are waiting for the fire to ignite the incense, waiting for perfume to be made into bombs. "Then Jesus told his disciples a parable to show them that they should always pray and not give up," Luke says in Luke 18. Jesus tells about a widow who nagged a judge into granting her plea. He tells the parable after instructing His disciples about the seeming endless delays and

diversions, the wearying, faith-eroding slowness and then shocking sudden-
ness of the coming kingdom. And after He's spoken, they have one response:
"Where, Lord?" Where is this kingdom? Where is the evidence of all this
coming to be?

Jesus tells them the parable to encourage prayer in the interim as the main
work they engage in during the time of waiting. Jesus sums up the story this
way:

> Listen to what the unjust judge says. And will not God bring justice
> for his chosen ones, who cry out to him day and night? Will he keep
> putting them off? I tell you, he will see that they get justice, and
> quickly. However, when the Son of Man comes, will he find faith on
> the earth? (vv. 6–8)

Prayer is just that: crying out day and night without seeing justice and
continuing anyhow. The danger is that in waiting so long for Jesus to answer,
our unbelief bests our belief, and we stop waiting, stop hoping, stop praying,
and just get on with other things. Or we turn to other forms of belief—superstition, magic, the modern relics and elixirs and amulets and alchemies proffered on the back page ads of tabloids. We move to borderland.

Teach us to pray. Well, then, pray this: *Thy Kingdom come, Thy will be done,
on earth as it is in heaven.* Now there's a prayer that is not going to be answered
in a day, a week, maybe in our lifetime, not in fullness. It's taken two thousand
years of praying so far, and still it hangs fire. It could take two more. Or it
could be answered tomorrow. Today.

To pray well is to cultivate holy patience and perseverance. It is to practice holy waiting, which means often to keep on praying in spite of the poor
results. "They that wait upon the LORD shall renew their strength," Isaiah says.
"They shall mount up with wings as eagles; they shall run, and not be weary;
and they shall walk, and not faint" (40:31, KJV).

Two details in particular fascinate me about this verse. The first is that
waiting is, in God's paradoxical economy, not the cause of weariness, but the
pathway to renewal. God intends for waiting to invigorate and replenish us
rather than debilitate and deplete us. He desires that it would have exactly the

opposite effect it often does. But how so? Only if waiting is actually a shortcut or catalyst for some deep purpose of God, something intimately close to His heart, something tightly aligned with His creational and redemptive purposes. We generally want miracles: the deaf to hear, the blind to see, the lame to walk, the hungry to be filled. God, obviously, wants those things, too. But is that all He wants, the most He wants? Is that all prayer was intended to be: an instrument for getting that, making it happen? If so, prayer is, as I've said, a flawed tool, prone to breakdown, jamming, and backfiring like an old barrel-loaded musket, and usually hitting short of the target or wide of the mark when it is working.

What God wants most is for us to be like His son, Jesus—as Paul puts it, transformed into Christ's likeness with ever-increasing glory (2 Corinthians 3:18). But Paul says that early in his second letter to the Corinthians, and then goes on to describe the shape his own transformation into glorious Christlikeness has taken: overwhelming sorrow, persecution, hardships, torture, hunger (4:8–12; 6:3–10; 11:23–12:10). He has been waiting for the fire to fall from heaven. In many ways, 2 Corinthians reads like a diary of unanswered prayer, a litany of unresolved traumas, dilemmas, fiascoes, disasters. Paul builds this theme until its climax in chapter 12, where he recounts his experience with unanswered prayer: "There was given…a messenger of Satan, to torment me. Three times I pleaded with the Lord to take it away from me. But he said to me, 'My grace is sufficient for you, for my power is made perfect in weakness….' That is why, for Christ's sake, I delight in weaknesses, in insults, in hardships, in persecutions. For when I am weak, then I am strong" (vv. 7–10).

Paul learns in the place of unanswered prayer a deeper answer to prayer: grace. Through utter neediness and brokenness, he learns utter dependency upon God. He learns God's sufficiency in his own weakness and suffering—sufficiency not to remove the weakness or the suffering, but to be present within it.

He learns to be more like Christ, the suffering servant, the one who conquers through weakness.

He learns all of that through waiting. *Those who wait on the Lord will renew their strength.* Waiting is one of God's primary appointed means for becoming like Jesus. And its main expression and posture is prayer. Prayer is the womb we curl into, the dark, closed, often silent place where we are formed in Christlikeness, where strand by tangled strand our willfulness and selfishness is unraveled and stitch by painstaking stitch the Spirit's work is knit together in us.

The second detail that fascinates me is Isaiah's threefold promise to those who wait. They shall rise up on wings as eagles; they shall run and not grow weary; they shall walk and not faint. Actually it's not so much the promises themselves that fascinate me as the sequence of them. The promises culminate, not in eaglelike soaring, but in pilgrimlike trudging: walking and not fainting. According to the conventions of Hebrew poetry, the sequence of ideas should progress from the lesser to the greater. So we would expect the sequence of promise here to be reversed: Waiting on the Lord allows us to walk and not faint, to run and not grow weary, to—yeah!—rise up on wings as eagles. That is far more dramatic, climactic, inspiring, spectacular. It is the miracle we hope for. Any of us can walk. That is commonplace. What we really want is to fly.

But Isaiah—well, God—sees it otherwise. We may want wings, but what we really need is to walk without falling down—to plod through blistering heat, chilling cold, drenching rain, scathing storm, over dreary flatness or tangled thickets or rocky gorges, through swampland and badland and no-man's-land. And to do it all in steadfastness, undeterred. To go deeper into the holy wild, farther from borderland, and to not faint.

Not long ago I was in Mexico, where I had a trivial but vivid lesson in this. My wife bought me for my birthday a session of parasailing—a parachute ride, five hundred feet up, at the end of a rope pulled by a speedboat. Initially it took some courage to strap on the thin harness and entrust myself to the cords and silk of the parachute; to the rope that joined the harness, umbilical-like, with the boat; to the competency and alertness of the boat driver; to the mechanical soundness of the boat. But after my first brief moments of panic, it was all sheer escapade, a playful, elegant thrill that ended too soon. I was soaring on wings as eagles.

Later in the heat of the day, my wife and I went for a walk on the beach. On a whim we decided to try to walk to town, about two miles away. At first it was good: walking barefoot on a sandy beach in front of posh hotels. In the background, beyond the stone walls and screen of palm trees, we could hear the splash of pool water, the laughter of swimmers, the clink of glasses. But then the hotels gave way to empty, littered lots, and the sand became strewn with garbage. Amidst crushed pop cans, plastic bottles, chunks of Styrofoam, and food wrappers were condoms, hypodermic needles, broken glass, dog deposits. We put our sandals on. The sand gave way to rocks, difficult to walk on. The happy, lazy tourists gave way to angry-looking locals who sat in groups, drinking and eyeing us menacingly. Some vendors approached us to sell something, but they weren't nearly as friendly, engaging, willing to be put off, as those back at the hotels. The sun's glare skewered us. The air's humidity mobbed us. Stones cut between our feet and sandals. Our mouths were parched.

We had gone too far to turn back and felt too weary and wary to go forward.

But we continued on until we reached the town. There we rested and drank ice-cold water.

The soaring was much easier than the walking. The soaring required less endurance. At first it felt like the greater accomplishment, the heroic facing down and overcoming of obstacles, the literal and figurative act of rising above. But in retrospect, it was the lesser task, the more ordinary one.

Indeed, what is more amazing—Elijah calling down heaven's fire and routing the prophets of baal, or his willingness to press on in the face of a hateful, death-dealing queen and king bent on his destruction? What is more amazing—healing the lame, the blind, the sick, or caring for them, with vigilance and diligence and genuine love, day after day after day? What is more amazing—the crippled man taking up his mat and walking, or his living with faith and hope and thankfulness in his skin-blistering, blood-clotting immobility until the day death comes? What is more amazing—the star running back who's just scored the winning touchdown in the championship thanking God on national television, or the old man with Parkinson's disease thanking God in his musty, lonely apartment? Does soaring on eagle wings ever rank in its miraculousness with walking and not fainting?

William Willimon tells a story of a friend who attended a conference where the speaker exhorted the audience to love Jesus. This was fine, of course, but he defined that love as committing radical and subversive acts; challenging entrenched evil in corporations, government, education; taking on all the societal Goliaths. Willimon's friend leaned over to the person sitting beside him and whispered, "I know a woman who's a single mother. Her daughter is severely mentally and physically handicapped. Every day, all day, that mother's time and energy and attention is taken up feeding, caring for, washing, dressing and undressing her child, holding her through her fits of pain and her muscle spasms, trying to understand and respond to her inarticulate grunts and jerks. That's about as radical and subversive an act of love for Jesus as she can manage."[1]

To walk and not faint. To spoon-feed that child every meal, every day, every week, every month, every year for the rest of her life. To plead with the Lord to take the thorn away, and to hear in response, "My grace is sufficient for you. I am present, more and more, in your weakness. Every day I am transforming you more into My likeness. One day, people will hardly be able to tell the difference between us."

Between making perfume and making bombs, that is God's truest answer to our prayers.

Teach us to pray, O Lord.

You'll have to wait.

HOW DO WE PRAY THEN? I AM MAKING THE ARGUMENT THAT PRAYER requires a willingness to wait. But I am also saying that waiting requires a willingness to pray. Waitless prayer breeds cynicism, and soon prayer is abandoned or becomes lifeless, duty-bound gesture, like the Queen waving. On the other hand, prayerless waiting dries up into boredom, and soon the waiting becomes mere idleness or gives way to mindless busyness. The holy habits of waiting and praying—to see these, in fact, as a single discipline, each buoying up the other—are needed if we are to stay clear of borderland.

There are two ancient practices that give shape and substance to the life of waiting and praying. One practice is praying the Psalms. The other is praying without ceasing. There are, of course, many other forms and attitudes we want to cultivate in the life of prayer and many excellent books that guide us in that. But I am interested here in giving the life of prayer a deeprootedness. And to do that, these two ancient practices are unsurpassed.

The Psalms are the prayers that God's covenant people have birthed out of their celebration and anguish, their hope and hopelessness, their anger and forgiveness, their captivity and exile and conquest and triumph. They track a path through the vastness of human emotion, its tundras and its jungles, and direct all of it Godward. What do you do with your hatred, bitterness, ecstasy, weariness, heaviness, longings, disappointments, despair, and desires? To whom can you entrust all that? Centuries of wisdom tell us that the Psalms give form to and language for the fullness of our lives. They give us containers that allow us to offer our lives, distillate and undiluted, to God. They help us to bring all we are—our holy, disheveled, desperate selves—to all of God. They are gathering places, repositories, where the mundaneness and tragedy and glory of being human can be sorted out and given back as worship. As prayer.

The best and wisest way to do this is to pray a Psalm each day, in the order you find them. It doesn't matter if the emotional tenor of the psalm matches your own for that day: It has in the past and will in the future. And anyway these are community prayers, not just for us or about us. They are also vehicles for intercession. Psalm 137—a prayer of angry grief, a cry for gruesome vengeance—may be outside your particular needs today. But someone in Vietnam may need it, and your prayer is a Spirit work on their behalf, an imaginative act of entering into their pain. It is, in fact, incense in God's throne room, raw material for bombs.

Lift these Psalms to God. It is one way to wait as you pray, and pray as you wait.

THE SECOND ANCIENT PRACTICE IS TO PRAY WITHOUT CEASING. Paul calls us to this and connects it with being joyful always and giving thanks in all circumstances—with doing God's will (1 Thessalonians 5:16–18). In other words, he connects unceasing prayerfulness with being connected to God *no matter what* is happening to us, around us. It is the secret to centering all of our lives in the purposes of God. It is the essence of the practice of the presence of God.

Unceasing prayer is a cultivated attentiveness to the God who is always and everywhere with us. We explored this in chapter 15: the holy habit of speaking all our words, thinking all our thoughts, taking all our actions, in the mindfulness that God hears, knows, sees. Praying without ceasing, then, is not so much something *we do*. It is a way *we are,* the way we inhabit our skin, move in the world. It is simply being awake to the reality that, though we can't see it, we know by faith it is there.

Admittedly I practice this inconsistently. I am prone to long stretches of utter obliviousness to God: where Jesus walks on the road with me, and all I do is complain about His not being here. But I can attest to a growing skill—still halting, still makeshift, but a skill nonetheless—in unceasing prayer. So I can, at least roughly, describe it from the inside.

It is a constant *awareness*. It is a continual, though usually silent, dialogue. It is a fixed habit of mind, a conscious and deliberate gesturing toward and response to God that after long practice becomes unconscious and instinctive.

My wife's cousin Lois is deaf. I have only met her two or three times. Each time it has been in large gatherings, and each time she has been with her mother. Both are fluent in sign language. So while a vigorous, loud and many-sided conversation goes on all around, Lois and her mother—without any sense of awkwardness, without a break in the flow of conversation—sign to one another. Their agile hands twirl and flutter in a dance of arcane meaning that then gets translated into language we all understand. When I saw that, I thought, *Ah, yes, that is what praying without ceasing is like.* It is the conversation that goes on with another, without word and as everyone talks around us, that is both part of yet also separate from all other conversations.

If I were to try to communicate with Lois through sign language, it would at first require all my effort. It would be a slow, unwieldy business. I wouldn't be able to participate in any other conversation at the same time. I would be tempted to give up. To get to that place of fluency, there would need to be many painstaking hours of learning the language.

The habit of setting aside time to pray and the practice of praying without ceasing are connected in like manner. Praying in our closets teaches us the language that can be then practiced with fluency elsewhere. Ceasing—ceasing our coming and going, our buying and selling, our working and playing—in order to pray is what prepares us to pray without ceasing.

But if we don't begin and keep at the habit of praying without ceasing—the conversation with God always, everywhere—we soon lose the very thing we worked so hard to acquire. This is like the man who learns sign language from books but never uses it in conversation.

Praying without ceasing is the fruit and sap of all prayer: what keeps it alive and what makes it worthwhile. Because, above all, it is what makes God's presence real to us.

It's what makes the waiting more than bearable: It makes it holy ground.

WILLIAM WILLIMON TELLS ANOTHER STORY. A MAN HE KNEW WENT to Russia in the late seventies, at the height of the Cold War. He was sent as part of a delegation from the World Council of Churches to investigate and report on the state of the Christian church under an atheist regime. The man was not impressed.

"The church," he told Willimon dismissively, contemptuously, "is just a bunch of little old ladies praying." Just a bunch of perfume makers.

Willimon told that story in the early nineties, when statues of Stalin and Lenin—the patron saints of atheistic Russia—lay toppled, ready to be crated for storage or quarried for stone.[2]

Beware little old ladies praying. Secretly they're revolutionaries who make Bolsheviks look like kindergartners. They comprise a veritable bomb-making factory.

Pray the Psalms—offer your whole life before God. Pray without ceasing—bring your whole life into the presence of God.

For now it's incense.

But one day, in the hands of the God who is not safe but good, the fire will fall, and everything will become as it was meant to be.

Chapter Twenty-Two

LET'S PARTY

L ast summer Cheryl and I looked after our neighbors' dog, Max, for a week while they went camping. Max is a high-strung beastie, all sinewy muscle and hair-trigger nerves. Walk too close past Max's house and suddenly you hear the wild clatter of claws scrambling over vinyl decking—he races down, down, down the deck stairs, bolts across the backyard lawn, slams up against the fence, and starts bounding straight up into the air like Michael Jordan sailing hoopward, yelping as though he's being administered bone-rattling jolts of electric shock.

Kids from the neighborhood, walking by, sometimes come up to my neighbor's fence just to see Max's circus act. Whenever I get a new pile of wood to split and stack, Max hurtles over to the fence where I'm working and barks with a voice so shrill it almost splits the wood for me. It's hard for me to warm up to Max. I've thought more than once about having an "accident" with Max involving my splitting maul or a stray piece of alder.

But his family loves him. They're crazy about him.

This is the dog we had to look after. The routine was simple enough. In the morning let Max into the backyard and give him water. In the evening let him in the house with water and food, and leave the bathroom light on. The first night I told Cheryl—me being a servant and all—that I'd do the routine. I went over and let Max in from the backyard. To my surprise, he put up no fuss. He came straight in and lay down on the carpet. I got busy. I set his food and water out. I went down the hall to turn on the bathroom light. When I got back, Max wasn't there.

"Max," I called. No answer. I checked the other rooms. "Max," I said. No Max.

Then I noticed it. I'd left the front door open. I pictured what was now happening—Max, the wild, half-mad creature, drunk with newfound freedom, running, killing cats, chasing cars, fighting dogs, biting children, digging gardens, and lifting his leg on every car tire, fence post, and cedar hedge in a five-mile radius.

I started running through the neighborhood: "Max! Max! Max!" I asked everyone I encountered if they had seen this wiry dog. I commissioned neighborhood kids to find him. I went back several times and checked the house again, checked every far dark corner. I yelled myself hoarse.

Two hours later I returned home deflated, defeated. I went to bed. I lay awake for the longest time, listening to dogs yip and yelp, far and near. Twice I got up, dressed, and went to where I heard the barking. Nothing. I checked my neighbors' backyard—I had left the gate open a crack hoping that Max would sneak back during the night. Nothing. Once about one o'clock, I even went back in the house and searched it again. Nothing. I began to imagine the stricken faces of my neighbors' children as they were given the news: "Now, children. Sit down. Here's a box of Kleenex. Mommy and Daddy have some very, very, very sad news. Max is gone. Mark wasn't being careful and he let him out of the house last night. Yes, Pastor Mark. Children, I don't think our Max will be coming home again...."

I woke—if ever I slept—early and went straight over to Max's yard. Still nothing. I decided I should go into the house and get the phone number for the campsite where the family was staying. I braced myself to tell them the devastating news. I opened the door. At the top of the stairs, guess who stood there wagging his tail?

Max.

I never thought I'd be happy to see Max. But right then, I could have kissed him. On the lips.

JOY. HOW DELIGHTFUL, HOW LIFE-GIVING, IS JOY. AND ALL OF US know what it is to have joy burst upon us, to expect the worst and get the best, to taste the sheer exhilaration of tragedy turned to triumph, loss turned to gain, night become morning. We all know what it is to open the door and see Max at the top of the stairs, wagging his tail. We've all experienced joy.

Since most of us have had the *experience* of joy, let's focus on the *discipline* of joy. Now that sounds like a contradiction. Joy as a discipline? I have *to work* at this? How is that? Isn't joy something you either feel—or don't? Isn't it something that arises within us naturally—or doesn't?

Not exactly. The apostle Paul, sitting in a prison cell with a death sentence hanging over him, wrote, "Rejoice in the Lord always. I will say it again: Rejoice! (Philippians 4:4). He commands rejoicing. In 1 Thessalonians, Paul puts the command even more succinctly: "Be joyful always" (5:16). A command? Well, yes—joy is serious business. "Let us fix our eyes on Jesus," the writer of Hebrews exhorts, "The author and perfecter of our faith, who *for the joy set before him* endured the cross, scorning its shame, and sat down at the right hand of...God" (12:2, emphasis mine). Jesus died for joy.

You wouldn't have guessed it to watch Jesus set His face like flint and march down to Jerusalem. You wouldn't have guessed it to behold Jesus' sweat falling to the ground like drops of blood, pleading with the Father in Gethsemane to take the cup away. You wouldn't have guessed it to see Jesus, thirsty and bloody and haggard, hanging from the cross crying, "My God, My God, why have You abandoned Me?" You wouldn't have guessed that He did it for joy.

But He did. He did it because on the other side of that desert of God-forsakenness and suffering beckoned promised land, clean and bright. Jesus glimpsed the fullness of redemption, the delight of reunion, the ecstasy of welcoming the newborn, and just the glimpse of it sustained Him through the long, harrowing night.

He did it for joy.

So yes, joy is a discipline. It's the holy habit of setting something before ourselves. "Since, then, you have been raised with Christ, set your hearts on things above.... Set your minds on things above" (Colossians 3:1–2). All the moments of joy we can imagine—a child coming into the world, rain after the drought, a doctor's report that there's no cancer, finding Max wagging his tail at the top of the stairs—each of them, all of them, are little glimpses of heaven. The joy we feel at those moments is the smallest foretaste—a mere touch on the tongue, the faintest echo, a whisper grazing the ear—of what we will experience in technicolor and surround sound in heaven. It will be infinite joy without taint or diminishment, sustained for all eternity.

The discipline of joy is setting before us that reality that eventually defines all reality.

Jesus said He gives us His joy and desires that our joy would be complete. The Lord is deeply and passionately committed to our joy. Where did we get the idea that religion is a stiff, dull, flat business, all pursed lips and knitted brows and gloomy outlooks? Where did we get that portrait of the religious type as sour, dour, brooding, scolding? How ever did we forget to dance and laugh and play—and live?

We see religion, of course, as gloominess in the Pharisees and religious rulers of Jesus' day. The people came into town alongside Jesus, singing and skipping and clapping their hands. "Shut these people up," the chief priest ordered. Jesus said, "If they remain silent, the rocks themselves will sing." The Pharisees accused Jesus of hanging out with all the wrong people, going to all the wrong parties. He eats with sinners, they said, aghast. They called Him a drunkard and a glutton.

And look at Jesus. There was some basis to their complaints. His first miracle? Turned water into wine at a wedding where the guests were already so loosened up you could have given them soda and vinegar and they wouldn't have known the difference. He kept comparing Himself to the groom at a wedding feast, said that now was the time to party. He always seemed to be eating and then sleeping. He kept describing heaven like a huge fandango: loud music, lots of fattening food, drinks, dancing, singing.

The religious leaders of the day hated it, as too often they do today. They found Jesus irreverent, frivolous, irresponsible, a threat to public order and decency. *Stop that dancing! Stop that laughing! Stop that singing! Stop that eating! Stop that playing! Stop having fun! Stop it! Stop it! Stop it!*

Do you want to imitate them?

THERE IS ONE PERSON COMMITTED TO YOUR JOYLESSNESS. THAT would be...*Satan*. C. S. Lewis, in *The Screwtape Letters,* imagines for us the devil's view of joy. The book is a series of letters from Screwtape—a senior devil—to his nephew Wormwood, a demon in training. Screwtape writes Wormwood advice on a range of issues as to how a demon should keep people from coming to Christ, and how, if the demon fails in that, to keep them from being free and effective in Christ. In one letter, Screwtape writes about joy and the emotions and activities related to it. (Naturally, when Screwtape says "the Enemy," he means God.)

> Fun is closely related to joy—a sort of emotional froth arising from the play instinct. It is of very little use to us. It can sometimes be used, of course, to divert humans from something else which the Enemy would like them to be feeling or doing; but in itself it has wholly undesirable tendencies; it promotes charity, courage, contentment, and many other evils.

Screwtape goes on to discuss jokes and flippancy—generally, jokes are bad unless they trivialize the sacred, and flippancy is good because it does precisely this. But then Screwtape gets down to joy:

> You will see joy among friends and lovers reunited at the eve of a holiday. Among adults some pretext in the way of jokes is usually provided, but the facility with which even the smallest witticisms produce laughter at such times shows that they are not the real cause. What the real cause is we do not know. Something like it is expressed in much of that detestable art which the humans call Music, and something like it occurs in Heaven—a meaningless acceleration in the

rhythm of celestial experience, quite opaque to us. Laughter of this kind does us no good and should always be discouraged. Besides, the phenomenon is of itself disgusting and a direct insult to the realism, dignity, and austerity of Hell.[1]

Joy is *an acceleration in the rhythm of celestial experience.* Joy is *a direct insult to the realism, dignity, and austerity of hell.* If you think—as popular lore has it— that hell is the party place where you get to slap the backs and tousle the hair of all your pals, drink a Budweiser and dance the hokeypokey with them, you've got your addresses seriously scrambled.

The party's up above.

Down below? Grim, sour solemnity. Long, scowling faces. Endless scolding speeches. Much wagging of the finger, knitting of the brow, quibbling over minor points. Rivalry. Hostility. Envy. The very last place you'll find a party is in hell.

In an article on the Russian literary scholar Mikhail Bakhtin, Alan Jacobs discusses the ruthless soviet leader Joseph Stalin and notes that the one thing above all that Stalin couldn't bear was laughter—especially the idea that some-one, anyone, would laugh at him. You see it in the empire he created around his ego. It was such a gray, grim, mirthless business. Even the so-called cele-brations he staged were dark ponderous affairs.[2]

Laughter—just good bone-shaking, belly-jiggling, light-in-the-head laughter—is a sure sign of health. The only one who hates it is Satan and all his wanna-bes.

SO WHAT DO WE HAVE? GOD IS FULL OF JOY. JESUS IS FULL OF JOY. His desire is to have His joy in you and for that joy to be complete. Paul com-mands you to rejoice and to be joyful always. Those who don't know how to rejoice and resent everyone else doing it are the Pharisees and their gang. And the one person dead set against your joy is the devil.

So what are we going to do about it?

I say we party.

The discipline of joy, the discipline of partying is a holy habit of celebra-tion. It's a discipline because true celebration is deciding purposefully to rejoice and making every effort to do so. Celebration is the practice of lifting our eyes from our preoccupation with all the work we have to do and the trouble we're in and the money we owe and the reputation we strive to keep—to lift our eyes from all that and set them on things above. It's training ourselves, in the midst of and in spite of all that might be amiss, to see heaven: *an acceleration in the rhythm of celestial experience.* It's the discipline of setting joy before us so that we might throw off everything that hinders and run the race marked out for us—that we might endure and not lose heart and not grow weary.

It's so easy to grow weary in life. And it's so easy to grow weary in our spiritual lives. All these disciplines! Fasting. Praying. Serving. Confessing. Studying. As the writer of Ecclesiastes said, much study wearies the bones. *Oh, Lord, I need some refreshing. I need a break. Give me a break.*

Okay. Go party.

That's how I read the Bible. There are more than sixty references in Scripture to celebration and all but one or two of them are positive. Most of them are *divine commands* to go party. Exodus and Deuteronomy and Numbers read like a string of invitations to a nonstop whirlwind of festival: "Celebrate the Feast of Unleavened Bread.... Celebrate the Feast of Harvest.... Celebrate the Feast of Weeks.... Celebrate the Passover.... Celebrate the Feast of Tabernacles.... Celebrate." These were not quiet, sedate, well-mannered little tea parties. They were raucous, shout-at-the-top-of-your-lungs and dance-in-the-streets, weeklong shindigs. The heart of our Father God welcomes the prodigal home, shouting to His servants, "Bring the fatted calf and kill it. Let's have a feast and celebrate!"

That's our God. You read this stuff enough, you start to get the sense that God is looking for just about any excuse to fire up the barbecue and invite the neighborhood over. In Nehemiah, the priest Ezra reads and explains the law—the Bible—to the people in Jerusalem, and as they listen they weep. Nehemiah gets up and says, "This day is sacred to the LORD your God." Good. So what do we do on a sacred day, on a holy day? He continues: "'Do not mourn or weep.... Go and enjoy choice food and sweet drinks, and send some to those who have nothing prepared. This is a day sacred to our Lord. Do not grieve, for the joy of the LORD is your strength.' Then all the people went away to eat and drink, to send portions of food and to celebrate with great joy, because they now understood the words that had been made known to them" (8:9–12). It went on for seven days.

What do you do on a day sacred to the Lord? You party. *Do you now understand the words that have been made known to you?*

In fact, in Deuteronomy 14 we hit up against a variant teaching on what the tithe—the tenth of our income—is really for. Most of the Bible's teaching on the tithe is that it is for the Levites—basically, the pastoral staff (I've yet to have sufficient courage to press this point home with my church board). Deuteronomy 14 instructs about giving to the Levites, but adds this:

> Be sure to set aside a tenth of all that your fields produce each year. Eat the tithe of your grain, new wine and oil, and the firstborn of your herds and flocks in the presence of the LORD your God at the place he will choose as a dwelling for his Name, so that you may learn to revere the LORD your God always. But if that place is too distant and you have been blessed by the LORD your God and cannot carry your tithe (because the place where the LORD will choose to put his Name is so far away), then exchange your tithe for silver, and take the silver with you and go to the place the LORD your God will choose. *Use the silver to buy whatever you like: cattle, sheep, wine or other fermented drink, or anything you wish. Then you and your household shall eat there in the presence of the LORD your God and rejoice* (vv. 22–26, emphasis mine).

Take 10 percent and have a party. That's the word from God.
Do you now understand the words that have been made known to you?

I KNOW WHAT YOU'RE THINKING: *THIS FOOL DOESN'T KNOW WHAT he's talking about. He doesn't know who he's talking to. Come live inside one of my days, Mr. Preacher, Mr. Writer. See then if you feel like celebrating. I've got so many messy, mixed-up things going on in my life, so much trouble and rubble, it would be forced and false for me to shake loose and have fun.*

My response? Have you already forgotten what celebration is? It's glimpsing heaven. In Lewis's words, it's *an acceleration in the rhythm of celestial experience.* It's turning the volume up. When you really get a peek at what God is preparing for you, it's pretty hard to stay down in the mouth. And what I'm arguing is that celebration is precisely taking that peek. We celebrate in order to tear back the veil that keeps us from seeing heaven.

In Larry Crabb's book *Connecting,* he tells about a friend of his who grew up in an angry family. The family members, taking their cue from the father, were always sniping, griping, arguing with one another. Any minor accident at the table was met by a withering blast of mockery or scolding. Down the street from where he lived was a big old house with a huge front porch. In that house lived a happy family: Laughter, singing, lively friendly banter were always spilling from the house. When this man was about ten, he took to excusing himself from the dinner table as soon as he could without being yelled at. He would run down the street, hide under the large porch, and just listen to the happy, laughing, loving talk of the family.

"Imagine," Larry Crabb said to his friend. "Imagine one day the father of that family discovers that you're sitting under his porch. He sends his son to invite you in, to come sit at the table with them, to feast with them. Imagine you accidentally spill your water. The father roars with mirth. 'Bring him more water,' the father says. 'And a dry shirt. I want him to enjoy this meal.'"[3]

So much of our life is, literally and figuratively, lived with that angry family. Celebration is not just sitting under the porch of the happy family, it's sitting at their table.

So how can you play when you have so much work? How can you celebrate when you have so much to lament? I turn the question around: How can you not? Don't you want to join the laughing family at their table? Don't you long for, don't you need something in your life on a routine basis that reminds you what it's all about, that keeps you in the race, keeps you from losing heart?

It's a discipline. It's a holy habit. The Old Testament scholar Walter Brueggeman points out that many of the psalms begin as lament and end as proclamation and celebration. They start as groans and flower into hallelujahs. Many of these psalms, indeed, were shaped out of wounds and disappointment—out of missing God, not finding Him. But somehow, the psalm itself—the act of raising one's voice and gazing heavenward—becomes the vehicle for fresh hope. What began as a diary entry from borderland transforms into a field dispatch from the holy wild. Brueggemann calls such psalms the psalms of the "great nevertheless." It is praise birthed not out of victory and prosperity, but out of defeat and dread. The praise is an act of defiance and faith. It is a bold refusal to let the trouble that surrounds us be bigger than God who comes to meet us.[4] It is Habakkuk's prayer:

> Though the fig tree does not bud
>   and there are no grapes on the vines,
> though the olive crop fails
>   and the fields produce no food,
> though there are no sheep in the pen
>   and no cattle in the stalls,
> yet I will rejoice in the Lord,
>   I will be joyful in God my Savior.
> The Sovereign Lord is my strength;
>   he makes my feet like the feet of a deer,
> he enables me to go on the heights.
> (3:17–19)

Nevertheless.

IN *THE LAST BATTLE*, THE FINAL BOOK OF C. S. LEWIS'S *CHRONICLES of Narnia*, the children, along with a huge gathering of people and animals and creatures of all description, move in pilgrimage deeper and deeper, higher and higher, into Aslan's country. At the beginning of the book, the children were riding on a train. They heard a loud violent noise and were suddenly whisked into Narnia. Here's the scene:

> They found themselves walking together—and a great, bright procession it was—up towards mountains higher than you could see in this world even if they were there to be seen. But there was no snow on those mountains: There were forests and green slopes and sweet orchards and

flashing waterfalls, one above the other, going up forever....

The light ahead was growing stronger. Lucy saw that a great series of many-colored cliffs led up in front of them like a giant's staircase. And then she forgot everything else, because Aslan himself was coming, leaping down from cliff to cliff like a living cataract of power and beauty.

Aslan turned to them and said:

"You do not look so happy as I mean you to be."

Lucy said, "We're so afraid of being sent away, Aslan.... You have sent us back to our own world so often."

"No fear of that," said Aslan. "Have you not guessed?"

Their hearts leapt and a wild hope rose within them.

"There *was* a real railway accident," said Aslan softly. "Your father and mother and all of you are—as you used to say—dead. The term is over: the holidays have begun. The dream has ended: this is the morning."

And then the truest vision of both homecoming and all things made new breaks in on them:

And as he spoke, he no longer looked to them like a lion; but the things that began to happen after that were so great and so beautiful that I cannot write them. And for us this is the end of all the stories, and we can most truly say that they all lived happily ever after. But for them it was only the beginning of the real story. All their life in this world and all their adventures in Narnia had only been the cover and title page: now at last they were beginning Chapter One of the Great Story, which no one on earth has read: which goes on for ever and ever: in which every chapter is better than the one before.[5]

That's a little glimpse, a little taste on the tongue, of what awaits those who know Jesus Christ.

What should we say in response to all this?

Let's party.

RISE AND GO

In 1996 the staff at Bridger Wilderness Park in Wyoming posted some of the suggestions that had been returned to them by park visitors. Here are a few:

1. Trails need to be reconstructed. Please avoid building trails that go uphill.
2. Too many bugs and leeches and spiders and spider webs. Please spray the wilderness to rid the area of these pests.
3. Please pave the trails so that they can be plowed of snow during the winter.
4. Chairlifts need to be in some places so that we can get to wonderful views without having to hike to them.
5. The coyotes made too much noise last night and kept me awake. Please eradicate these annoying animals.
6. A small deer came into my camp and stole my jar of pickles. Is there a way I can get reimbursed?

7. Escalators would help on steep sections.
8. A McDonald's would be nice at the trailhead.
9. Too many rocks in the mountains.[1]

PLEASE AVOID BUILDING TRAILS THAT GO UPHILL. RID THE AREA OF *pests. Escalators would help. Too many rocks in the mountains.*

The ancients had a word for this: sloth. Sloth wasn't just laziness. It was boredom and bone-weariness, the heavy-limbed, heavy-lidded listlessness struck into us by the heat of the noonday sun. It was *acedia:* a death of purpose, a loss of wonder. The wildness of the wild stretches out and towers up in all directions, but we miss it, whining for a chairlift, pining for a Big Mac, chafing at the bugs, stumbling over rocks.

This is being stuck in borderland.

I hope you want off. I hope you want to venture into the holy wild, with all its danger and wonder and beauty. But one thing is for sure: It will not come cheap or easy. If we are going to walk that road to Emmaus and see, hear, and rejoice in Christ who walks with us, we will have to *walk,* one step after the other, and we will have to watch and listen with care and with shrewdness. We will have to *practice* His presence. And there are no shortcuts to that, no escalators in the steep sections, no artificial removal of obstacles and annoyances. It takes discipline—the steady, daily cultivation of holy habits.

If we were to gather suggestions from most North American Christians about how to improve the Godward life, we might get a list with items like this:

1. Give us quick, effective formulas for prayer.
2. Dispel our doubts without ever making us touch wounds.
3. Remove our wounds and disappointments.
4. Explain mystery, simply.
5. Take the risk and the work out of obedience.
6. Give us a God who's safe.

THE BORDERS OF BORDERLAND EXPAND INFINITELY THAT WAY. "YET all experience is an arch wherethrough/ Gleams that untraveled world whose margin fades/ Forever and forever when I move."[2] Trying to reach the holy wild by means of an escalator, trying to live with a God we insist be nice, safe, docile, domestic, who hands us life smooth and tidy and sterile, is to watch the margins of that untraveled world fade "forever and forever when I move."

In part 1 of this book, we explored what I called our "Jonah heart"—our impulse to flee the God who seeks us—or our "Peter heart"—our temptation to send away the God who comes near. We do this because we know, as Jonah and Peter knew, that God isn't safe. "Arise and go to Nineveh," He might say. "Come, follow Me," He might command.

So we refine an instinct for avoiding God. We perfect the art of the side-step. We live in borderland—the place between being saved and being sanctified, between coming to Christ and actually walking with Him. There are, we saw, many things that reinforce borderland living, many excuses we make for staying stuck there.

But we only break the habits of borderland dwelling by replacing them with other habits, holy habits. There are no tricks and gimmicks for living with the God who is not nice but who is good. There are no escalators in the steep sections.

You'll have to walk the whole way.

I BEGAN THIS BOOK WITH A STORY, A WALKING STORY THAT LUKE tells of two disciples walking the road to Emmaus, who meet Jesus unawares. I end with another walking story, also from Luke, about ten lepers stuck in borderland, who meet Jesus fully aware:

Now on his way to Jerusalem, Jesus traveled along the border between Samaria and Galilee. As he was going into a village, ten men who had leprosy met him. They stood at a distance and called out in a loud voice, "Jesus, Master, have pity on us!"

When he saw them, he said, "Go, show yourselves to the priests."
And as they went, they were cleansed. (17:11–14)

JESUS WALKS THE BORDERLAND, ATTENTIVE TO THE CRIES OF THOSE who want off. "Jesus, Master, have pity on us." He does have pity, but it's not the simpering, pampering thing we often call pity. It is bristling and blunt and hard: "Go, show yourselves to the priests." This is a bold and dangerous command: They're to travel from the leper colony at borderland to the temple in Jerusalem in one audacious move. This command from the lips of any other man would have been a death sentence, an invitation to lawbreaking, an act of taunting defiance. But these men must know that coming from Jesus, it's a pledge of healing.

And as they went, they were cleansed. Much of what this book is about is caught in that simple, elegant pronouncement. *As they went.* Our cleansing from the numbness in us, the loss of feeling and the decay that comes with it, occurs *as we go,* as we walk out what Jesus has told us to do. "If you hold to my teaching, you are really my disciples," He said to His disciples in another place. "*Then* you will know the truth, and the truth will set you free" (John 8:31–32).

I envision it being morning. Maybe Jesus has been alone in the solitary place, praying. And now He's hungry, heading for a village to buy bread fresh and hot and thick-crusted, paddled out from a stone oven. The sun is a splinter of brightness at the edge of the gaunt landscape. Huge, dark, sharp-edged shadows strew the earth. And sudden as the rush of spooked birds taking wing, voices cry out: loud, desperate, urgent. *"Have pity!"* Jesus shades His eyes against the sun's widening gleam, looks around. *"When he saw them,* he said, 'Go....'"

And they're off. Running, running, amazed to be running. They feel a surge and tingle in bones and flesh that have been long dead like sticks, a dizzying headlong flood of strength, burning and washing all at once. They could run like this all day, run and not grow weary. They look down, each of them, and see what they have wanted for so long and so badly that they've been almost afraid to hope for it: Hands and feet whose flesh was once cracked and stubbed and ashen now have a ruddy smoothness. A wholeness. One counts his toes: *Ten! All ten!* Another brushes the tips of his fingers together, and thrills at the sensation that flits down his nerves. One steps on something sharp, cutting, and laughs: He *felt* that.

And they keep running.

But one stops. *Go, show yourselves to the priests.* But right now, that seems secondary at best.

> One of them, when he saw he was healed, came back, praising God in a loud voice. He threw himself at Jesus' feet and thanked him—and he was a Samaritan.
>
> Jesus asked, "Were not all ten cleansed? Where are the other nine? Was no one found to return and give praise to God except this foreigner?" Then he said to him, "Rise and go; your faith has made you well." (Luke17:15–19)

MARTIN LUTHER DESCRIBED WORSHIP AS ONE LEPER RETURNING. I would go further. This, I think, is the shape of the holy life. This—returning to praise Jesus, to throw ourselves at His feet and thank Him—this is what makes the difference between *just being cleansed* and living out a faith *that makes us well.* Borderland is filled with former lepers who remember nostalgically, like old war veterans swapping barracks stories, the day they met Jesus and He cleansed them. But somehow, they never walked in it very far. They never continued, step by step, day by day, in the faith it stirred and confirmed and expressed. They never cultivated the holy habit of returning, wonder struck, to praise and to thank and to use all their renewed strength to offer their bodies as living sacrifices. They showed themselves to the priests but forgot to throw themselves at the High Priest's feet.

Where are the other nine? I would imagine in borderland again, complaining, doubting, disappointed, guilt-ridden, bored. Talking about the good old days. Waiting for the next vacation.

Stuck.

Only the one who keeps looking for Jesus, wherever He's found, really gets to rise and go, made well by faith.

NOTES

INTRODUCTION

1. Some people have overliteral minds. Mine tends to be over*literary:* Books clutter it.

2. Mark Twain, *The Adventures of Tom Sawyer* (Toronto: Bantam, 1981), 214–5.

PART ONE

1. Sigmund Freud, *The Future of an Illusion* (London: Hogarth Press, 1978).

CHAPTER TWO

1. C. S. Lewis, *The Lion, the Witch and the Wardrobe* (New York: Puffin Books, 1978), 75.

CHAPTER FIVE

1. Interview with Os Guinness, *Books and Culture* (July/August 1998): 17.

2. Barbara Tuchman, *A Distant Mirror: The Calamitous 14th Century* (New York: Ballantine Books, 1978).

CHAPTER SIX

1. Michael O'Brien, *Father Elijah: An Apocalypse* (San Francisco: Ignatius Press, 1996), 561.

2. John Updike, *Roger's Version* (New York: Knopf, 1986), 80–1.

CHAPTER EIGHT

1. Personal letter from Bonnie Middlemiss to the author, September 2000.

2. Ibid.

CHAPTER TEN

1. Letter to *Focus on the Family,* (1992).

PART TWO

CHAPTER THIRTEEN

1. Mark Twain, *The Adventures of Tom Sawyer* (Toronto: Bantam, 1981), 124.

2. John Ortberg, *The Life You've Always Wanted* (Grand Rapids, Mich.: Zondervan, 1997), 51.

3. See Dallas Willard, "Taking God's Keys," *Leadership* (Fall 1998): 57.

CHAPTER FOURTEEN

1. Brother Lawrence, *The Practice of the Presence of God* (Springdale, Pa.: Whitaker House, 1982), 8.

2. Isaiah 28:10.

3. William Shakespeare, *As You Like It,* Act II, Scene 1.

4. Elizabeth Barrett Browning

CHAPTER FIFTEEN

1. Marshall Shelley, *Leadership* (Winter 1997): 130.

CHAPTER SIXTEEN

1. See, for example, R. W. Southern, *Western Society and the Church in the Middle Ages* (New York: Penguin Books, 1970), 240ff.

2. Frank McCourt, *Angela's Ashes: A Memoir* (New York: Scribner, 1996), 292–3.

3. Richard Foster, *The Celebration of Discipline* (San Francisco: Harper and Row, 1988), 146–7.

4. Greg Asimakoupoulos, *Fresh Illustrations for Preaching and Teaching*, ed. Edward K. Rowell, (Grand Rapids, Mich.: Baker Books, 1997), 27.

5. This story, perhaps apocryphal, is in wide circulation.

CHAPTER SEVENTEEN

1. David Riesman, *The Lonely Crowd* (New Haven, Conn.: Yale University Press, 1950).

2. Robert Benson, *Between the Dreaming and the Coming True* (San Francisco: HarperSanFrancisco, 1996), 110.

3. Ben Patterson, "Holy War," *Leadership* (Spring 1999): 120.

CHAPTER EIGHTEEN

1. From Richard Foster, *The Celebration of Discipline* video, Tape 1.

2. Richard Foster, *The Celebration of Discipline* (San Francisco: Harper and Row, 1988), 48, 51.

3. See Dallas Willard, *The Spirit of the Disciplines: Understanding How God Changes Lives* (San Francisco: HarperSanFrancisco, 1988), 1–10.

4. C. S. Lewis, *Mere Christianity* (New York: Collier Books, 1960), 89–90.

5. Cornelius Plantinga, *Not the Way It's Supposed to Be: A Breviary of Sin* (Grand Rapids, Mich.: Eerdmans, 1995), 35.

CHAPTER NINETEEN

1. David Grossman, "Trained to Kill," *Christianity Today* (10 August 1998): 30–9.

2. Dr. Bockmuehl died of cancer in 1989.

3. *Illustrations for Preaching and Teaching*, ed. Craig Brian Larson (Grand Rapids, Mich.: Baker Books, 1993), 279.

CHAPTER TWENTY

1. John Ortberg, *The Life You've Always Wanted,* (Grand Rapids, Mich.: Zondervan, 1997), 97–8.

2. Ben Petterson, "A Faith Like Mary's," *Preaching Today,* Tape #87.

3. Cited in Ravi Zacharias, *Cries of the Heart: Bringing God Near When He Feels So Far* (Dallas: Word Publishing, 1998), 9–10.

4. Tony Campolo, *Carpe Diem: Seize the Day* (Dallas: Word Publishing, 1994), 193–4.

CHAPTER TWENTY-ONE

1. Source unknown.

2. William H. Willimon, *Peculiar Speech: Preaching to the Baptized* (Grand Rapids, Mich.: Eerdmans, 1992), 90.

CHAPTER TWENTY-TWO

1. C. S. Lewis, *The Screwtape Letters* (New York: MacMillan Publishing, 1977), 50.

2. Alan Jacobs, "The Man Who Heard Voices," *Books and Culture* (January/February 1996), 25.

3. Larry Crabb, *Connecting: Healing for Ourselves and Our Relationships* (Nashville: Word, 1997), 14.

4. Walter Brueggemann, *The Message of the Psalms: A Theological Commentary* (Minneapolis: Augsburg, 1984), 51ff.

5. C. S. Lewis, *The Last Battle* (New York: Puffin Books, 1978), 164–5.

EPILOGUE

1. "Escalators Anyone?" submitted by Mark Neifert to *Leadership* (Summer 1999), 75.

2. Alfred Lord Tennyson, "Ulysses."

ACKNOWLEDGMENTS

THIS BOOK IS STOLEN. TO WRITE IT, I HAVE PILFERED OTHERS' ideas, robbed family and friends of my time and attention, and commandeered the creative energy and shrewd insight of dozens of busy people. These brief pages are a modest attempt to repay the debt.

I have had the honor of being a pastor now to two congregations, people who have been bighearted enough to receive me with grace and thankfulness and only minor complaints. You have been—in all your greatness and fallenness, your willingness and stubbornness, your pursuing God and fleeing God—a mirror of my own likewise qualities. You have continually forced me to be not just true, but real. That this book is not academic speculation but living testimony owes much to you.

My literary agent Ann Spangler found me like a baby in the bulrushes and whisked me into the courts of the kings. Her earthy wisdom, genuine encouragement, unshakable integrity, and unflinching toughness have been excellent tutelage for a bumpkin like me. When I think of her and the work she does, a reworked line from The Band's song "Up on Crippled Creek" comes to me: "With my manuscript, she sends me; when I start to freak, she amends me; I don't have to speak, she defends me—a writer's dream if I ever did see one."

The people at Multnomah Publishers are a wonder. They like their work so much it's almost a crime to pay them for it. Bill Jensen's enthusiasm—for books, classical music, river fishing, his family, life—is a beautiful buoyant thing, floating on the deep like a good dry fly. Keith Wall, my editor, somehow managed to do radical surgery on the book—at times dividing joints and marrow, or simply cutting away the fat—and made it sting like only minor scratches. Heather Kopp did some eleventh hour chapter shuffling and title-mending that helped bring the book's many ideas into greater coherence and sharper focus. Don Jacobson, Multnomah's president, has paid me the high

honor of being more interested in the condition of my heart than in the prof-
itability of my prose. Through leadership like that, the kingdom shines. And
there are many more people whose creativity and industry and faithfulness
have made the creation of a book not a weariness in the bones as Ecclesiastes
says it is, but a delight of the heart.

Many friends have given special encouragement to my writing. If I start
naming them, I'll miss some—and then won't I hear about it! You know who
you are. Thank you, each and all.

I have had the privilege of a good family. My dad, who died in 1996, taught
me things that, like buried treasure, I keep digging up and getting rich by. One
of them was a love for words, their magic and power and beauty. My mother
has always believed in me and never tired of telling me so. My brother, Adam,
and sister, Jennifer, have been a lifelong blessing—we've been able to avoid that
nasty thing called sibling rivalry and simply been one another's cheerleaders.
And I am perhaps one of the few men on earth who has in-laws I like to boast
about and who do the same for me. Kay and Bill, Randy and Bob, thank you
for always making me a son and a brother, never an outsider.

My wife, Cheryl, and my children, Adam, Sarah, and Nicola—all to whom
I dedicate this book—keep bringing me light and bringing me into the light.

First, last, and most, I thank my Lord Jesus Christ. You found me when I
was far from You and keep inviting me to open my eyes and see You on the
road beside me, keep calling me into and meeting me in the holy wild. Thank
You that You forgave my sins and that You continue to forgive my Jonah heart
and chase me down wherever and whenever I try to run. More and more, You
are showing me the wisdom of being still and knowing You are God.

Shalom.

MARK BUCHANAN
OCTOBER 2000

The publisher and author would love to hear your
comments about this book. *Please contact us at:*
www.multnomah.net/yourgodistoosafe

THE HOLY PLEASURES OF A DANGEROUS FAITH

ISBN 1-57673-889-2

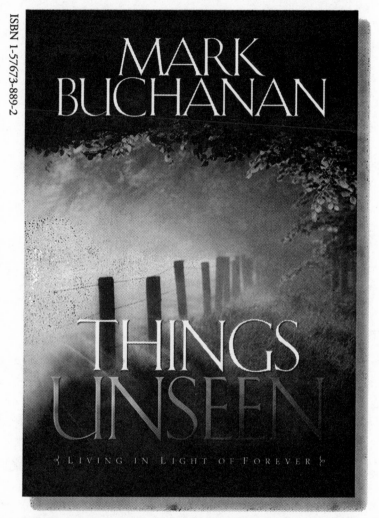

Here's a thoughtful, probing exploration of why Christians get stuck in the place of complacency, dryness, and tedium—and how to move on to new levels of spiritual passion! Buchanan shows how the majority of Christians begin their spiritual journey with excitement and enthusiasm—only to get bogged down in a "borderland"—an in-between space beyond the "old life" but short of the abundant, adventurous existence promised by Jesus. Citing Jonah, he examines the problem of "borderland living"—where doubt, disappointment, guilt, and wonderlessness keep people in a quagmire of mediocrity—then offers solutions…effective ways to get unstuck and move into a bold, unpredictable, exhilarating walk with Christ. Inspired writing!